MASTERY

Also by Tony Wagner

Learning by Heart: An Unconventional Education

*Most Likely to Succeed: Preparing Our Kids for the
Innovation Era,* coauthored by Ted Dintersmith

*Creating Innovators: The Making of Young
People Who Will Change the World*

*The Global Achievement Gap: Why Even Our Best Schools
Don't Teach the New Survival Skills Our Students Need*

*Change Leadership: A Practical Guide to Transforming Our
Schools,* with Robert Kegan, Lisa Lahey, Richard Lemons,
Jude Garnier, Deborah Helsing, and Annie Howell

Making the Grade: Reinventing America's Schools

How Schools Change: Lessons from Three Communities

MASTERY

Why Deeper Learning Is Essential in an Age of Distraction

Tony Wagner & Ulrik Juul Christensen

with contributions from Sujata Bhatt

BASIC BOOKS

New York

Basic Books
Hachette Book Group
1290 Avenue of the Americas, New York, NY 10104
www.basicbooks.com

Printed in the United States of America

First Edition: September 2025

Published by Basic Books, an imprint of Hachette Book Group, Inc. The Basic Books name and logo is a registered trademark of the Hachette Book Group.

The Hachette Speakers Bureau provides a wide range of authors for speaking events. To find out more, go to hachettespeakersbureau.com or email HachetteSpeakers@hbgusa.com.

Basic books may be purchased in bulk for business, educational, or promotional use. For more information, please contact your local bookseller or the Hachette Book Group Special Markets Department at special.markets@hbgusa.com.

The publisher is not responsible for websites (or their content) that are not owned by the publisher.

Print book interior design by Amy Quinn.

Library of Congress Cataloging-in-Publication Data
Names: Wagner, Tony, author. | Christensen, Ulrik Juul, author.
Title: Mastery : why deeper learning is essential in an age of distraction / Tony Wagner, Ulrik Juul Christensen; with contributions from Sujata Bhatt.
Description: First edition. | New York : Basic Books, [2025] | Includes bibliographical references and index. |
Identifiers: LCCN 2024059579 | ISBN 9781541601925 (hardcover) | ISBN 9781541601932 (ebook)
Subjects: LCSH: Mastery learning. | Motivation in education. | Student growth (Academic achievement) | Continuing education. | School-to-work transition.
Classification: LCC LB1031.4 .W34 2025 | DDC 371.39/4—dc23/eng/20250205
LC record available at https://lccn.loc.gov/2024059579

ISBNs: 9781541601925 (hardcover), 9781541601932 (ebook)

LSC-C

Printing 1, 2025

In Memory

Esmond Harmsworth, our literary agent at Aevitas Creative, died suddenly just after we completed this book. From the very beginning, Esmond contributed enormously to the development of the book in essential ways. Reading multiple drafts and consulting with us on numerous occasions, he went above and beyond what anyone might expect of an agent. He did an extraordinary job of shepherding us to the finish line with a steadying hand and delicate diplomacy. Without Esmond's great skill and dedication—his true mastery of his craft—this book would not have been possible. We shall miss him greatly.

Contents

INTRODUCTION

THE CLASSROOM LOOKED like any other, in any high school across the country. Students sat at desks in rows, listening to a teacher giving out instructions and then trying to follow them. There wasn't much to distinguish this class from, say, geometry, where students had to memorize formulas, or English with its grammar drills. Except this was a journalism class, and the students were expected to put out a six-page newspaper on a typewriter.

That was the scene at Palo Alto High School in California when Esther Wojcicki first observed the class in 1984. What most struck her was that the students didn't seem motivated by what they were learning and doing—or, more to the point, what they were supposed to be learning and doing.

"I realized that the reason the kids were so unmotivated was because they didn't feel that they were responsible for the paper," Wojcicki recalled for us. "The teacher was the one in charge of the school newspaper, just as the previous teacher had been."

As the new journalism teacher, Wojcicki wanted to change that paradigm—a power shift. "I wanted the kids to *own* the paper," she said.

Today we know that creating agency is one of the most important ways to motivate learning. Learner agency refers to the level of control, autonomy, and power that a student experiences in an educational situation. It encompasses the student's involvement in their own learning process, allowing them to make meaningful choices, take ownership, and respond to their educational experiences. Wojcicki intuitively understood the importance of learner agency.

Wojcicki is widely known by many titles: educator, journalist, and author. Her best-selling book *How to Raise Successful People* draws on her experiences teaching high schoolers using the TRICK model: trust, respect, independence, collaboration, and kindness. Her book also gives a nod to the fact that Wojcicki and her husband raised three highly accomplished daughters: Susan, former CEO of YouTube; Janet, a researcher and professor of pediatrics at the University of California, San Francisco; and Anne, cofounder of 23andMe.

Among Wojcicki's most notable accomplishments, though, is having changed the approach to learning within the Palo Alto journalism program. She empowered the students by giving them control over the newspaper—reporting, writing, and editing—including peer-to-peer feedback and coaching. She was there to guide, counsel, and support, but she made it clear that they were responsible for the final product.

Within a year of Wojcicki taking over the journalism class, enrollment in the program doubled and kept growing. During her tenure until her retirement in 2020, the program expanded in every direction—more than one hundred students, additional faculty, and a broader editorial scope. Currently, *The Campanile* (the name refers to an Italian-style bell tower) publishes eight to ten print issues each academic year. The newspaper, which is both in print and online, has three sections: news and opinion, lifestyle and science/tech, and sports. Readership includes not only students and faculty at Palo Alto High but also the community.

The program is now housed in a twenty-five-thousand-square-foot media arts building, and when *The Campanile* staff is on deadline, it's buzzing with activity. The physical expansion of the program is impressive, but it's not the point of this story. The turnaround in the journalism program was not due to the latest technology or even the dedicated building. The secret ingredient, Wojcicki told us, was passion.

"It's having a project or an idea that you're passionate about," she said. Add to that "collaboration and a sense of community," and the journalism students at Palo Alto have learned more than writing and editing skills. "It made their lives richer," she continued, "because the number one skill they leave with is that they believe in themselves—they believe they can do anything that is set in front of them."

Passion and purpose were dominant themes in our conversations with three of Wojcicki's former students: Adora Zheng, Ujwal Srivastava, and Kai Vetteth. In college when we spoke with them, the students enthusiastically recalled the creative and collaborative experience of helping to produce *The Campanile*, despite the long hours during production.

"I think if another teacher had said that every couple of weeks you're going to stay for three days after class until eleven or twelve at night—just working continuously on one product for the student body to read—I probably would have said no," said Kai, who, after graduation from Palo Alto High School in 2020, went on to the University of Chicago. "But I think it speaks to the degree to which this model empowers students."

Kai described students willingly going "above and beyond"—to get more interviews for a story, to write and rewrite their articles, and to help younger students who were new to the paper. "I don't think that was driven by grades," he said. "It was driven by setting your own goals and working to achieve them."

Ujwal, who graduated from Palo Alto High School in 2019 and then went to Stanford, credited the journalism experience with teaching "more hands-on problem-solving, communication, collaboration skills," as well as another life skill: responsibility. "Students get to decide what types of articles they're going to write, how they're going to lay them out on the pages, and who they're going to interview as sources," he said.

Adora, a 2021 graduate of Palo Alto High School, described how prepared she felt when jumping into the student-run newspaper at Georgetown as a freshman and being promoted to desk editor. "I felt very prepared for that role. And I'm forever going to be appreciative of Woj [the students' nickname for Wojcicki] for her way that she prepared me and the experience that I had in that class."

The Secret Sauce of Mastery Learning

Listening to Wojcicki and her students talk about the journalism program, we were struck by their enthusiasm and commitment. This is the kind of energy that is most often reserved for things like the school play, marching band, or sports. So, what made the difference?

When we asked Wojcicki, she summed it up succinctly. "It has to be product based." In other words, the students were not just memorizing facts or cramming knowledge, the way they might in, say, history or math. They were gaining knowledge and developing a broad base of skills (from writing to teamwork) and using it to produce a product—namely, a newspaper.

This is what makes the Palo Alto journalism program a prime example of mastery learning. No more learning for the sake of accumulating knowledge in preparation for a test or to become a human hard drive of information. Mastery learning enables you to accomplish something—from flying a plane or operating a nuclear power plant to playing the cello, scoring a goal in soccer, or, for young children, decoding words so that they can read and learn on their own.

From electricians to beauticians, from plumbers to pilots to physicians, there are countless examples of learning where people acquire knowledge and skills and meet defined standards of proficiency so that they can do things that matter to them. Mastery learning enables you to achieve a goal that matters to you or your family, community, or employer.

Here's another shorthand way to think about mastery learning: it is the opposite of what passes for learning in schools and most workplaces today. In these environments, learners spend time acquiring information and then getting tested and graded on their ability to retain it, without understanding why this knowledge is important. Nor do they acquire the skills they need to use the knowledge they've been asked to memorize. Lacking both a purpose for their learning and the skills needed to use this knowledge, most of it is quickly forgotten.

There are three indispensable and interrelated components that define mastery learning:

1. **Teaching**: The focus of learning shifts from mere content knowledge acquisition to the development of essential and enduring cognitive and character skills needed for work, citizenship, and personal growth.
2. **Assessment**: The measurement of learning is based on learners showing evidence of being able to use the skills and knowledge they have learned.
3. **Motivation**: The development of individual interests, intrinsic motivation, and character skills becomes an integral element of the learning process.

Across learning settings and subject matter, a mastery learning approach encompasses *what* you must learn—both content knowledge and skills—*how* you best learn, and *why* you must learn. We all learn at different rates and even in different ways. A key to a mastery approach is understanding each individual's learning pace. Another essential aspect is motivation. Learners are far more motivated to acquire knowledge and skills when they understand the purpose of what they are learning, when they have set their own learning goals, or when they are pursuing a passion. This is what we referred to earlier as learner agency. Wojcicki's students understood why they needed both knowledge and skills, and they could make real choices about what news to cover, whom to interview, and so on. Their motivation did not stem from wanting to pass a test and get a good grade. It came from knowing that they had to put their names on a public product, and they wanted it to be something that they could take pride in. In short, they had both choice and voice as learners, key aspects of an intrinsic motivation for learning. Mastery learning, then, defines a completely different approach to learning.

What if learning everywhere—for students and adults alike—was mastery learning? What if a high school or college diploma was a collection of required and elective licenses or merit badges—to borrow a concept from scouting—that students earned by demonstrating real proficiencies rather than merely by serving their seat time and passing some multiple-choice tests? For example, it would be the difference between spending a specified number of hours sitting in a class and then passing a test on the parts of speech and grammar rules, versus having to demonstrate proficiency in many forms of oral and written expression to earn an English credit. What if adult learning, as well, was about mastering new skills and knowledge and so adding to what you can do in the world?

If we were to move to such a different system, what would mastery-based learning look like at each of the different grade levels and for adults? How would you assess mastery learning? How could time spent learning be differently organized to make way for mastery learning? Most importantly, what difference might mastery learning make for individuals and for society?

These are some of the critical questions we explore in this book.

Why Mastery Learning Now?

We believe there are three essential purposes of education: to prepare all young people for productive work, for an active and informed civic life, and for personal growth, health, and well-being. All three are needed to enable our young people, our society, and our species to not merely survive but to thrive.

These goals have long been accepted in the United States and elsewhere as givens. They are foundational, and few would argue with them. What many people may not see, however, are the profound changes that make attaining each of these three education goals both more challenging and more important than ever.

The first is the radical restructuring of work. With increasing numbers of routine jobs being offshored or automated, higher levels of skills are a prerequisite for the jobs that remain. In an age of innovation, the employees in greatest demand are creative problem solvers who can generate new ideas, products, services, or solutions to address the pressing issues of our time. The assembly-line work that remains has also been totally transformed. Factory workers today are in teams that manage automated processes; they no longer labor in isolation on repetitive, mindless tasks. Even entry-level jobs in the service sector now require problem-solving and people skills.

The second is the challenge of preparing young people for citizenship and civic engagement in an increasingly complex and polarized world. The digital age and now the increased use of artificial intelligence (AI) have led to a dramatic increase in the spread of misinformation, fake news, and divisive content. Young people need to learn how to critically evaluate sources, understand bias, and differentiate between untrustworthy and reliable information. Young people also need an understanding of the challenges such as climate change and growing inequities in our communities, our country, and our world. Tomorrow's citizens need to master the skills that will enable them to actively participate in civil discourse and civic life—respecting differences, volunteering, seeking common ground, and working with others to solve problems together.

Finally, there is the challenge of the mental and physical health of our young people today. With the increased use of social media, cyberbullying and peer pressure are significant emotional challenges for many adolescents. Mental health professionals report that rates of anxiety and depression among this age group are at an all-time high. Educators increasingly describe young people as addicted to their smartphones and unable to concentrate for any length of time. Too many young people today get very little exercise, have poor nutrition, and are overweight. Students need new knowledge and skills that will strengthen their social-emotional muscles as well as their physical muscles to thrive in today's world.

Given these profound changes, mastery learning is not just a nice-to-have or something for only a few kids. Mastery learning becomes the way that we prepare young people for work, citizenship, and personal growth and health in the twenty-first century. Mastery learning is also the way adults can best be equipped to adapt and contribute to a rapidly changing world.

The Skills that Matter Most

There is now a great deal of agreement on the skills most needed today. For his 2008 bestseller, *The Global Achievement Gap*, Tony Wagner, one of the authors of this book, interviewed business, civic, education, and military leaders across the globe and summarized the competencies that they considered essential. He called them the Seven Survival Skills for the Twenty-First Century. They are:

1. Critical thinking and problem-solving
2. Collaboration across networks and leading by influence
3. Agility and adaptability
4. Initiative and entrepreneurship
5. Effective oral and written communication
6. Accessing and analyzing information
7. Curiosity and imagination[1]

Some individuals and organizations have different lists that may prioritize other skills, and they may refer to them as "life skills" or what Tim Taylor, cofounder and CEO of America Succeeds, calls "durable skills," but there is general agreement on the ones that matter most. Since the publication of Tony's book, many people have come to refer to the essential skills in an abbreviated form as "the four Cs": critical thinking, communication, collaboration, and creative problem-solving. Less frequently mentioned are character skills—what we call the fifth C. Character skills such as initiative, grit, self-discipline, curiosity, and empathy can and must be developed, as they are essential to becoming a productive human being who can engage in the lifelong learning that our rapidly changing world demands.

While learning foundational knowledge is still important, we argue in this book that teaching and assessing proficiencies in the five C's are more important. Progression through school should no longer be based on your age and whether you have attended classes for the requisite time to get a credit. Rather, you should be required to demonstrate increasing mastery of essential skills and dispositions as you progress through the different levels of learning.

Mastery takes up where *The Global Achievement Gap* left off. We begin with a brief review of the history of mastery learning and a more detailed discussion of its elements. Then, we explore in greater depth all the ways our traditional education system falls short and why mastery learning is essential today. In the following chapters, we take you to a wide variety of schools—from kindergarten to graduate school—where this new learning is happening. We also show how the mastery-based approach is used in a variety of adult learning environments, from medicine to aviation, sports, and corporate offices. Along the way, we explore some of the challenges and trade-offs in transitioning from a time-based to a mastery-based system. We also explain the new alternatives to computer-scored standardized tests that assess important skills, as well as how teachers must be differently prepared. Finally, we consider the system and policy changes needed to take this different paradigm of education to scale.

The new education imperatives are clear, the innovative models exist, and the time is now. This book is a vital call to action and a road map that points the way toward a dramatically better education for everyone. Whether you are a manager, educator, parent, student, or concerned citizen, *Mastery* is for you.

CHAPTER 1

What Is Mastery Learning?

The History of Mastery Learning

How do you know if someone has learned something, or become proficient, or is on the way toward achieving some level of competence? For millennia, humans have intuitively understood the importance of answering this question.

In hunter-gatherer and agrarian societies, people determined each other's proficiency by their performance. Could they make a pot or weave a basket that held the grain? Cultivate plants? Bring back sufficient fruit and nuts or wild game for meals? Children worked side by side with their parents and other adults over a period of years, gradually becoming more capable with practice and coaching.

Beginning in eleventh-century Europe, a new system of teaching and assessing competence evolved, called the guild system. Guilds emerged from craft associations and fraternities that were common in medieval towns and cities. These associations were formed by skilled craftsmen to protect their economic interests and to regulate the quality and quantity of their products. Over time, these associations evolved into more formalized guilds that had greater power and influence.

Guilds were organized around a hierarchical system of apprentices, journeymen, and masters. Apprentices were young boys who worked for a master craftsman in exchange for training and room and board. Journeymen were skilled craftsmen who worked for wages and were free to travel and work in different cities. Masters were highly skilled craftsmen who owned their own workshops and employed apprentices and journeymen. In time, as they progressed, these apprentices and journeymen might become masters in their own right—sometimes surpassing even the masters who had trained them.

During the Italian Renaissance, a teenage boy was apprenticed to an artist named Andrea del Verrocchio at his renowned workshop, where the boy received training in painting, sculpture, and technical drawing. That teenager was none other than Leonardo da Vinci. Like most apprentices to master artists, da Vinci helped Verrocchio with his commissioned artworks—an accepted practice at the time. Eventually he became a paid collaborator.

When da Vinci painted what is considered his first masterpiece, *Annunciation*, he proved himself to be a master painter.[1] Today, that painting hangs in the Uffizi Gallery in Florence, Italy. By this masterpiece, da Vinci proved what he could do by applying all he had learned and practiced, just as apprentices in various trades have done for centuries.

The guild system began to decline in the eighteenth century with the rise of industrialization and the emergence of factory production. By the mid-nineteenth century, it had largely disappeared. However, many of the principles of apprenticeship and mastery that were central to the guild system continue to shape the training of skilled workers such as plumbers, electricians, and carpenters.

This is true in some white-collar professions as well. The path from an undergraduate to a graduate student to a PhD candidate to an assistant, associate, and finally a full professor represents a kind of modern-day guild system. And the method of testing doctoral students is through oral exams, in which students are required to defend their thesis to earn a degree. The medical profession represents another kind of guild system, where most future physicians progress from being students, to interns, to fellows, to licensure.

Andreas Schleicher, an education researcher with a global reputation and currently the director for education and skills and special adviser on education policy at the Organisation for Economic Co-operation and Development (OECD), offered a concise definition of mastery in the context of lifelong learning. "We used to learn to do the work, and now learning *is* the work," he told us. "For me, that's what mastery is about. Do you have those cognitive, social, and emotional prerequisites to continue to learn, unlearn, and relearn—expand your horizon, question the established wisdom of your time?"

Mastery plays a part in so many types of learning where a standardized test would be meaningless. This is especially true in jobs and professions where it is critical to know how to do something competently. Think about pilots, doctors, and astronauts—the outliers when it comes to building mastery because of the life-and-death consequences involved. The pilot needs to handle engine failure, the surgeon needs to remove an appendix, and an astronaut needs to dock a capsule on the International Space Station. The same need to build and demonstrate mastery applies to musicians, actors, and craftspeople. Think of the carpenter who needs to construct a load-bearing wall or put a roof on a house.

Among many professionals today, licenses, credentials, and badges are often earned by showing evidence that knowledge and skills have been acquired. Physicians, pilots, and plumbers must demonstrate proficiency to get licensed. So do beauticians and electricians. And now a growing number of employers are beginning to use badging or "microcredentials" for hiring and promotion.

If that sounds familiar, it should: many of us or our friends earned badges in childhood.

Scouting: Earning Badges and Awards

Since the beginning of the twentieth century, young people have worked to earn badges in scouting, first in the United States and then eventually around the world. There are two major scouting organizations in the United States, and while they are similar, they are independent and separate. Scouting America (what used to be called the Boy Scouts of America) and Girl Scouts of the USA both offer opportunities to earn merit badges in specific categories such as outdoor activities, sports, and science, technology, engineering, and mathematics (STEM). Both assess a variety of cognitive and character skills, and the badges earned attest to a young person having demonstrated proficiency—what we would call mastery—in particular areas.

Scouting America offers a camping merit badge, where scouts must learn first aid; demonstrate proficiency in the use of a compass, maps, and GPS; and master basic camping skills such as how to handle an axe, build a fire, pitch a tent, and so on. Additionally, they need to camp out for a total of twenty days and successfully plan and lead a multiday trip. Finally, they must discuss what they have learned about personal health and safety, survival, public health, conservation, and good citizenship.[2]

While some of the skills that must be mastered to earn this badge can be measured by a onetime standardized assessment, such as a first aid test, the majority can only be assessed by the scoutmaster and other adults who are looking at a scout's overall performance over time. They use their observations to coach for improvement until the performance standards for the badge are achieved.

Dr. Kari Rockwell, CEO of the Girl Scouts for several counties in New York State and herself a former Girl Scout, explained the importance of badges. As she told us, they build not only competence in a particular area but also confidence, a quality that speaks to mastery. "Badges really help to build confidence in areas that girls in many cases are not confident in. And we encourage our troop leaders and our program personnel to really level the playing field for girls, so that every girl has a chance to be successful and earn a badge."

The Gold Award is the highest honor badge, where Girl Scouts "change the world by tackling issues they are passionate about to drive lasting change in their communities and beyond while they learn essential skills that will prepare them for all aspects of life."[3] In contrast to completing a one-and-done community service project, a Girl Scout pursuing the Gold Award spends a minimum of eighty hours developing a plan, forming and leading a team, and implementing and evaluating a long-term project to address a problem in her community. She also needs to collect and present evidence of the impact of her project. Examples of completed projects include building a database of service-learning opportunities for students, creating a community garden to grow fresh produce for a local food pantry, advocating for a state bill that funded menstrual products in schools, and making videos to explain distracted driving.[4]

In many respects, mastery learning re-creates the badging experiences described above in the classroom, where students combine skills and knowledge to meet well-defined and authentic standards.

The Threads of Mastery Learning

Throughout this book, we offer many different examples of mastery learning. We found elementary school students not only demonstrating their newly acquired skills but also talking about their strengths and weaknesses as learners in front of their teachers, peers, and community members. We had discussions with high school and college students who described how their basic mastery of cognitive and character skills has enabled them to become competent and accomplished adults.

We sat down with administrators and thought leaders at the state and national levels for whom the change to mastery learning is a mission. Indeed, for some, it has meant putting their careers on the line to creatively disrupt an ossified education system so that their students can acquire the skills that enable them to use their learning in the world.

Finally, we learned about varieties of adult mastery learning through conversations with individuals in many fields, from scuba divers and airline pilots to athletes and physicians.

Before venturing down those pathways into the stories, let's take a deeper look at some of the aspects of mastery learning.

In the Introduction, we introduced the concept of learner agency: the capacity to lead or direct one's own life. One of the most eloquent spokespeople for this concept is Tom Vander Ark, CEO and founder of Getting Smart and former director of education grant making for the Gates Foundation. He has visited over 2,500 schools across the globe. He told us, "The outcome that I'm most interested in these days is agency! The sense of knowing yourself, understanding your interests and skills, the causes you care most about, where and how you want to act on the world." Vander Ark continued, "I think the most important and overlooked objective of mastery learning is to create an environment where learners own the targets, where learners are clear about what's important in the environment. They understand with a sense of priority what the learning goals are, what their developmental priorities are."

Another way to understand agency is to know its opposite: passivity and powerlessness. Most students today don't feel that they are masters of their own learning. They cannot make any meaningful choices about what or how to learn. Many have little sense of their own interests or needs. Even worse, many believe their fates and futures are fixed, beyond their control.

The first essential aspect of mastery learning, then, is giving students real choices about what they learn. Yes, all students need to learn research skills, for example, but if the teacher gives them a choice of what to research, everything changes. The paper or presentation that they subsequently create is a product that reflects who they are and what they care about. They have also been able to make creative choices about how they present what they've learned. As learners, they have both a real choice and an authentic voice. As you will see, there are many ways to give students of all ages both choice and voice, and so promote learner agency.

Practice is an essential element of mastery learning, but it is a frequent misconception that lots of practice leads to better performance. We argue that vast amounts of practice—and much of the drilling that you find in classrooms—is completely futile. Why? Because it is *mindless* practice.

Expertise is built very differently, with *deliberate practice*. This term was coined by the late K. Anders Ericsson, a Swedish psychologist and researcher, to explain the secret of how people can improve their skills to the point of achieving mastery. In the process, Ericsson changed the way people think about becoming an expert performer in anything.[5]

Ulrik Juul Christensen, one of the authors of this book, first met Ericsson in 2001 at a conference where they were both presenters. It was clear that Ericsson's research on expert performance was complementary to Ulrik's study of how learning occurs. What followed from that initial conversation was nineteen years of discussions and friendship, until Ericsson's sudden death in 2020.

Ericsson's findings leveled the playing field for improvement and introduced the possibility of people achieving higher levels of performance than they had dreamed possible. As Ericsson discovered, it's not about talent or having a rare gift. In his words, "Consistently and overwhelmingly, the evidence showed that experts are always made, not born."[6] As he also stated, "A lot of people want to be the very best they can be. The deliberate practice notion has kind of opened the possibility that people can achieve higher levels of performance than they previously thought possible."[7]

The key to unlocking this potential is the nature of deliberate practice. It is not just doing the same thing over and over. Rather, deliberate practice identifies weaknesses that can be addressed by incorporating feedback from a coach or teacher to get better.[8] *Adjust this. Try that . . .* It's what musicians, athletes, and other top performers do so they can overcome weaknesses and close the gaps in their performance. Most important to this discussion, deliberate practice is not just for those peak performers; it is also at the core of any kind of mastery learning.

A key component to deliberate practice is a feedback loop. Sports offer a great example for both youth and adults. In fact, sports and other avocational pursuits are where we are most likely to have personal experience with mastery learning, particularly as adults. Driven by passion and the desire to improve our skills, we strive to get better, whether at playing a musical instrument or hitting a ball.

Practicing countless hours will not bring about improvement if the technique is incorrect. In fact, the result may be more harm than good. Incremental improvement to the point of mastery requires deliberate practice, with its focus on feedback, coaching, and adjustments.

Baseball, tennis, golf, soccer, and other highly commercial sports were early adopters of hardcore statistics and analytics. In each sport, performance at all levels can be broken down into subcomponents and evaluated. Advanced technology is deployed to show how a player is hitting or kicking a ball, as well as the resulting ball flight and spin. These technologies have transformed how players practice, because now they have a feedback loop that tells them the results of the changes they are making.

For example, golfers used to be taught to knock down on the ball to "trap" it against the turf, generating backspin that would slow down the roll of the ball when it landed on the green. Today, radar measurements of the ball's flight and spin show that what really matters is the angle of the clubface and the forces generated when the ball is hit.

In learning any skill, feedback loops are essential for mastery learning to occur. Measurement and performance analytics are used to support learning so that mastery occurs through ongoing iterations. Granted, human nature being what it is, most people want to hear more about what they're doing well. And deliberate practice in the pursuit of mastery could be viewed in a negative way: identifying what you have *not* learned or having someone point it out to you. In school, that would mean accepting a low grade and moving on to the next assignment.

But in mastery learning, the point of identifying something that a learner cannot do is to close the gap toward proficiency. *I want to be able to do A, B, and C. With deliberate practice, I see that I need to work on X and Y to get there.* Instead of being penalized for not yet having developed a level of mastery, the learner uses knowledge of that gap as a vital tool for growth.

In mastery learning, the outcome or goal is constant: proficiency for everyone. What varies is the time it takes to get there. As mentioned earlier, this is in sharp contrast to traditional learning, where time is constant. In most classrooms around the world, there is a fixed amount of time for all learners to complete an activity or take a test.

This difference has a monumental impact on how learning environments should be designed. For example, Ulrik has worked with mastery learning systems and tens of millions of learners across a wide variety of subjects and age groups. Across that population of learners, the time needed to reach the desired level of proficiency can vary widely. In some cases, the learners who make the slowest progress—but who still get to full proficiency—need eight to ten times as long as the fastest learners.

In addition to deliberate practice, for learners to pursue mastery learning they need to develop a growth mindset. This concept was popularized by Carol Dweck of Stanford University. She defines a growth mindset as believing that one can continuously develop new abilities, versus a fixed mindset, where the presumption is that one's abilities are determined at birth.[9]

People with a growth mindset believe they can improve if they're willing to invest the time and effort.[10] Another difference between a growth versus a fixed mindset is how someone handles failure. In her studies, Dweck found that some students fell apart in the face of failure, while others seemed to become engaged. "They woke up, they said 'I love a challenge,' they said things like 'I was hoping this would be informative.'"[11] People with a growth mindset are more willing to take risks and stretch themselves. As a result, when they experience failures, they see them as stepping stones on the path to learning.

This kind of failure as learning is very different from the failures students experience in schools. The latter can be paralyzing or stigmatizing. In contrast, failure with a growth mindset informs the learner. Indeed, throughout our lives, most learning occurs as a process of trial and error. No one accuses a young child of "failing" because they fell the first time that they tried walking or riding a bike. The same should apply to the adult who is learning to play a sport or a musical instrument—or who is trying to learn a new procedure or technology in the workplace. In mastery learning, the only real failure is the failure to try.

Having a growth mindset is far more than an inspiring way to think. In a world where challenges are going to be more numerous, with more complex problems to solve, a growth mindset is essential to being able to adapt.

A growth mindset has an impact on all aspects of learning. Consider an experiment conducted by researchers working with high school math students. The students were encouraged to picture their brain like a muscle that could grow stronger and smarter. As they embraced this way of thinking, lower-achieving students improved their grades, and more students enrolled in advanced mathematics courses.[12]

Traditional education systems for learners of all ages are often mere sorting machines, where students' abilities and the time given to learn something are both fixed. The quick learners get the best grades, and the slower learners get left behind. With a growth mindset, the assumption is that all learners will develop and progress with practice and feedback.

Together with a growth mindset, grit is a critical ingredient needed for mastery learning. Psychologist Angela Duckworth of the University of Pennsylvania has been a pioneer in research on grit and wrote a best-selling book on the topic. She describes grit as a combination of passion and perseverance. The more grit people have, the more likely they will see failure as a learning experience rather than a setback.[13]

Duckworth views grit in the context of goals that take a long time to achieve (although what constitutes a "long time" varies from childhood to adulthood). Overall, though, people who are "grittier"—those who stay with something to get better at it—tend to be those who love what they do "and stay in love with what they do over extended time periods."[14] This is why Duckworth says that passion is such an important component of grit.

Gritty people are also more likely to depend on others—not less. As Duckworth observes, those with grit ask for help and rely on coaches, mentors, and teachers. They seek collaboration because that is the most efficient way to progress toward their goals. "Grit sounds like being a strong individual who figures things out all by themselves," Duckworth writes. "But gritty people try to find other people to make everything they're striving to accomplish *easier*. It's very much about developing relationships, being vulnerable, saying what you can't do, and then, with the support of other people, figuring out how to do it."[15]

Duckworth believes that character spans three dimensions: "Strengths of heart," including the capacity for empathy and gratitude for strong personal relationships; "strengths of will," such as resilience and self-control to propel achievement; and "strengths of mind," or curiosity, for independent thinking.[16] We call these qualities of character *skills* because they can be learned and practiced.

Dweck's and Duckworth's work also suggests to us a dynamic interrelationship between the development of cognitive skills, such as critical thinking, communication, and creative problem-solving, and character skills, such as a growth mindset, grit, and the ability to work collaboratively and accept feedback. One needs these character skills to develop essential cognitive skills.

Duckworth mentions another thread needed for putting mastery learning into practice, and it is essential for developing grit and adopting a growth mindset: curiosity.

Stefaan van Hooydonk, the founder of the Global Curiosity Institute, also believes in the power of curiosity to encourage discovery and unlock innovation. "Curiosity requires self-awareness and intentionality—being proactive, focused, and disciplined," he said.

An author and researcher, Van Hooydonk founded the Global Curiosity Institute after a career in executive education in several large global companies. His last role was chief learning officer for Cognizant, managing learning for more than three hundred thousand associates around the world.

Van Hooydonk told us that curiosity can lead people in two directions. On one path, they push more deeply into a particular area. They become specialists in areas they are already good at. There is certainly nothing wrong with becoming a specialist; indeed, every organization needs them. However, there can be a danger if being a specialist appeals so much to someone's ego that they are reluctant to become a novice in new areas, he said.

The second path follows where curiosity leads. People look beyond what they already know and explore new, unfamiliar areas. "A broad-based person is happy saying, 'I don't know, but let's find out together.' The higher up one goes in an organization, the more they need broad-based curiosity," Van Hooydonk told us.

Curiosity carries an extrinsic payoff, such as the reward for taking on a more skilled role. Equally important, there are intrinsic benefits, starting with the satisfaction of self-improvement.

"If you are doing the same thing for too long, your curiosity is going down. Your mastery is at peril," Van Hooydonk said. "The moment you start thinking you know it all, you are moving from confidence to arrogance. Your curiosity comes down again. Mastery needs constant feeding with challenges that become bigger and bigger."

University of California psychology professor Alison Gopnik's research on how infants learn has revealed the extent to which curiosity is a fundamental driving force in human development.[17] The problem is that most traditional schooling inhibits this innate trait. Curiosity is schooled out of us with learning that is more about test prep and fear of failure than about inquiry. In such circumstances, students become obsessed with getting the right answers versus asking their own questions.

Few people understand that this inhibition has serious effects on economies around the world. Innovation and entrepreneurship in all their forms are increasingly the real engines of economic and social progress. Companies and governments that are entrepreneurial and can innovate will thrive; those that can't will fall behind. This demands curiosity and a trial-and-error approach, where all "failures" are considered essential steps in progressing from 1.0 to 2.0. Given all the ways that schools thwart curiosity and instill fear of failure, it should come as no surprise that many large companies and organizations around the world struggle with creating cultures that support innovation and entrepreneurship.

The good news, though, is that curiosity is a muscle that can be strengthened over time. It begins with taking students' questions seriously, and we will see many examples of this in a wide variety of classrooms profiled throughout the book.

At the highest level, innovation is a form of adult disciplined play: following your curiosity, exploring, experimenting. If any organization knows about the intersection of innovation, learning, play, and passion, it's LEGO. The Danish company is the iconic maker of the colorful plastic bricks that snap together into ingenious models.

We asked Bo Stjerne Thomsen, head of educational impact for LEGO, to explain what he means by the term "hard fun." His answer provides an important piece of the puzzle for the future of learning. "Hard fun is better than just 'fun,' because it's more exciting, engaging, and rewarding to test boundaries, overcome challenges, and learn new skills," he told us.

In other words, hard fun rewards the effort. Esther Wojcicki's students were having hard fun. They were deeply engaged in learning and work that had a clear purpose.

This contrasts with "easy fun," which is a lot like eating empty calories that do not promote growth and development. Easy fun does not support the development of long-term grit—that combination of passion and perseverance—that needs to be the spine of modern educational architecture.

A New Paradigm

When fully implemented, mastery learning incorporates all the essential elements that we've described: a focus on the knowledge and skills that enable the learner to accomplish important goals, learner agency that gives students real choice and voice, deliberate practice, a growth mindset, grit, and the development of other character skills. Curiosity and hard play are vital as well. Mastery learning builds skills and competencies that make a difference beyond just one grade or satisfying graduation requirements and getting into college. Mastery learning truly lays the foundation for lifelong learning.

In schools and organizations around the world, mastery learning is taking root as a new paradigm—a focus on making sure that learners have what they need not just to get a job but also to lead a life of meaning, engagement, and purpose. In upcoming chapters, we take you to schools and adult learning environments where the practices of mastery learning and new approaches to assessment and accountability are being developed. All are engaged in what we call education R&D, research and development aimed at creating an education system that is adapted to the needs and aspirations of the twenty-first century. No one model is perfect, and few combine all the threads we have described, but there's something to be learned from each.

Before we go into these new learning environments, however, we need to more clearly understand how our current education system fails to prepare young people for work, citizenship, and personal growth and health in the twenty-first century. We need to clearly answer the question: Why change?

In the next chapter, we'll hear from someone who has become a true believer in mastery learning because of her own life experience, the failure of traditional learning to prepare her for life, and how she charted a new course for herself and her son.

CHAPTER 2

The Case for Reinventing Our Education System

I N MANY WAYS, Monique Little represents a quintessential American Horatio Alger story—in her case, a young woman who came from "humble beginnings," as she told us, and rose into the middle class with a bit of luck and a great deal of grit and determination. She grew up in a suburb of Cleveland and attended public school there. Her father was a steel mill worker who, after being laid off, became a stay-at-home dad, while her mother worked as a licensed practical nurse. What her parents wanted for her, more than anything else, was that she go to college. And so Monique was an achiever from an early age.

Today, Monique, a forty-eight-year-old African American single mom, works as a security analyst for a successful start-up car-shipping company called RunBuggy. "I'm responsible for vulnerability management and threat intelligence," she explained.

How she got there, however, is a journey into mastery learning, as Monique triumphed despite her formal education, not because of it.

Her story begins with her high school experience, where she lettered in band, was on the dance team and student council, and served as vice president of the National Honor Society and president of the Foreign Language Club. She worked part-time as a tutor. In her junior year, Monique joined INROADS, a national nonprofit organization that offers underrepresented youth a pathway from high school to college. Through INROADS, Monique was able to get an internship at a local bank directly after graduation.

Monique's alma mater, Warrensville Heights High School, currently enrolls about five hundred students, and 99 percent are Black. According to GreatSchools, an education nonprofit that assesses school quality, the high school's 2021 graduation rate was 89 percent, but only 17 percent of graduates went on to an in-state college or a vocational program, and 23 percent of those who did were required to take one or more remedial courses.[1] "The school is known more for vocational education programs than for academics," Monique said.

What the data do not tell us is what percentage of those students who started college or a vocational program actually graduated. Nationally, in the year 2000, 31 percent of eighteen-to-twenty-four-year-old Black students were enrolled in college.[2] But fewer than half of them ended up with a bachelor's degree.[3] And yet that is exactly what Monique did. She graduated from Wittenberg University, a small, Lutheran-affiliated liberal arts college in southwest Ohio, in 1997.

Monique learned skills such as teamwork and time management through her extracurricular activities, but her academic courses did not prepare her for college. She didn't even know the basics of sentence punctuation.

Monique majored in Spanish, minored in math. She appreciated that her college, with an enrollment of only 1,300 students, was "a happy little bubble" in many ways. She felt that, due to Wittenberg's diverse student body, she learned to be more open-minded. Students were able to have honest conversations about racism—conversations that she knew weren't likely to happen in a large state university.

"Wittenberg is the only place where I have had a truly open and honest conversation among white people about racism. There was a girl in our dorm who had grown up in the South. She was raised to believe that we [Black people] were different on the inside from her. One night, we all sat down in the hallway and talked. There was no yelling. There was no screaming. There was no fighting. There was no disrespect. It was just her sharing. She didn't hate us. It was just so shocking to hear because this girl was our friend. She liked us, and we liked her."

As much as Monique appreciated these aspects of college life, her list of what college didn't do for her is long, and her recounting of it was painful to hear.

"I went to a small private college with people that had gone to the best high schools in the state. We all came out with the exact same degree, into the exact same workforce that wanted us to have five years of work experience. But all we had was our four years or so of college."

Monique was on her own to acquire the life skills that could help her in the future. "I had to take the initiative and go to the career center and do mock interviews. They weren't required. Nobody tells you how to budget your money, how to balance your checkbook." And although she learned things in her classes, they often felt like checking a box. "In college, you get piles of expensive books, you work hard to pass a bunch of arbitrary exams, and then you get a degree. . . . In many ways both my high school and my college degrees were merely certificates of attendance—no skills. The only difference between high school and college is that the books are bigger. All college prepares you for is more academia."

The real-world training that was available, Monique said, was impractical for a student like her. The internships that were available "were unpaid. As a student, that's not affordable. You really don't come out with any type of work experience other than whatever you might have done in college. Any job you take has to be entry-level."

What Monique did graduate with, though, was crushing debt. "I have a ton of debt—$96,000! Wittenberg was $20,000 a year at the time. I had $4,000 a year in scholarship and some grants. I didn't understand a lot about the loans when I took them out. There wasn't anyone to teach me about finances. So, I consolidated my loans, which made everything worse, because I'm paying interest on the interest that had already accumulated." Her loans were in default at one point but have been mostly deferred for hardship. She is just now able to start paying them off.

"I still remember my exit interview for the loans. A woman came to campus to talk to us, and I'll never forget what she said. 'I just made my last loan payment!' And she smacked her hand on the counter she was so pleased. She was easily forty-five or fifty years old, and I was twenty-three. I remember thinking to myself, *So I'm going to be paying these for almost thirty years. That's a mortgage!* I cried as I walked home because it felt so impossible. Now I've reached that age, and I still have this huge debt."

Monique is hardly an exception. The total student loan debt in the United States is now more than $1.75 trillion, and that doesn't count the debt that many parents assume to enable their kids to go to college. Today, more than half of all students leave school with debt, with the average being about $29,000 per individual. Those between the ages of twenty-five and thirty-four account for about $500 billion in federal student loans, with the majority in this group owing between $10,000 and $40,000. But this is not just a problem for recent college graduates. Borrowers between the ages of thirty-five and forty-nine collectively owe more than $620 billion. This age group has the highest number of borrowers who owe more than $100,000 in loans. Student loan debt follows many into retirement and ordinarily cannot be discharged through bankruptcy. More than 2.4 million borrowers aged sixty-two or older owe a collective $98 billion in student loans.[4]

Monique explained that she graduated from college with no "marketable skills." This was certainly a significant factor in her accumulating debt over the next twenty years, as it is with many college graduates. Lacking skills, far too many young people right out of college are forced to accept low-wage jobs, and their earning potential suffers throughout their lives. However, student debt is part of the bigger picture of profound changes in the economy over the last forty years.

After graduating from college, Monique enrolled in City Year, an AmeriCorps program that brings together young people from diverse backgrounds—from high school dropouts to Ivy League grads—for a year of intensive community service. "I still carry a lot of my City Year experience with me, the whole idea that idealism can combat cynicism," Monique explained. She went on to tell us about some of the other important takeaways from her City Year experience.

"I worked alongside high school dropouts and learned that many people have so many different skills and talents that are sometimes overlooked because of their background or the choices they have made. It doesn't make them any less intelligent or any less of a hard worker or any less of a creative or innovative person. City Year taught me that, and I've not forgotten it."

Monique's first job after City Year was as a customer service representative at a bank. She was hired because of her internship at her local bank after high school. "I figured this is how you get your foot in the door. And you still get to serve people." But she soon became disillusioned. "When I look back, it was a kind of trap. Every job that I had after that was in customer service, and they all operated in the same way. You have all these metrics. They tell you that if you meet these metrics, then you can become a team lead or post out to another job. But the rules change a little bit here and there," and advancing is not as easy as it seems.

Monique spent the next twenty years moving from one call center to the next, always making $17 or $18 an hour, never getting promoted. Her bosses focused only on the metrics. "How many calls did you take today? How long were you on the call? They never looked at the surveys that my customers left. They didn't look at the fact that I did things correctly. The things that I valued—serving my customers—they didn't seem to think were very important." In this environment, Monique could not move up the ladder, but she didn't know where else to go. "I felt that the only job skill I had was that I was bilingual. And where is the best place to use that skill? In a call center. I didn't know how to gain any other skills."

Monique was in therapy at the time, and she and her therapist would spend the last fifteen minutes of every hour session looking for jobs. In one session, she mentioned that she used to like computers and originally was a computer science major. Her therapist said that her nephew had completed a program called Per Scholas.

Per Scholas changed Monique's career and life path not only because of what she learned—in-demand technical skills, as well as critical thinking and creative problem-solving—but more importantly *how* she learned. Per Scholas takes a mastery learning approach. It aims to bring every student to competency and to do so with a high rate of success.

Founded in 1995 in South Bronx, New York, Per Scholas is a nonprofit that provides tuition-free technology training to unemployed or underemployed adults for careers as information technology (IT) professionals. It offers a twelve-to-fifteen-week intensive program centered around a variety of courses that lead to different industry-recognized certifications in IT. In addition to this technical training, about 25 percent of the curriculum is focused on career coaching and career development skills: communication, working in team settings, engaging with peers. It currently serves about four thousand students a year in nineteen different locations around the country and has graduated nineteen thousand students since its inception. About 65 percent of the students are men, and 85 percent are people of color. Many come from economically disadvantaged communities.

We spoke at length with Plinio Ayala, who has been president and CEO of Per Scholas since 2003, to learn more about the program. "The story is very similar for a lot of our students," he explained. "Whether they have a high school diploma, some college, or even a college degree, what they have learned in their education experience is not translating to relevant skills that lead to a job. . . . What we're hearing from folks with some college background is 'I learned more in twelve weeks in your courses than I did in four years of college.' I think it is a failure of our education system."

Ayala went on to describe that failure. "Traditional education institutions are not built to work with the corporate sector to fully understand what it is that they need, and are not nimble enough to adapt curricula to stay relevant to all that's changing in technology. . . . That there should be alternative pathways to postsecondary education is a mindset that we are trying to create among public officials, policymakers, and investors."

Most for-profit job training programs have an extraordinarily high dropout rate and often do not teach the skills that lead to a better job. The Per Scholas graduation rate is better than 85 percent, and most graduates land good jobs shortly after graduation, because its courses offer a great deal of hands-on experience. Even more important, Per Scholas continues to offer job counseling and upskilling courses for two years after their students graduate. For Ayala, the goal of the program shouldn't merely be to get graduates into an entry-level IT job that pays $50,000 a year. He wants his graduates to go on to better and better paying jobs so that their meager life savings are not wiped out by a disaster—such as another pandemic—and so that they can contribute to wealth creation in their communities.

"The truth is that I was poor," Ayala told us. "I grew up with two meals a day, if we were lucky. Electricity getting shut off because we couldn't pay it. It was really bad. But at the time I didn't know better. I thought that was the way life was. Now I know better. I know that in a lot of these communities, the opportunities just don't exist. You get all of these Americans, millions of them, waking up every day, saying, 'I'm just going to try and find something that could change my future,' and they can't find it."

Monique graduated from Per Scholas in 2018. "I got a college degree in five years. I did Per Scholas in ten weeks, and there is absolutely no comparison to the level of learning that I got from Per Scholas. I feel better about completing the program than I do about my college degree." Monique compared the experience to boot camp; she learned not just important job skills but also about the breadth and strength of her own abilities. "Per Scholas changed my life, and my son watched it happen. He saw where we were before. He sees where we are now. That's my favorite part, because he knows that if he decides he doesn't want to go to college, there are other things that he can do and still be successful."

The Bigger Picture

Monique did everything that our society says she should do to have a good job and a good life. She worked incredibly hard in high school, attended a good college, and earned her bachelor's degree. And yet, were it not for Per Scholas, she would likely still be marginally employed, stuck in a dead-end job, struggling financially and emotionally. Is hers a unique or unusual story?

As of July 2024, the unemployment rate of recent college graduates was 4.6 percent.[5] But the more important number is the percentage of college graduates who are *underemployed*. The Federal Reserve Bank of New York defines underemployment as "working in a job that typically does not require a bachelor's degree"—for example, working in a call center, a job that pays marginal wages. As of June 2024, it was estimated that 40.5 percent of recent college graduates were underemployed in the United States.[6] A recent study that tracked the career paths of college graduates found that 52 percent were in jobs that did not make use of their credentials. And most remained underemployed even a decade after graduation.[7]

Underemployment is not a problem only for recent college graduates. According to data cited by the Federal Reserve Bank of New York, the underemployment rate for *all* college graduates ages twenty-two to sixty-five has remained between 32 percent and 34 percent since 1990.[8] One reason this underemployment hasn't negatively impacted the overall economy is because parents are picking up the slack. Recent research revealed that two-thirds of US adults receive parental financial support into their forties.[9]

What's gone wrong? Why is a college degree no longer a guaranteed ticket to a good job and the middle class? We have already pointed out that far too many college grads go into the workforce with no marketable skills. But there is an additional answer to this question, one that is relatively obvious for anyone who's followed trends in college tuition costs versus salary increases. For the forty years between 1980 and 2019, the cost of college increased 169 percent, while the median salaries of four-year college graduates ages twenty-two to twenty-seven during that same period rose only 19 percent.[10]

These data explain the squeeze in which many college graduates find themselves: huge student loan debt while earning an income that barely enables them to do much more than pay the monthly interest. The millennial generation has been pejoratively referred to as "the Peter Pan Generation" who "refuse to grow up: No mortgage. No marriage. No children. No career plan."[11] But the simple fact is that increasing numbers of young people simply can't afford the things that older middle-class Americans take for granted as a part of the good life.

It turns out that Monique's story is typical for many her age. What makes her story different is that she found a way out.

A Historical Context

The squeeze we're describing does not explain why so many college graduates have been underemployed since at least 1990, earning salaries that do not even qualify them for the middle class. It turns out that the underemployment trend is a symptom of much larger changes. To learn why so many seemingly well-educated Americans are not thriving, we need to better understand the fundamental transformations in our economy that have taken place over the last forty years. These broader trends make so much of the education people are receiving obsolete.

One fundamental change is globalization. Thomas Friedman brilliantly depicted the impact of globalization on the US economy in his 2005 bestseller, *The World Is Flat*. He describes a world where a growing number of countries have highly skilled workers who are at least as well educated as those in the United States. American workers, both white-collar and blue-collar, must now compete with workers in other countries for good-paying jobs.

For much of the twentieth century, the United States had the most highly educated workforce in the world. After the devastation of World War II, few countries were able to compete economically with the United States. This one simple fact goes a long way toward explaining the dramatic rise of the US middle class between 1950 and 1975. But near the end of the twentieth century and increasingly into the twenty-first century, much of the world has caught up with the United States and even surpassed it, in terms of both worker productivity and a highly educated labor force.

Globalization has two distinct elements. The first is the exporting of good-paying manufacturing jobs from the United States to countries that pay lower wages, a trend known as offshoring. In the forty years between 1980 and 2020, manufacturing jobs as a percentage of the total US labor market declined from 22 percent to 9 percent. In 1979, which was the peak of manufacturing employment in the United States, there were nineteen million people who had factory jobs. By 2020, that number had dropped to about 12.8 million, a 35 percent decline.[12]

What happened to these displaced factory workers? One answer is that many have simply dropped out of the labor market altogether, as Monique's dad did. Others have found minimum-wage jobs in the service sector: grocery clerks, warehouse employees, Walmart greeters. A growing number of economists and analysts argue that the recent political turmoil in the United States and around the world is directly attributable to the anger and despair that these displaced workers feel. Many in this group believe that their countries' leaders have ignored their plight.[13]

People who have good-paying jobs have benefited greatly from the lower costs of a wide variety of consumer goods, which are now made in China, India, Vietnam, and elsewhere. But the impact of globalization on young people who have earned a high school diploma or have some college education has been severe. Median wages for young adults between twenty-two and twenty-seven who have less than a college degree have declined by 12 percent since 1980.[14]

A second characteristic of globalization is increasingly impacting our college graduates. The advent of the Internet, with fiber-optic cables moving data at the speed of light around the world, and the increasing importance of computer and workflow software have combined to enable a global white-collar workforce to compete with US college graduates. To give a couple of examples, your accountant might be local, but much of the behind-the-scenes tax preparation work is more likely to be done in Bangalore than in Boston. And while your X-rays are taken locally, they could very well be read overnight in any country that has lower wages than the United States and a skilled workforce, with the results electronically delivered to your physician the next morning. Jobs in call centers, like the ones where Monique worked, have been replaced by customer support centers in low-wage areas in India and the Philippines.

Different Skills for the Future

Automation and AI are expected to grow exponentially in the coming decades. The breakthroughs in AI are a consequence of finally cracking the code of how to make computer networks learn, gather, and organize knowledge in substantially the same way that college graduates do. The disruption in the labor market will be more severe than what we've seen over the last forty years—likely more transformational than ever before in history.

Economists continue to argue over the extent to which the lost jobs will be replaced by an equal number of new jobs, as was the case during the industrial era. But even if this holds true, the newly created jobs will require very different levels and types of skills. For example, designing, programming, and repairing robots will be great jobs in the future. Prompt engineering—developing and curating content using large language models like GPT-4—was a discipline that did not exist before 2023. These new job categories will be highly skilled jobs that will demand a radically different education.

While the examples cited above are obvious and predictable, it is much more uncertain to what extent—and how—most white-collar jobs could be affected. According to an August 2023 Gallup survey, 72 percent of Fortune 500 corporate human resource officers foresee AI replacing jobs in their organization *in the next three years.*[15] Predictions on the percentage of both blue- and white-collar jobs that will be lost to machines in the coming years range from 9 to 47 percent.[16]

In a world where infinite amounts of knowledge are available with just a few keystrokes, white-collar professionals may find that all the knowledge they've spent years acquiring no longer gives them a competitive advantage over computers. Mastery of skills such as collaboration, complex and creative problem-solving, and critical thinking may be the only guarantee for a job in the future.

New Criteria for Employment

With the economy's need for highly skilled employees, the criteria for employment are rapidly evolving. For the last seventy-five years or more, a bachelor's degree was considered evidence of employability for almost any white-collar job, other than in a specialized profession like law or medicine. The running joke in HR offices was that no one ever got fired for hiring a Harvard graduate.

Increasingly, that's no longer true. Google is an interesting case study in this evolution. Since its founding in 1998, Google has prided itself on only hiring the people they consider to be the smartest in the world. Believing that elite universities were the places to find the smartest talent, they tended to prefer interviewing students who had graduated from Ivy League colleges. They then offered jobs to the ones who had the highest GPAs and test scores and who could give clever answers to brainteaser questions like, How many golf balls can you fit into a 747?

Laszlo Bock was senior vice president of people operations and a member of Google's management team from 2006 to 2016, a time when the company grew from six thousand to seventy-two thousand employees. He began to look into the performance data of employees who had been hired using these criteria. In a 2013 *New York Times* column, Adam Bryant asked Bock what he'd learned: "One of the things we've seen from all our data crunching is that G.P.A.'s are worthless as a criteria for hiring, and test scores are worthless. . . . Google famously used to ask everyone for a transcript and G.P.A.'s and test scores, but we don't anymore. . . . What's interesting is the proportion of people without any college education at Google has increased over time as well."[17] As of 2021, only a little over two-thirds of Google employees have a college degree.[18]

By the time Bock left Google in 2016, the company was relying almost exclusively on a series of structured interviews to make hiring decisions, and they continue to do so today. They developed a common rubric that was used by all interviewers and asked questions like, "Describe a time where you've solved a difficult analytic problem." Bock recently told us that there was also far more diversity in the Google workforce as result of the changes in hiring practices, and that these workers were also much more productive than those hired by the old standard.

So, if a college degree is no longer a criterion for employment at Google, what is? What skills do you need to get a job there now? That was the question Thomas Friedman put to Bock in a *New York Times* interview in 2014.

"The number one thing we look for is general cognitive ability, and it's not I.Q. It's learning ability," Bock replied. "It's the ability to process on the fly. It's the ability to pull together disparate bits of information. We assess that using structured behavioral interviews that we validate to make sure they're predictive." These are precisely the skills that Monique learned at Per Scholas.

The second area, Bock said, is leadership, specifically what he called "emergent leadership," as opposed to more traditional forms of leadership, such as being president of a club at school. "What we care about is, when faced with a problem and you're a member of a team, do you, at the appropriate time, step in and lead. And just as critically, do you step back and stop leading, do you let someone else? Because what's critical to be an effective leader in this environment is you have to be willing to relinquish power."

In his conversation with Friedman, Bock also addressed the importance of displaying "ownership"—that is, taking responsibility to step in and solve a problem, while also having the humility of stepping back when others have better ideas. He called it "intellectual humility," without which people are unable to learn. That can be a fatal flaw for "successful bright people [who] rarely experience failure, and so they don't learn how to learn from that failure."

The last point that Bock made was in some ways the most surprising. He told Friedman that the least important attribute Google looks for is content knowledge and expertise. He told Friedman that if someone "has high cognitive ability, is innately curious, willing to learn and has emergent leadership skills," they can readily figure out what they need to know. Even more important, such individuals will often come up with fresh solutions that may not occur to those who have perceived themselves "experts" for some time and believe they already know everything that's important in their field. True top performers are humble, curious, and constantly looking for ways to learn and improve.

Bock was one of the first senior executives in a major corporation to look for evidence of competencies, rather than mere credentials, in hiring. According to a November 2022 report from the National Association of Colleges and Employers (NACE), the percentage of employers screening by college GPA as a part of the application process plummeted from 73 percent in 2018 to 37 percent in 2022. What do they look for now? "More than six in 10 of employers responding to NACE's Job Outlook 2023 survey are seeking evidence of a candidate's abilities to solve problems and to work in a team."[19] And a growing number of employers are no longer sorting out job applicants who do not have a four-year college degree. Here are just a few examples.[20]

- In 2016, Accenture launched an apprenticeship program, and 80 percent of the 1,200 hires from that program lacked a four-year degree. Now the company has expanded the program and aims to fill 20 percent of its US entry-level jobs—from application development and cybersecurity to cloud and platform engineering— through apprenticeships.
- In 2021, Dell Technologies began to focus on hiring from community colleges. It now hires students who have completed associate degrees, apprenticeships, or certificate programs.

- Bank of America no longer requires college degrees for most of its entry-level jobs.
- In 2022, Maryland became the first state to no longer require a four-year college degree for most state government jobs. As of June 2024, nineteen additional states had followed suit.

Creativity—rather than a college credential—has become the new competitive advantage. In an article for the World Economic Forum, tech entrepreneur Scott Belsky writes, "As our adoption of automation increases, creativity is set to become ever-more important" because it is a "uniquely human trait that no algorithm can replace."[21] In the World Economic Forum's *Future of Jobs Report 2023*, employers ranked creative thinking second only to analytic thinking as the most needed workplace skill, and they expect that the need for creative thinking will continue to grow as more analytic tasks are done by AI.[22]

When employers talk about the need for creativity, they are not suggesting that every employee needs to be artistic. They have a much broader definition in mind. In *Forbes*, author Amy Blaschka explained why creativity is the number one so-called soft skill employers now seek: "Creativity is the ability to perceive the world in new ways, to find hidden patterns, to make connections between seemingly disparate things, and to generate innovative solutions. . . . Every role at every level can use soft skills to solve problems in innovative ways. It simply requires adjusting your mindset to see the possibilities and allowing your curiosity to take over."[23]

Resilience, flexibility, and agility ranked third in importance—behind analytic and creative thinking—in the World Economic Forum report. The report summarizes these skills under the heading of "self-efficacy."[24] We look at these skills as essential aspects of mastery. You really cannot become proficient in anything important without them. They are essential not only for work but also for civic life and for personal health and well-being.

To summarize: Employers will increasingly be dependent upon a new set of cognitive and character skills that are far beyond the scope of what happens in most high schools and colleges today. This trend will continue to accelerate as AI is able to perform a greater variety of complex tasks that formerly required individuals with a bachelor's to do. The specific descriptions of the skills needed vary from one individual or company to the next, but all can be broadly summarized as variations of the four Cs: critical thinking, communication, collaboration, and creative thinking. Add to that character skills: the self-efficacy described in the World Economic Forum report, as well as other traits of character such as a sense of agency, grit, humility, trustworthiness, and empathy.

There are two reasons for the fundamental misalignment between the education most people receive versus what young people will need to get and keep a good job today and into the future. One problem is how learning is measured, and the other is what competencies are considered essential. An education system that prioritizes the acquisition of academic content knowledge over skills and primarily measures knowledge retention with machine-scored standardized tests simply does not prepare our students for work in the twenty-first century. Efforts to reform American education for the last century have served to make both problems worse.

The Failures of Three Education Reform Movements

Traditionally, the purpose of education has been to transmit a common body of knowledge and basic literacy and numeracy skills. When only a few people in a society were educated and the body of knowledge was constant and limited, things were simple. Teachers knew what pupils needed to learn, and in small learning settings they could tell whether their pupils had learned it.

Then, in the nineteenth century, the Industrial Revolution remade the world. Knowledge and populations exploded. Scale complicated everything. Systems had to be developed for mass education, and the architects of the new systems looked to industrial methods of standardization as a solution to the problem of designing learning for the masses. Three forms of standardization emerged: standard curriculum taught, standard time spent in school, and standard tests given.

The first problem was content, what to teach at scale. The Industrial Revolution created new types of white-collar work, which called for new specialized skills like stenography, bookkeeping, and mechanical drawing. High schools began offering courses on some of these new employment-ready skills, in addition to the usual nineteenth-century classes in Latin, Greek, English, the modern languages, and the natural sciences. Different high schools offered different courses; a student in Denver might be learning something vastly different from a student in Boston. For colleges, this was chaos.

In 1892, the National Education Association (NEA) convened ten university presidents and high school principals (famously called the Committee of Ten), chaired by Charles Eliot, the president of Harvard, to make sense of what schools should teach to prepare young people for life and especially for college.

The committee agreed that all high school students should receive the same education, essentially a classical academic liberal arts education that prepared them for college regardless of whether they planned to attend. This included a standard sequence of courses, pared down from the existing hodgepodge of classical disciplines and vocational offerings, where learning would be determined via standardized units of time for both high school and college course credits. In short, the committee doubled down on the knowledge of the past as a response to a rapidly changing present.

The second problem was how to measure learning at scale. The unit of measurement they landed on was time: seat time served. A

Carnegie unit, the standardized unit for courses in high school, or the credit hour, the college equivalent, are both measurements of time spent sitting in a classroom. A Carnegie unit is supposed to represent a total of 120 hours spent in a classroom learning in one subject. To graduate from high school, students need a minimum of fourteen Carnegie units: four years of English units and three years each in math and science, plus history and foreign language. After serving the prescribed amount of seat time for a high school or college course credit, students are then tested and graded on their capacity to retain the information to which they've been exposed. This system of quantifying learning has been in place in the United States since the turn of the twentieth century, and variations of a time-based, memory-intensive system are widely used around the world.

This design became widespread when the newly established Carnegie Foundation for the Advancement of Teaching, whose board was also chaired by Eliot, created a fund in 1906 to provide retirement pensions for college professors. For colleges to be eligible to participate in this faculty retirement fund, which came to be known as TIAA-CREF, they had to agree to use the newly established standardized units of time for admission to college and for college course credit. They also had to agree to use the recommended course of study for high school students who sought admissions to college. By 1910, nearly all secondary schools in the United States used the Carnegie unit as a measure of coursework, and most now taught the same academic subjects in the same sequence.[25]

Unlike the time-based units of learning—which remain unchanged in our education system today, both in the United States and globally—the Committee of Ten's content design began to unravel early on. The committee had been convened to create order out of chaos at a time when high school enrollment was less than 2 percent of eligible young people. By 1920, though, high school enrollment was over 30 percent.[26] With immigration and population growth, the passage of child labor laws, and the hopes of parents looking for a better future for their children, ever more students were enrolling in high school, sitting in their seats for the prescribed amount of time and learning a classical academic curriculum that didn't necessarily prepare them to succeed. In the 1910s, education reformers went back to the drawing board to define the purpose of secondary education: What did young people need to learn, in what order, and to what ends?

The NEA convened a new committee, the Commission on the Reorganization of Secondary Education. In 1918 it issued an influential report, the *Cardinal Principles of Secondary Education*, that laid out the design of the comprehensive high school we know so well today. In many ways the *Cardinal Principles* report was forward-thinking; it explored how school could support young people in developing interests around work, citizenship, character, and even leisure. It argued for interest-based learning and differentiation, as well as a common foundation for all students. It proposed that school become a place for human development and the application of the principles of psychology to pedagogy. It suggested that students have the choice to explore vocations and be able to switch from one path to another, and it argued that vocational learning should be allowed to lead to college admission.[27]

You'll see many of these ideas in the schools we describe later in this book, schools committed to developing the cognitive and character skills that enable young people to become competent, thriving adults. These schools today are finally trying to fulfill some of the discarded aspirations the *Cardinal Principles* issued almost a century earlier.

What Went Wrong?

The *Cardinal Principles* report came out at a time when eugenics and other ideologies of superiority were dominant, and when World War I enabled a mass standardized testing industry that could be marshaled to support those prejudices. IQ tests were first developed by Alfred Binet for the French government when it created mandatory public education. These tests sought to determine which students would be "slow" in class, where slowness was seen as indicating lesser intelligence (but still better than "sick," which meant the student needed to be placed in an asylum). While Binet cautioned that motivation and other contextual factors should be taken into consideration when administering IQ tests, others were less careful. During World War I, governments adapted the test to classify millions of soldiers, and then psychologists at Stanford University turned it into a general intelligence test used to predict cognitive abilities.[28]

School administrators embraced the Stanford-Binet and other cognitive assessment tests to create the differentiation the *Cardinal Principles* called for. But instead of high schools where students could choose their own path through academic and vocational learning and human development, the comprehensive high school became a place for tracking, where students were placed in separate and unequal pathways in the same building—or in fully segregated buildings—based on biased characterizations of their cognitive abilities.[29] The most rigorous liberal arts academic pathway was reserved for one set of students, often identified as "gifted." A mass version of that pathway—but much more focused on rote learning, memorization, and recall rather than skills development—served the bulk of students. Practical vocational education was for outlier groups, while still others were placed into the lowest track, "special education." These tracks often coincided with race, class, and gender; middle-class white students dominated the gifted classes, while working-class students of color were shunted to vocational or special education. Education reform had failed once again.

We now know that time is a poor proxy for learning. The amount of time required to learn something varies widely from one individual to the next. A time-based system that demands all students march in lockstep to arrive at the same result at the same time leaves many students behind—students who might otherwise be able to master the course material, if given more time. As far back as 1971, education researchers such as Benjamin Bloom have proven that nearly all students can attain high levels of achievement if given adequate time and appropriate learning conditions.[30]

We also know that rote learning—prioritizing the acquisition and retention of academic content knowledge over skills development—doesn't prepare students for productive work, active and informed civic life, and personal growth, health, and well-being. The new education curriculum prioritized knowledge that was easy to measure with standardized tests over essential skills that require human judgment to assess.

We now understand the biases implicit (and sometimes explicit) in the world of IQ tests and other standardized assessments such as the SAT. However, with the growing demands for increased education accountability over the past forty years, the use of computer-scored, multiple-choice standardized tests and end-of-course exams for high school students has become even more widespread.

As the twentieth century marched on, the forces of change—what the Committee of Ten and the Commission on the Reorganization of Secondary Education were convened to respond to—continued to accelerate. Mass education became even more massive. In 1960, 41 percent of Americans were high school graduates, but by 1980, 74 percent were. As more students completed schooling and took standardized tests, some scores declined.[31] Meanwhile, other nations like Japan, South Korea, and China were growing their manufacturing base, creating competition for the United States. New technologies like computers began to shift the skills needed to succeed.

Modern Attempts at Education Reform

In 1983, yet another commission was convened, this time by Terrel H. Bell, the secretary of education. This group produced an alarming report, *A Nation at Risk*, about the disconnect between what our students were learning in schools and the need for a much more highly skilled labor force. From its first few paragraphs, the report was inflammatory and apocalyptic.

> Our Nation is at risk. Our once unchallenged preeminence in commerce, industry, science, and technological innovation is being overtaken by competitors throughout the world. . . . The educational foundations of our society are presently being eroded by a rising tide of mediocrity that threatens our very future as a Nation and a people. What was unimaginable a generation ago has begun to occur—others are matching and surpassing our educational attainments. . . . If an unfriendly foreign power had attempted to impose on America the mediocre educational performance that exists today, we might well have viewed it as an act of war. . . . We have, in effect, been committing an act of unthinking, unilateral educational disarmament.[32]

Commission members correctly recognized the problem of increased competition from countries around the world that were now educating a highly skilled labor force. But they totally misunderstood the root cause of the problem. They believed that high school education had become diluted, with too many students enrolled in vocational programs, general education courses, and health and physical education classes that were not academically demanding. They called for a return to a more strictly academic curriculum and advocated that students should be assigned more homework and have a longer school year.

Like the Committee of Ten ninety years before them, the commission prescribed educational reforms that essentially called for more academic "rigor," defined as more difficult courses, more homework, more required courses, more standardized testing, more accountability, and a reduction in choice and skills-based courses. Efforts to reform education in the forty years since then have continued to advocate—and increasingly mandate—the same solutions.

The commission's report gave rise to the so-called standards-based education reform movement. After a series of education summits involving meetings with governors and corporate leaders in the late 1980s and into the 1990s, states adopted legislation that called for high school students to take more academic courses to receive a diploma, including at least three years of math and science, and all course content became increasingly standardized. Standards-based reform efforts accelerated with the passage of the No Child Left Behind legislation in 2001. To receive federal dollars for education, this new law required states to regularly test all students at selected grade levels on literacy and math and to make the results public.

Finally, in 2009, with money that was a part of the American Recovery and Reinvestment Act, the US Department of Education developed a $4.35 billion competitive grant program, known as Race to the Top. As a condition for receiving grant money, states were now required to have clearly defined academic standards and use test scores to hold teachers and principals accountable for school improvements.

So, what do we have to show for these education reforms? While the tests currently used for accountability do not measure the knowledge and skills that matter most, they are nevertheless the coin of the realm that politicians and the media rely on to determine the effectiveness of education reform. Even by these flawed metrics, we have accomplished nothing in forty years of efforts to increase academic rigor. According to the National Assessment of Educational Progress—tests that are periodically administered to sample student populations across the country—reading scores have only increased 2.3 percent since the publication of *A Nation at Risk* in 1983. (And that's excluding the dip in scores that took place in 2022 because of the COVID disruptions.) Math improvements were only marginally better, showing a 10 percent improvement over forty years.[33]

One of the rationales for education reform—and especially for the passage of the 2001 No Child Left Behind Act—was to establish accountability systems that would pressure schools to address the achievement gaps between economically advantaged and disadvantaged students, across racial categories and students with disabilities. But these gaps have persisted over the past fifty years. By the end of high school, students in affluent communities are three to four years ahead of the most disadvantaged students.[34]

As a country, the United States has squandered billions of dollars on annual testing programs that do nothing to close the achievement gap. Meanwhile, proven programs that do make a real difference in closing this gap—quality universal preschools, better teacher preparation, more early interventions for struggling students, smaller classes, better access to counseling, so-called wraparound school programs that offer medical and social services to struggling families, and more support for disadvantaged students entering postsecondary programs—remain underfunded or nonexistent.

The Human Costs of Failed Reforms

The human costs of these reform efforts have been very high. According to a recent study, teachers' job satisfaction is at the lowest level in fifty years. The percentage of teachers who feel that the stress of their job is worth it has fallen from 81 percent to 42 percent in the last fifteen years. Interest in the teaching profession among high school seniors and college freshmen has declined 50 percent since the 1990s, and the proportion of college graduates who go into teaching is at a fifty-year low.[35] About 13 percent of teachers quit or move every year, and it is estimated that between 40 and 50 percent of new teachers leave the profession within five years.[36] Teacher evaluations tied to student test score results, salaries that haven't kept up with inflation, controversies around mask mandates, school disruptions due to COVID, and now culture wars in communities and school board meetings over what should be taught continue to take a very heavy toll on teachers.

Teachers aren't the only ones suffering. The impact on students' motivation for learning may be the most serious consequence of forty years of educational reform. According to a national Gallup poll, the longer students spend in our K–12 schools, the more disengaged they become in their academic work. While 75 percent of fifth graders report being engaged in their schoolwork, that number declines every year thereafter until reaching a low point for eleventh graders at just 32 percent.[37] And since the COVID pandemic, it appears that more and more students can't find a reason to go to school. According to a 2023 *New York Times* editorial, "More than a quarter of students were chronically absent (meaning they have missed more than 10% of the school year) in the 2021–22 school year, up from 15 percent before the pandemic."[38]

The absentee problem is worst in high-poverty schools, where "nearly 70% experienced chronic absenteeism in 2021–22, up from 25% before the pandemic."[39] However, student disengagement is a problem even in high schools where more-privileged students understand that how well they perform will directly affect their college choices. New Trier Township High School in Illinois is a highly competitive public school that serves some of the country's most affluent communities. According to the same *Times* editorial, chronic absenteeism at New Trier "got worse by class, reaching nearly 38 percent among its seniors."

A 2013 study conducted by Jerusha Conner and Denise Pope looked at levels of academic engagement among students attending fifteen so-called high-achieving secondary schools, where nearly all graduates go on to college. They found that two-thirds of students at these schools "are not regularly 'fully engaged'" in their academic schoolwork; that is, they do not regularly report high levels of affective, behavioral, and cognitive engagement. Although most students report working hard, few find their schoolwork engaging, and many see no real value in what they are required to learn. According to Conner and Pope, this lack of full engagement is associated with more frequent school stress and higher rates of cheating.[40]

One of us, Tony, has conducted numerous focus groups with young adults who are three to five years out of high school. He asks them in what ways high school prepared them the most and the least well for whatever they are doing now. The majority of students have told him that time spent in high school classrooms was time wasted. A young woman who had attended one of the most academically prestigious public high schools in her state echoed Monique's complaint about her high school when she said, "The one thing I needed high school to teach me was how to write, and they totally failed." Another said, "I usually forgot the stuff I had to study for tests in high school the next day, but it didn't really matter because we started over with the same course content in my freshman year of college." However, many students greatly appreciated their out-of-classroom experiences. "The high school learning experience that I truly value was my time spent as the editor of the school newspaper," one young man said. "I learned how to work on a team there, how to meet deadlines, and how to edit and write."

Most high school students today are under tremendous pressure from parents and teachers to achieve, to work harder. In December 2021, Surgeon General Vivek Murthy warned of the "devastating effects" of the mental health crisis among the young. According to Murthy, the suicide rate for Americans ages ten to nineteen jumped by 40 percent from 2001 to 2019, while emergency room visits for self-harm rose by 88 percent. He went on to tell the *New York Times*, "Young people tell me they feel caught up in hustle culture . . . that they felt that they were being asked to chase certain objectives— getting a job with a fancy title, making a lot of money, becoming famous, acquiring power. And not only did many of them say that they were exhausted, but they weren't sure that was going to bring them happiness."[41]

Our young people know their education is failing them. In the spring of 2023, Gallup surveyed more than two thousand students in fifth through twelfth grade at public, charter, and private schools and asked them to grade their schools on a range of issues. Students gave an average grade of a C+ for how well their schools teach about potential careers, foster excitement about learning, and teach in ways that adapt to their learning needs. Schools also earned an average grade of C+ for how well they support mental health.[42]

Few young people see any purpose in what they are learning. They don't see a connection between their schoolwork and their future. The nature of most high school academic work revolves around memorizing copious amounts of information for the sole purpose of passing a seemingly endless array of tests, and the increased number of required academic course credits has left students with far fewer choices of elective courses. With more homework and more required academic courses, students also have much less time for the extracurricular activities that do promote active engagement and encourage the development of cognitive and character skills: sports, the arts, school clubs and publications, and volunteering in the community.

What About Civic Engagement?

Thus far in this chapter, we have focused on how our education system has failed to ensure that young people leave school with the skills they need to get and keep good-paying jobs and the ways in which education reform efforts have not addressed this problem. But lack of preparation for work is not the only outcome that concerns us. Developing students' interest in and capacity for civic engagement is, in our view, an equally important education outcome.

Thomas Ehrlich has served in the federal government during the administrations of six presidents and as president of Indiana University, provost of the University of Pennsylvania, and dean of Stanford

Law School. He has published numerous books and is considered one of today's leading authorities on civic engagement. Ehrlich defines civic engagement as "working to make a difference in the civic life of our communities and developing the combination of knowledge, skills, values, and motivation to make that difference. It means promoting the quality of life in a community, through both political and non-political processes."[43]

Ehrlich goes on to explain: "A morally and civically responsible individual recognizes himself or herself as a member of a larger social fabric and therefore considers social problems to be at least partly his or her own; such an individual is willing to see the moral and civic dimensions of issues, to make and justify informed moral and civic judgments, and to take action when appropriate."[44]

Traditionally, this category of learning has come under the heading of "civics education." Robert Putnam, author of the bestseller *Bowling Alone: The Collapse and Revival of American Community* and another leading authority on civic engagement, explained to us in a recent interview that civics education had its roots in the Progressive Era. "It was a big part of the conception of how Americans should be raised," he said.

Putnam went on to say that the "high-water mark" for civics education was in the late 1950s. He recalled for us growing up at that time in Port Clinton, Ohio, and "taking the course Problems in Democracy, learning about public speaking, and shadowing the mayor." However, during the Vietnam War era, distrust in government became widespread, and critics of civics education claimed that such courses were mere government brainwashing. Required courses in civics education declined steadily through the 1960s.

The pendulum began to swing back in the latter part of the twentieth century, but with the increased pressures and testing for literacy and numeracy, today there is far less time being spent in schools on civics education and social studies than was the case twenty-five years ago. According to a 2022 report from the American

Bar Association, "This neglect of social studies and civics is directly linked to decades-long education policies at the state and federal levels mandating testing of basic literacy (reading and math) through funding incentives. Specifically, and as a direct consequence of education policy, civic education has been chronically underfunded, both federally and locally. Currently, the federal government invests a mere 5 cents per K–12 student [on civics education] compared to $54 per student for science, technology, engineering, and mathematics." The report goes on to declare, "The evidence makes clear that decades of decline in both the quality and the quantity of civic education have contributed significantly to the discord, dysfunction, and widespread disengagement plaguing our nation today."[45]

In recent years, some states—now nineteen and counting—have tried to address this shortcoming by mandating yet another test that high school students must pass to graduate: a multiple-choice civics exam based on the citizenship test that all immigrants take to become US citizens. The state tests draw from a battery of one hundred civics and history questions that the US Citizenship and Immigration Services uses. The tests are entirely focused on memorizing answers to questions like:

- How many amendments does the Constitution have?
- How many US senators are there?
- What is the name of the current president of the United States?
- What is one reason colonialists came to America?
- Who lived in America before the colonialists arrived?
- Who wrote the Declaration of Independence?[46]

Critics of this approach to civics education argue that the test does nothing to assess comprehension of the information and creates a further barrier to high school graduation.[47] We think the problem is far worse. Students who take such tests don't necessarily know how laws are made or what the Bill of Rights stands for. Nor do they have to show understanding of some of the complex issues facing us today, such as climate change and economic and social inequities. Such tests tell us nothing about whether students feel some responsibility to their communities or plan to volunteer. And because the high school curriculum is so disempowering for most students, with few opportunities for choice and voice, many also lack a sense of agency or efficacy that would enable them to act effectively and responsibly in their communities.

We asked Monique, whom you met earlier in this chapter, how her high school had prepared her for civic life. At that time, the state of Ohio required all seniors to take a civics class. Monique doesn't remember anything she learned (despite liking the teacher), but she does remember that registering to vote was a requirement of the class.

More than any lesson learned in a classroom, a far bigger influence on Monique's involvement in civics and local government was her mother. "She was a driving force in teaching me the importance of being involved in the community. When I was a teenager, she was volunteering for a candidate for city council, and my friends and I went door-to-door for him. I didn't know anything about politics or the city council then. I just knew that my mom and dad voted in every single election. They always talked about how important it was."

Her sense of civic engagement was further strengthened at Wittenberg, where students were required to complete a certain number of community service hours to graduate. "Wittenberg's motto is, 'Having light, we pass it on to others.' So we were sort of indoctrinated to be kind to people, to care about other people. But it's a Lutheran university." Only about 9 percent of all college students attend a religiously affiliated college, and only a very small percentage of colleges mandate any form of community service as a graduation requirement.[48]

Her college experience, as well as the example of her mom, influenced Monique's decision to do community service with City Year right after college. "I like helping people," she said simply.

Following in her mother's footsteps, Monique teaches her son about civic engagement. "I don't know how to make children be civically engaged beyond making them care about somebody other than themselves," Monique said. She takes her son with her to the polls and makes sure he knows why she does it; she also helps him understand the importance of reading and researching ballot questions. Finally, she has started encouraging her son to do community service. "I want it to become a habit for him." The skills required for civic engagement are the same as those needed for productive work in the twenty-first century. To be a contributing and engaged member of a community, you need to think critically and creatively, work collaboratively, communicate effectively. But these intellectual qualities, while necessary, are not sufficient. You need character skills. You must "lead with humility," as Laszlo Bock said. You also must care, as Monique explained so well. Both are aspects of mastery.

Education for Personal Health and Well-Being

There is general agreement that education should also help students cultivate the knowledge, skills, and habits they need to lead a healthy life, though the focus has traditionally been on physical rather than mental health. The first public school physical education requirement dates back to 1855. Now nearly every state requires at least some physical education, though the amount of time spent in these classes has been cut significantly due to budget constraints and the perceived need to spend more time on math and reading to boost test scores. Sadly, in most schools these days, what gets tested is all that gets taught.

Like the work that has been done to create education standards for math and literacy, efforts to create health education standards began in 1995 and have been continuously revised. The 2024 revision includes eight standards:

1. Use functional health information to support health and well-being of self and others.
2. Analyze influences that affect health and well-being of self and others.
3. Access valid and reliable resources to support health and well-being of self and others.
4. Use interpersonal communication skills to support health and well-being of self and others.
5. Use a decision-making process to support health and well-being of self and others.
6. Use a goal-setting process to support health and well-being of self and others.
7. Demonstrate practices and behaviors to support health and well-being of self and others.
8. Advocate to promote health and well-being of self and others.[49]

These are excellent standards, and they are accompanied by performance indicators for elementary, middle, and high school students. More than thirty-six states have formally adopted them, but actual instruction—let alone assessment of outcomes—is another matter entirely. Like the rhetoric around civics education, there is an enormous gap between aspiration and implementation.

While students may learn the basic physical health and wellness facts in such classes, their ability to retain and apply this knowledge to how they live is very limited, suggesting that much of what passes for health education is ineffectual. (Stunningly, as of 2020, there have been no long-term studies of the impact of K–12 health education curricula on health literacy or health outcomes, according to a National Academy of Medicine discussion paper.)[50] Students may be taught what proteins and carbohydrates are, as well as the importance of limiting sugar in one's diet, for example, but data show that very few students practice good eating habits. One piece of evidence speaks volumes: Obesity has reached epidemic proportions among American adolescents. According to the Centers for Disease Control and Prevention, more than 22 percent of American adolescents are obese.[51]

Increasing numbers of young people rely on social media for all their health information. With the growing prevalence of misinformation online, the ability to distinguish credible from noncredible sources becomes essential. Unlike more specific outcomes of health education, students' ability to critically assess digital sources of information has been extensively reviewed in recent years. One groundbreaking study was conducted by the Stanford History Education Group. *Evaluating Information: The Cornerstone of Civic Online Reasoning* studied the abilities of 7,804 middle school, high school, and college students to assess the credibility of online information sources.

The authors discovered that the problem of digital illiteracy was even worse than they'd assumed. "When we began our work we had little sense of the depth of the problem," they write. "Our first round of piloting shocked us into reality. Many assumed that because young people are fluent in social media they are equally savvy about what they find there. Our work shows the opposite. . . . When it comes to evaluating information that flows through social media channels, they are easily duped."[52]

But misinformation isn't the only Internet risk to students' well-being. Addiction to social media is now a growing threat to the health of our youth. The most recent Gallup data found that American teens spend about five hours a day on social media.[53] According to a 2023 US Department of Health and Human Services report, "Adolescents who spend more than three hours per day on social media face double the risk of experiencing poor mental health outcomes, such as symptoms of depression and anxiety. . . . Social media may also perpetuate body dissatisfaction, disordered eating behaviors, social comparison, and low self-esteem. . . . Additionally, 64% of adolescents are 'often' or 'sometimes' exposed to hate-based content through social media." The report goes on to say that over half of teenagers admit that it would be hard for them to give up social media.[54]

Summing up the latest research in a March 2024 article for *The Atlantic*, psychologist Jonathan Haidt writes: "Something went suddenly and horribly wrong for adolescents in the early 2010s. . . . Rates of depression and anxiety in the United States—fairly stable in the 2000s—rose by more than 50 percent in many studies from 2010 to 2019. The suicide rate rose 48 percent for adolescents ages 10 to 19. For girls ages 10 to 14, it rose 131 percent." He also reports that "similar patterns emerged around the same time in Canada, the U.K., Australia, New Zealand, the Nordic countries, and beyond."[55]

The use of smartphones became widespread during these years. Haidt believes that adolescents' use of these devices directly contributes to their increased levels of anxiety and depression by rewiring childhood and replacing play-based activities with excessive screen time and social media use. He argues that the widespread adoption of smartphones contributes to constant social comparison, bullying, reduced face-to-face interactions, and disrupted sleep patterns. (Haidt's 2024 book, *The Anxious Generation: How the Great Rewiring of Childhood Is Causing an Epidemic of Mental Illness*, elaborates on the themes of his *Atlantic* essay and has become an international bestseller.)

Clearly, learning to think critically about sources of digital information is necessary but not sufficient for digital literacy. Students must be taught how to navigate the digital world safely and responsibly. This includes understanding the algorithms behind platforms, recognizing clickbait, and discerning between real news and fake news. Students need to learn online etiquette, the implications of their digital footprint, and the benefits and drawbacks of social media. Finally, students must learn to use social media in constructive ways, such as showcasing their talents or participating in online communities aligned with their interests.

We asked Monique to reflect on how she acquired the essential knowledge, skills, and character for personal growth and health. "Not in school," was her short answer.

Monique told us that she took the required physical education classes in middle and high school, where she played games like dodgeball, but she learned nothing about health and wellness in school. She finally came to understand how to take care of her body as an adult by becoming certified as a personal trainer.

"When I think about character, resiliency, personal growth, those are things that came from home," she told us. "We were raised with a sense of resiliency. But it was from a negative standpoint, very much race related. Because you're Black and you're a woman, you're going to have to work twice as hard to get half as much."

She continued, "Many people say character should only be taught at home. But what if parents don't have a good character? Schools have to do more."

What Monique Wants for Her Son's Education

At the conclusion of our several conversations with Monique, we asked her to reflect on the education that her son, Reuben, is getting in his gifted-and-talented public high school program. She had a lengthy list of concerns.

"He doesn't have a government requirement. He hasn't had a gym or health class yet either. The health class is only one semester, and there's no way that they can teach you everything that you need to know about your health in half a year of school."

Along with those gaps, Monique told us that "he's not being challenged. His assignments don't seem to be developing any skills, like study and organizational skills. He hasn't had to write a single essay yet. He's not being taught to think critically. . . . I have sat in on the school's instructional leadership team meetings and have listened to them talk about what could be happening with kids that have poor grades. These are gifted and exceptional kids, and they're just not being challenged."

Were there any bright spots in Reuben's high school experience so far? "Band!" Monique exclaimed. "He came in second place in a flute competition. Band teaches him discipline, but also teaches him how to work with a group. . . . They take band seriously because who wants to play in a concert and sound ridiculous, right? So they keep each other in line. He doesn't do that in any other class."

Monique's observation about the importance of an extracurricular activity for her son's learning and development reflected her own high school experience—as well as what high school graduates had reported to Tony in the focus groups described earlier in the chapter. It is also consistent with the findings in Jal Mehta and Sarah Fine's recent book, *In Search of Deeper Learning*, in which they report on the results of their six-year study of the best American high schools. According to Mehta and Fine, the dominant pattern of instruction in most classes was rote transmission: worksheets, multiple-choice questions, and teachers lecturing. The notable exception was in those few classes where students had to produce something, most often in extracurricular activities such as band, drama, school publications, and art.[56]

Reinventing Education

In this chapter, we have learned about the essential cognitive and character skills now required to enable students to make choices and act on them for productive work, civic engagement, and personal health and well-being. We have analyzed how a learning system focused almost exclusively on the memorization of academic subject knowledge has failed to equip generations of students with the skills they most need, and how it continues to leave our most disadvantaged students behind. We have also described how the so-called education reforms of the last forty years have failed to address these problems and have negatively impacted both teachers and students.

Our century-old education system does not need more reforming. It needs reinventing. An education system that measures learning outcomes according to seat time served in the classroom and multiple-choice test results must be replaced by assessments of competencies and character, as well as demonstrations of the ability to apply knowledge and to create new knowledge, not merely to retain information. Finally, we believe that education must nurture intrinsic motivations for learning and contribute to individual health and well-being.

Mastery learning is the future of education in both schools and the workplace. This new system of education isn't just a vision. It is being actively developed in a growing number of communities across the country and around the world, as you will see in the pages that follow.

CHAPTER 3

Mastery Learning in K–8

A POSSE OF young children ages five through eleven are running around Baker Beach under the Golden Gate Bridge in San Francisco. They're students at a small private elementary and middle school called Red Bridge, and they laugh and squeal and chase each other. They sing, they tumble, they do all the things young children do when they're on a school trip at a beach.

Then the teachers ask them to take out paper and pencils and look carefully at the bridge towering in front of them. The students move their heads this way and that, put small fingers out to test scale. They begin to draw. Some notice the many parts of the bridge: towers, piles, deck, suspension cables. Others also see the waves or the clouds or the seagulls in the air and the boats in the bay. Each drawing is roughly similar but also completely different based on each child's personal curiosity, as well as their powers of observation and their skill in the techniques of drawing (line, shape, shading, perspective, color). The teachers ask questions that help the children sharpen their powers and skills.

The class, one they participate in twice per week, is called Observation, and it's one of their five core academic subjects. They observe on neighborhood walks and field trips as well as inside the school building. They observe the natural world, their own bodies and emotions, patterns in how they interact with each other. They observe each other's observations, drawings, and writings, and give each other feedback to help sharpen their observation and execution skills.

Observation is so central to the school that Red Bridge hired an Observation teacher. The job description read, "You will be responsible for planning experiences that deepen students' ability to observe the world around them and represent what they see in words or art. . . . The goal is to train the eye to see the world and reflect it back through a variety of media including drawing, sculpting, mathematical analysis, written word, lab report and more." Observation class is foundational to scientific understanding, creative expression, and human relations. It's also an exercise in slowing down, intentionally designed as an antidote to the attention-deficit-inducing world we currently live in.

Everything at Red Bridge is thoughtfully constructed to develop humans who can thrive in this moment and future times of rapid change. Humans need the ability to make choices that support productive work and an active and informed civic life. They also need to have the will and skills to cultivate and sustain themselves, their health, and their well-being. Red Bridge takes its role in developing thriving humans very seriously.

Its team has taken a close look at how primary schools operate. And they've chosen to redesign almost all the elements that you or your grandparents or their grandparents might recognize as "school."

The Elements of School

If you were to enter the Red Bridge building when school wasn't in session, you might not immediately know that it's a school. The space and its furniture look nothing like the hard wooden or plastic chairs and rows of graffiti-scratched metal desks in traditional classrooms.

Instead, the furniture is lightweight, comfortable, and flexible, not unlike the work environments of San Francisco's start-up and tech offices. Everything can easily be reorganized into different configurations based on the needs of the moment. Inviting rugs and large cushions, soft chairs, wheeled desks and tables, movable whiteboards, and materials bins can be organized into large or small rooms.

The space is designed to promote creating and collaborating rather than to maintain order and control. Unlike in most schools, Red Bridge's fifty-four young people have the choice of how to configure space to meet their varying needs. When they are in the building, you see them all over the place, sprawled with a book in beanbag chairs, writing on the whiteboards in small conference rooms, tucked in quiet corners working on their laptops wearing noise-canceling headphones.

Let's move on to the curriculum. In the nineteenth century, the Committee of Ten, as described in Chapter 2, decided that school should focus on the classical and modern subjects most of us took in school: math, science, languages, history, and so on. These core subjects, as familiar to our grandparents as they are to us, are all academic content.

Red Bridge instead focuses on five core academic skills: communication, computation, critical thinking, world studies, and of course observation.

A teacher—though at Red Bridge, teachers are called learning guides—does not stand at the front of the room lecturing about how to communicate or do computation. Academic skills are developed through application. You grow your capacity to communicate or observe by actually doing things in the world, usually in collaboration with others.

In each of these curricular areas, the school's focus is first on teaching young people to learn how to learn, with rigor as well as personal and community expectations of excellence. The students are not taught how to memorize and regurgitate academic content for a test. To enable this, the day is organized into a flexible timetable that includes chunks of time for specific activities that build work habits and academic skills and activities such as deliberate practice.

During the daily deliberate practice block, for example, students choose which habit or skill they need to or want to focus on. They choose with intention, often in consultation with their adult learning guides. In contrast, in traditional school, the teachers mandate exercises and assignments to be completed, turned in, and graded, either as classwork or as homework.

In a traditional school, cohorts of children of the same age slog through the calendar year, squirming in their seats for a required amount of time, masking boredom, and, as research shows, growing increasingly disengaged. After 180 days of seat time, the batches of students are promoted to the next grade, unless they spectacularly fail to meet certain requirements.

These requirements may or may not have anything to do with what the students actually learned that year. Grades are given for content knowledge, but they are not a measure of whether a student knows the content or has made progress in the development of character skills. Attendance, behavior, and missing assignments all can lower numerical grades. Sometimes extra credit is created to push young people through. At one of our children's high-performing schools, for example, students could boost their grade by bringing in tissue boxes for the classroom supply closet.

At Red Bridge, there are no age-based grade levels that corral students together for twelve successive 180-day school years. There is no social promotion or tissue box extra credit. There are no one-and-done tests to measure achievement.

Instead, students are grouped by personal mastery, their individual capacity to drive their learning independently. This means, can they consistently develop, reflect on, and maintain work habits like goal setting, time management, focus, initiative, and collaboration? As students mature, the expectations and demonstrated behaviors (or "look-fors") for these habits grow increasingly sophisticated. The school calls these personal-mastery-based groupings "autonomy levels." Every autonomy level has children in a wide range of ages. Autonomy level one, for example, might include five-to-seven-year-olds.

Red Bridge has no grades or report cards. In addition to guiding the curriculum, Red Bridge's teachers have weekly one-on-one coaching conversations with their students to support them in their ups and downs as they reach for greater autonomy levels. Twice a year, students—or learners, as Red Bridge calls them—can go to their learning guides and initiate a promotion process to the next autonomy level. The learners make a case for their readiness for promotion based on evidence they have gathered in their portfolios about the consistency and quality of their own work and skill habits.

And all of this starts at the ripe old age of five.

Cognitive and Character Skills for All Students

What enables someone to thrive in a world rushing headlong into the unknown? When knowledge, work, and even how humans relate to one another are in flux, what remains stable? Heraclitus 2,500 years ago, in a much less turbulent time, answered, "Change is the only constant." This has never been more true. What enables humans to thrive is their competence in adapting to change, which means learning all throughout their lives.

Learning how to learn—in other words, mastery of the cognitive and character skills that enable a person to lead themselves (and others) toward meaningful goals and choices through success, failure, and change—becomes the pathway to a productive, engaged, and healthy life.

It's never too early to get on this pathway. From the earliest years of schooling, as Red Bridge shows, you can embark on a journey to develop ever more sophisticated and durable personal mastery and, along with it, grow your competence to do things in the world.

But it can't be taught in a one-off class only for some students.

In traditional school, most likely high school, you might have an elective in psychology or leadership that helps you with personal mastery. If you get into trouble, you might have sessions with a counselor who helps you with goal-setting and self-management skills. That's unlikely, though, given student-to-counselor ratios; the average ratio in grades K–8 in US schools ranges from 613:1 to 787:1, depending on which state you live in. That means one adult helping with personal mastery for 787 young people.[1] Elementary and middle schools employ a variety of curricula that support durable cognitive and character skills, but most often they're done for a few minutes a few times a week, if there's time.

In our current education system, development of personal mastery is at best an add-on. More often, it's simply not taught.

A Mastery System

Schools like Red Bridge that are looking at what our economy and society need right now understand that every child requires this type of learning. It's not an accessory or a nice-to-have but rather the core purpose of education, around which everything else should be designed.

The entire system that is school—from schedule to school year to teaching and learning to the roles of adults to curriculum and assessment—needs to be redesigned to enable this personal development. That ambitious task is what the team at Red Bridge is taking on.

Red Bridge focuses first and foremost on developing agency, which the school defines as "the ability to set meaningful goals and have the will and skill to achieve them." Having a sense of personal agency is essential for personal health and well-being, as well as for individuals to feel they can make a difference in their community.

The school's founder, Orly Friedman, described the approach. "Our mastery system makes this happen. It allows students to make choices about what they're working on. It allows for students to shine in different areas, but it still ensures that they cover the basics. When students are able to work at their own pace toward really deeply understanding or being able to do something, then it allows our schedule and other elements to come together."

In response to some of the inadequacies of the industrial model of learning, some instructors and schools have designed learning like an iTunes or Spotify playlist, but with a quiz at the end: Read this book or that one, watch this video or that one, at your own pace on your own time. Then, when you feel you're ready, take the quiz. If you pass, you get mastery credit. Some of these designs may insist that you complete specific readings or videos, while others only concern themselves with your ability to pass the test. You can follow their recommended path, or you can pick and choose how you get to the final destination: the test. With these innovations, it's irrelevant when, where, and how long it took you to learn the material. These programs have taken seat time out of the equation (though they still rely on the Carnegie unit to grant credit). What matters is that you passed the test.

Repeat this process for a certain number of courses, and you can be granted a credential.

In this design, mastery becomes a series of teaching inputs (the book, the video) and a student output (the test), which is very much like the traditional education system, except that each student can go at their own pace. The form of the output is still standardized (a test), and students have little to no say in how they demonstrate their learning.

To be clear, this is *not* what we mean by mastery learning.

In contrast, mastery at Red Bridge is built on a system of "mastery credits," which are demonstrations of what young people can do, not what has been taught by teachers or learning materials (inputs) or what is demonstrated by onetime assignments or assessments students have completed (outputs). Red Bridge's approach is both deeper and more individualized.

In life, you show your mastery of cooking by being able to create consistently delightful, flavorful dishes that make your family and friends beg for seconds. Over time, you may begin experimenting with creating your own concoctions. Your mastery continues to deepen and grow. Similarly, you show your (nonprofessional) mastery of home repairs by being able to fix things successfully, with less and less support from YouTube videos and more and more understanding of how to approach the problem. You show your mastery of the guitar by being able to play a greater variety of chords and songs, perhaps even with other people also making music. A soccer team shows its mastery of the game by being able to meld its individual players' strengths and skills into a collaborative, winning whole.

In all these situations, mastery cannot be standardized into a test. Demonstration of mastery is context dependent and may involve other people. In short, demonstrations of mastery are different for different areas. There are stages to development, and sometimes they involve collaborative mastery.

This is how Red Bridge approaches mastery credits. "In our math or computational thinking credits," Friedman told us, "we always want there to be an oral explanation because we think if you can explain something orally in math then you really deeply understand it." This is deeper than the math teacher saying, "Show your work." You need to be able to explain the choices you made to arrive at a solution and, gradually, as your learning gets more sophisticated, perhaps even the choices you didn't make.

"For character habits," Friedman continued, "we always want to have a piece of peer feedback." Character includes what you think and do in private, but even more so it's demonstrated via your behavior in the social sphere. Given that, it makes sense to include how your peers perceive and respond to you—and how you respond to their feedback—as evidence of your growing character.

In life, to feel a sense of mastery, you also have to have a sense of how you learn, what success feels like, and where you may want to develop and grow. As a cook, you may understand that your go-to skills are baking related and French. As you feel a sense of strength and mastery in relation to baking, you may choose to move on to sautéing and searing and exploring Indian spices. You are pursuing mastery based on your curiosity and choice as well as developing an internal compass of what mastery means.

Red Bridge wants its learners, from age five on, to know what this sense of growing and expanding mastery feels like. Before its learners sign up for an assessment of a skill, they're asked, "How do you know you'll be successful?" If they don't have an answer to this question, they're asked to spend some more time in deliberate practice until they feel they can answer it. Friedman explained why: "Our goal is to get students to not only think about what they're learning and why it's important, but also to recognize for themselves when they've reached a depth of understanding to be ready for assessment, to know what a deep level of understanding feels like, and what it takes to reach that level."

Designing a system to nurture and assess mastery is a complex undertaking, and mastery learning schools are works in progress. Friedman and some of her team got their start at Sal Khan's Khan Lab School, the brick-and-mortar experimentation space for his global digital Khan Academy. Friedman was head of the Khan Lab primary school, where she noted that while some students thrived in the self-directed mastery environment the Khan Lab School was building, others plateaued. Success wasn't directly related to academic ability but rather often coincided with work habits and developing that internal sense of mastery described above. She wanted to design a system that truly put character and work habits on an equal footing with other learning. She also wanted to build a school model that was replicable, rather than a one-and-done school that served a limited number of students.

Sujata Bhatt, who has been on Red Bridge's board since its prelaunch year, has seen firsthand how the team continues to learn as they design and improve their mastery system. The team grappled with questions like, *How do you measure traits like kindness that are an ongoing process?* and *How do you create a credit system based on mastery, not seat time?* They continued to develop the work-habits curriculum and iterated on how mastery is expressed and assessed. They explored which modes of demonstration match up best with parts of the curriculum. Through all this design, they learned from and responded to the learners in their care. Now, as they expand into middle school, they are reassessing these design questions with older children as well as newcomers who have not grown up in the culture of the school. Throughout this journey, they have also been documenting their methods and sharing them with other schools, including public schools.

How Learning Works in a Mastery System

At Red Bridge, for more complex learning, students participate in the design of their demonstrations of mastery. They have the freedom to get wildly creative and introduce their individual interests into the process. You don't just learn to pass a test; you design the test—or rather, the demonstration of mastery—in ways that are interesting to you and that let you keep learning.

When we visited the school, a group of young learners were finishing up a multiweek exploration of roly-poly bugs. They had become curious about the little gray creatures, also known as pill bugs or potato bugs, on one of their neighborhood walks. The learning guides encouraged the young learners' curiosity: to observe the bugs, photograph them, sketch them in detail, record their observations about the bugs' behaviors, and discuss what they noticed.

The learners, a pod of seven- and eight-year-old girls, thought that roly-poly outer shells looked a lot like lobster tails and armadillos. Through research, they learned that their observation was right. Roly-polies aren't insects; they're in the arthropod family, just like lobsters and armadillos. The discovery led the girls down a very academic rabbit hole of how scientific classifications (kingdom, phylum, etc.) work.

This particular group of girls all happened to be budding fashionistas. When it came time to wrap up the arthropod explorations, they decided they wanted to demonstrate their understanding of form and function by each designing a piece of clothing that incorporated the overlapping yet flexible plate structure of crustacean shells. They designed the clothing, sewed it, and figured out how to construct shell armatures, practicing a whole set of skills including academic skills, character habits, and work habits.

They then decided to model their creations in a formal fashion show, complete with invitations and guests, which itself led to learning and practicing a bunch of cognitive and character skills: goal setting, communication, critical thinking, time management, organization, and collaboration.

This learning journey, an adventure really, exemplifies how mastery learning and assessment work at Red Bridge. It can be sparked by student curiosity, which the teachers then bring forth, amplify, and guide into a deeper learning experience. That deeper learning experience continues to be shaped by the students' personal interests and goals all the way through to the demonstration of mastery, which is truly what Bo Stjerne Thomsen of LEGO described in Chapter 1 as "hard fun."

Teachers support learners in their development of cognitive and character skills—in setting goals, applying and sustaining effort, growing persistence, managing time, and being open to feedback. They also support the young students in knowledge acquisition.

This mastery system is so much more than our traditional approach where: (1) the teacher teaches the predetermined, standards-based content; (2) the student learns the content, often for the sake of an upcoming test; and (3) the student takes the test or some other summative assessment that shows they remember the content—even though they may forget it in a day or a week.

The roly-poly investigation and fashion show will likely stay in the learners' memories for a long time. Even if those activities do not, the work and character habits they learned along the way—which they continue to build on for their entire time at Red Bridge—certainly will.

Character Skills

In the roly-poly example, we saw how observation is critical to learning and growth. This is why one of the core academic areas at Red Bridge is learning how to observe the world around you with ever more care and detail; it's critical for nurturing and sustaining curiosity.

Equally important is learning to observe and understand the world *inside* you. This internal observation and awareness are the foundations of character. Character Lab, cofounded by Angela Duckworth, the expert on grit we discussed in Chapter 1, defines character as "intentions and actions that benefit both the individual and others." Or, in even simpler language, character is "everything we do to help other people as well as ourselves."[2]

Anyone who's spent time around five-year-olds at a playground or birthday party knows well the volcanic mix of emotions, actions, and reactions that shape how they interact. One minute it's joy, the next it's jealousy or fear or rage, erupting like unpredictable magma. Adults scramble to contain the mayhem.

Now imagine a world where five-year-olds become fluent in understanding and managing themselves. It all begins with teaching them how to pay attention to their own emotions. Emotion is what happens in our bodies. Feelings are what happens when we become aware of emotions; they're our thoughts about our emotions.

Red Bridge's youngest students learn to consciously experience and observe the swirls of emotion that rise up inside their little bodies. With practice, they learn to name the feelings. They explore what triggers different kinds of emotions in themselves, how interactions can be nourished or hijacked by emotions, and how they can intentionally move themselves from one state to another.

When we visited, we saw the youngest students using a feelings chart with four color-coded zones—red, yellow, green, and blue—to describe what was going on inside them and what might be going on inside others. Each zone included a variety of feelings. Sick, tired, sad, and shy were in the blue zone. Out of control and angry were in the red zone. In between, in yellow, were frustrated, scared, uncomfortable, and nervous. The green zone included happy, focused, and awake.

We witnessed a five-year-old boy roaming around the room banging on things while the rest of the group sat in their circle to close out the day. Unlike what might happen in a more traditional classroom, the boy's behavior didn't disrupt the proceedings for the rest of the children. The teacher noted that he was in the red zone. A child offered that maybe he was feeling out of control. Other children expressed sympathy.

After all, each of them knew what it was like to be in the red zone. They had experienced it, named it, discussed it. They could draw on that knowledge to be empathetic to their classmate.

As part of receiving their "thoughtful communicator" mastery credit, the five- and six-year-olds in autonomy level one do a weeklong experience where each day they look back and reflect on the tone and word choice they used when they expressed a need or a want. Friedman told us about a girl who was really enjoying a writing block. When the learning guide told the student that writing time was over, the student calmly asked to be allowed to continue to write. The learning guide explained that she could write later during choice time if she wanted. At the end of the day, the student reflected that she didn't use a whining voice but rather a calm one when she asked for what she wanted. She was five. Friedman told us they get a lot of positive feedback from autonomy level one parents on how their child matures socially and emotionally.

Deliberate Practice

Red Bridge's learning system is based on deliberate practice, a concept learned from the work of K. Anders Ericsson, whom we referenced in Chapter 1. The last chunk of each day is set aside for deliberate practice of academic skills (reading, writing, and computation). In working on these academic skills, young learners practice work habits and character skills.

In the first half of the year, students work to establish routines that help them successfully meet their personal goals. They learn to describe what a goal is and how to monitor progress each day on a goal tracker. The goals can be academic or related to personal mastery. The students are taught that both are necessary for growing.

By practicing a growth mindset, the students begin to understand that learning is a process, not a one-and-done. They learn how to learn, or what Laszlo Bock of Google called learning ability. They also practice sharing, taking turns with talking time, asking clarifying questions of each other, incorporating each other's feedback into revisions, and making group decisions—all critical components of what we call cognitive and character skills and what Bock called emergent leadership.

Bock explained that a crucial part of emergent leadership includes knowing when to step back. Nikita Khetan, the lead teacher at Red Bridge, who helped design the school with Friedman from its earliest days, told us a story about a six-year-old embracing this skill, which, by the way, many adults have a hard time with.

One year, during the semiannual promotion process, a six-year-old and his learning guides felt he was ready to move to the next level. Khetan explained, "In our early autonomy levels, work habits are separated from content and academic areas like communication and computation. But there is a component in our work habits of being able to read at a certain level—the idea being that to drive your own learning and take ownership of your own learning, you have to be able to read basic information and directions on your own."

During their conversation about promotion, the learning guide showed the boy the sorts of directions and informational text that autonomy level two students were expected to navigate on their own. The student hesitated. He found them difficult. He felt sad and disappointed, but he decided what was best for him. He said, "You know what, I think I need some more time to work on my reading."

When you start at five, mastery can develop quickly. Friedman told us a story of what happened when the school had to close for the first time due to a COVID outbreak. (They called it a "snow day" for fun, since it never snows in San Francisco.) By the end of that snow day, she said, "I had received emails independently from two families. Each parent had the same story: Their child had decided to make their own learning plan for the day. They'd written out a schedule on paper or a whiteboard and followed the schedule they set for themselves."

In stark contrast to the student disengagement described in Chapter 2, the young Red Bridge students had chosen to transform a COVID "snow day" into a learning day. Their parents were impressed, the students felt satisfied, and learning happened without a teacher standing over them. The students were six and seven years old.

What Parents Want

Red Bridge works to create an intentionally diverse student body and has developed an innovative pay-what-you-can tuition model to enable greater access. Most of its learners, however, come from high-achieving parents who thrived in traditional schools. We wondered how they felt about a program where the focus on academics almost feels secondary to agency and character development.

Khetan pushed back against our either-or premise. "We're creating internal scope and sequences for each of our core content areas," she explained. "For academic areas like computation or reading and writing communications, we've developed four different stages: the emergent stage, early stage, middle stage, and late stage. These stages pull from the critical standards in the Common Core and enrich them with other resources." The school is not, in short, sacrificing academics but rather designing them differently, and the detailed annual parent satisfaction surveys show that parents are overwhelmingly happy.

Friedman did tell us that some parents have wondered when their children will learn the sorts of things they learned when they were in grade school—content like the fifty states and their capitals. A curiosity-driven curriculum design could easily collapse under the weight of more and more requests for specific content. Imagine another family wanting to include the countries of the world or the history of San Francisco or any of a million other things. In fact, this is part of what makes public schools unwieldy. As the world changes and schools try to keep up, we keep adding more and more without subtracting anything until there's more mandated content than there are hours of the day in school, and legislatures keep passing laws to mandate even more.

The Red Bridge team arrived at an elegant solution that honored the parent requests, student interest, and the mastery-based design of the school. They zeroed in on the underlying cognitive competency rather than the content.

When you memorize material, instead of focusing on the specific content, why not focus on your capacity to memorize? Isn't that what you want to grow and what will serve you in the future?

The Red Bridge team is now creating set of mastery credits that they're calling memory credits, which students can earn by consistently being able to memorize things like the states, poems, the periodic table, or the first hundred digits of pi. They're also creating a separate set of speed credits (e.g., for rapid fluency with multiplication facts or keyboarding speed or running races).

Unless they relate to core academic skills like math fluency, these mastery credits are not considered foundational and necessary for everyone. They're an example of how the school continues to tinker to meet the needs of the individuals it serves. The teachers hadn't originally considered learners who are motivated by the desire to build speed or memorization, but given the curiosity of the little humans in front of them, they found a way.

The crediting system at Red Bridge, unlike time-based Carnegie units, is individualized to meet the needs and interests of individual learners choosing their own path to developing enduring mastery. In addition, a memory credit or a speed credit can provide interesting and relevant information about the learner's growth and development to "next step" organizations like high schools, colleges, and employers. No high school cares whether you've memorized the state capitals, but one may be intrigued by a middle schooler who has a towering stack of memory credits.

Creative Agency Versus Performative Compliance

As it does with students, Red Bridge's mastery system activates teacher agency and creativity. The teachers are codesigners of the school in partnership with the leadership team. Unlike in traditional schools, where professional development is usually mandated and designed by the administration, teachers at Red Bridge are trusted to direct their own learning. Each receives a learning stipend they can use to develop themselves as they see fit. Khetan, for example, was using hers to take a continuing education class on creative writing at Stanford.

Except for in a few hundred teacher-powered schools across the nation, these practices are very much at odds with how we train and expect our teachers to behave, and how we expect them to train young people to behave.[3]

Teachers in traditional schools—like children—are often expected to comply. They're subject to control and discipline. This can happen at high levels, like rigid, unrealistic curricular pacing plans that dictate that teachers teach a new concept or skill each day, regardless of whether the students have mastered it. There are also scripted curricula that teachers are expected to parrot almost word for word. On a trivial level, in some schools, teachers *have to pay* the school to wear jeans and sneakers to work on Fridays.[4] Contrast this with the Silicon Valley tech bros who are paid millions to run companies wearing jeans and sneakers. Is it any surprise that teachers who are treated this way then build classrooms that are also based on compliance and discipline?

Teachers are often taught that classroom management depends on creating strict teacher personas: "Don't smile till Christmas" is a common piece of advice for new teachers. At Red Bridge, color charts help even the youngest students name and understand their emotional states so they can learn self-regulation. In other schools, color charts are used to discipline young children. If the teacher puts your name into the red zone, for example, you're in trouble and will face punitive consequences until you perform the behaviors expected of you.

Perhaps the most egregious examples of compliance-based classrooms are in "no excuses" charter schools such as Success Academy, KIPP, and Uncommon Schools, whose aim is to create academically rigorous environments for children from high-poverty Black and Brown communities. Over the past two decades, to deliver high performance on standardized tests, these school networks—which operate elementary, middle, and high schools in mostly urban locations around the country—have created elaborate systems of classroom management. Teachers use extrinsic carrot-and-mostly-stick motivational methods that include demerits and detentions. Although the term "no excuses" was originally meant to apply to adults ("there are no excuses for your students not succeeding"), it also became the standard for young children who were subjected to experiences directly opposite of Red Bridge's nurturing of agency as the foundation for academic and life success.

While Red Bridge promotes self-regulation through empathy, understanding, reflection, and deliberate practice, the young children at these no-excuses schools are taught to SLANT: Sit up straight, Lean your body toward the speaker, Ask and answer questions, Nod your head yes and no, and Track the teacher with your eyes.

Teaching SLANTing necessitates complicated behavior management systems that are the opposite of intentional mastery. These systems require teachers to give students demerits and infractions, which result in privileges like recess and field trips being taken away.[5] In an article in *Education Week*, Joanne Golann and Mira Debs, professors at Vanderbilt and Yale, respectively, told the story of a Latina mom whose daughter Esmeralda attended one of these no-excuses schools. She was disciplined for humming in class. Then she was disciplined for laughing during a fire drill. One consequence she faced: wearing a yellow shirt to school the next day, the school's equivalent of a scarlet letter of public shaming. She was also forbidden from talking to her peers.[6]

All this control is done to build a pathway to success: strong behavioral compliance to get strong math and language skills as demonstrated by standardized test scores year after year until you arrive at college acceptance. Start with the youngest children and drill and discipline them so that eventually they will get accepted into college and thereby have improved life outcomes.

But a system largely based on discipline, control, and extrinsic motivation doesn't work in a world with exponentially increasing choices and complexity.

KIPP's own website demonstrates this path to success is not working, even on the terms the school sets for itself. The website poses a question, "Are our students climbing the mountain to and through college?" The data they publish there say: not so much.

Based on 2019 data, 94 percent of Kippsters graduate from high school, on par with the 90 percent national average. Eighty-two percent enroll in college, much better than the 62 percent nationally. But then the gap emerges. Only 34 percent of KIPP students complete college, fewer than the more than 40 percent nationally. Put another way, 82 percent of the no-excuses-trained Kippsters go into college but only 34 percent make it out; 48 percent do not succeed in college.[7]

Succeeding in college—and in life—means navigating an increasing number of ever more complex choices relating to productive work, an active and informed civic life, and personal growth, health, and well-being, all often accomplished in collaboration with other humans (and AI and robots as well).

SLANT doesn't train you to be comfortable with choice making or complexity or collaboration. SLANT doesn't grow agency or passion or curiosity. Red Bridge's intrinsic-motivation-based personal mastery system does.

Orly Friedman and Nikita Khetan explained to us that it's hard to find teachers who have the mindset and skills to operate in a relationship- and mastery-based school. Our schools of education aren't currently designed to produce teachers who can step right into Red Bridge, and teachers who have grown up in the last two decades of education reform have a difficult time transitioning into a wholly different approach to teaching and learning.

Friedman, Khetan, and other Red Bridge teachers also acknowledge that the mastery system is exhausting. As the initial designers of a school that is constantly responding to the needs of its community, they're building the plane as they fly it. They're doing R&D for new assessment systems. They're doing outreach and recruitment and storytelling. Red Bridge aligns its salaries to the nearby unionized public school districts, so it pays its teachers well. All these things require fundraising, which is yet another workstream.

And of course, first and foremost, they're putting so much work into the personal development of each and every young human in their care. The first time we spoke with them, the teachers were creating Red Bridge's narrative progress reports, their way of documenting and sharing learners' growth with their families. Traditional report cards are now mostly done online with pull-down menus of comments, which teachers find grueling and soul killing. Red Bridge's beautiful slide-presentation progress reports, co-constructed with each child, create a different kind of exhaustion and take a lot of time. As the school grows, something will have to give. In fact, the school is instituting a paid sabbatical system to give teachers the opportunity to take a break.

Before coming to Red Bridge, Khetan worked in a large urban district, a charter network, and the Khan Lab School. She's been at Red Bridge since before it opened and so has been working on its design and teaching for five years. Daily, she finds herself both exhilarated and exhausted.

Despite the exhaustion, she declared, "I just can't imagine being in a system where there isn't a teacher whose job it is to get to know each child really deeply one-on-one and be looking out for all aspects of them . . . where it isn't the goal of the system to teach them how to take ownership over their lives."

Hawaii: Embedding a Mastery System in Community

Red Bridge's greatest strength is redesigning school for developing personal agency, personal and social well-being, and intrinsic motivation through a mastery-based system. A loose network of seventeen public charter schools in Hawaii has been redesigning school to prepare young people to be civically engaged and contributing members of their communities. Just as Red Bridge's innovations can be adopted and adapted by other schools, the design the Hawaiian schools have developed can be applied in other contexts. Many communities are grappling with how local values and resources can play a role in reinventing the standardized model of school. The two Hawaiian examples we'll showcase explain how to do this.

In Hawaii, an incredibly diverse population and layers of often violent history coexist on a string of remote, geologically active islands during a time of deep ecological shifts. As the wildfires in

Maui in 2023 showed, community is a necessity, not a luxury. People have to be able to depend on each other, because institutions and systems break down in times of ecological crisis, and ecological crises are becoming more frequent. Meaningful learning in Hawaii has to create community and be embedded in community.

However, over much of the past 125 years, it hasn't been. In 1893, Hawaii's last queen was ousted in a violent coup led by US troops and white plantation owners, the islands were annexed by the United States in 1898 despite the objections of more than 50 percent of native islanders, and it became the fiftieth state in 1959. During this turbulent history, Hawaii's schools began operating on the same standard, industrial-era model the mainland used. In the ninety years between 1896 and 1986, the Hawaiian language was legally banned in the islands' public schools, and local community and culture played little to no role in how young people were being educated.

Unsurprisingly, students, particularly Native Hawaiians, were disengaged from their school system—one that actively disconnected them from their heritage and pushed them into special education, the penal system, or dropping out.[8] Then, beginning in the early 2000s, educators launched new charter schools that were Hawaiian–culture focused to try to repair the rift between the standardized model of schooling and local communities.

The Mind of the Navigator

One of those schools is Mālama Honua Public Charter School, a K–8 school on the Windward Coast of Oahu. The school has a diverse student body: 53 percent Native Hawaiian and Pacific Islander, 21 percent Hispanic, 16 percent white, 9 percent two or more races, less than 1 percent Black, and 50 percent low income.

At Mālama Honua you hear one word over and over again, *kuleana*. In Hawaiian culture, kuleana refers to "a reciprocal relationship between the person who is responsible, and the thing which they are responsible for."[9] It's a complex notion of responsibility that embraces the honor and privilege of being given or taking on responsibility. It also encompasses how you develop authority and accountability, and it includes a legal notion of rights and roles.

Like agency, kuleana is the sort of rich, multifaceted concept that can progressively grow more complex as you mature from a five-year-old child to a thirteen-year-old adolescent to a thirty-five-year-old adult. Kuleana is fundamental to personal mastery at Mālama Honua and many of the seventeen Hawaiian-culture-focused charter schools. The basic premise is that you grow yourself in relation to the responsibilities you take on: for yourself, for the community, for the land, and especially for the sea.

Mālama Honua's origin lies in the open seas. In the 1970s, the Polynesian Voyaging Society built native-style canoes and used traditional navigation techniques—no modern instruments—to sail the five thousand miles round trip from Hawaii to Tahiti. These voyages proved that the ancient Polynesians were intentional master navigators with a body of deep knowledge that could be used to sail into the unknown. They were not, as the history books said, folks who got into a boat and happened to drift 2,500 miles to Hawaii by accident. The Polynesian Voyaging Society expeditions were a key part of revitalizing Hawaiian native communities in the late twentieth century.

In Polynesian cultures, navigation was a form of service to the community. Islands often weren't large enough to support the food needs of their populations; the open seas were the only choice for getting enough sustenance or finding new territory to settle.

Out on the open sea, especially on a cloudy day and without the security of modern instruments, there's no way to know which way is which or how to decide where to go. There's just a vast expanse of endless possible directions and tiny you, floating, adrift without a compass.

Over centuries, the Polynesian navigators developed and mastered a body of knowledge to overcome the fundamental challenge of figuring out which way to go. They learned to observe carefully and read the patterns in the seas, bird and fish behaviors, the winds and stars, and any other data source available on the open ocean.

Even if they had written it down, navigation isn't knowledge you can read in a book, take a test on, and be certified as a master in. It's knowledge in action amid life-and-death situations that require working side by side with someone who already is a master, who can coach and guide you so that over time you develop your own ability to observe and process information and make good decisions. It needs to become second nature.

Knowledge + navigator + decision-making and wayfinding skills + responsibility to community in ways that matter to survival. All this came together in the minds of the Polynesian navigators.

The "mind of the navigator" is the metaphor Nainoa Thompson—a sailor, navigator, and cofounder of the Mālama Honua Public Charter School—used for the global education movement he launched. Many years after successfully completing the voyages to Tahiti in the 1970s, he came to see that the problems he was addressing in Hawaii were actually global in scale. Many cultures have been alienated from their histories and their local ecologies, their social and ecological well-being. As a result, individuals feel rudderless. In the mid-2010s, as he came to this global understanding, he and other Hawaiians began sailing traditional canoes on around-the-world voyages.

The name Mālama Honua means "care for the planet." The movement's aim is to redesign how humans interact with the earth. Thompson frames the earth of tomorrow as the island we're all currently, often unsuccessfully, navigating toward. For humans to be able to survive—to arrive at a successful, sustainable future—the earth needs for many more people, old and especially young, to be trained in the mind of the navigator.

To Thompson, this meant building an education movement based on values and people taking on kuleana, responsibility. Mālama

Honua, founded in 2014 as a "school of nature immersion," was his and his cofounder Robert Witt's attempt to turn the mind of a navigator into a formal Western institution that would be recognized and funded by the same Hawaii Department of Education that had banned the Hawaiian language for almost a century.[10]

Think Globally, Act Locally

To nurture and grow kuleana and the mind of the navigator in its young people, the school has designed a system that entails living into a set of community values: care, protect, preserve, good health and well-being, betterment, love, cultural service, benevolence. These are combined with a set of mastery competencies that we see over and over again, with slight variations, in innovative schools across the world: environmental awareness, communication and collaboration, global awareness, civic responsibility, ethical problem-solving, and confident cultural identity. Families everywhere are coming to understand that these are the universal character and cognitive skills their children need to thrive in a world of disruption and globalization.

Like at Red Bridge, academics at Mālama Honua at first glance seems secondary to character building and the five Cs. That isn't accurate. Again, as at Red Bridge, knowledge isn't for knowledge's sake. Mālama Honua views academics as knowledge young people learn and master to be able to do things in the world, to solve real problems and pursue real responsibilities in the community.

Every school everywhere sits in a neighborhood with histories, assets, problems that need solving, and adults with knowledge and wisdom. But traditional schools ignore this reality. Students are largely locked away in the school building for a set number of hours, separated from the richness and complexities of their neighborhoods.

At Mālama Honua, students are often out in the world. The school is two short blocks from Waimānalo, one of the most beautiful beaches on the planet and also one that has problems with vandalism, homelessness, and land-use battles. The school is close to saltwater and freshwater ponds and streams, mountains, ranches, rainforests, and reefs, all of which are stunning jewels and also fraught with social, ecological, and economic problems. These neighborhood locales, with their assets and problems, become classrooms for investigation and civic engagement.

At Mālama Honua, investigations are long term: units of study last a trimester or longer. In fact, the kindergartners spend the entire year exploring coral reefs. By going out to the reef regularly, students see patterns and problems. Teachers support the students in asking fundamental questions that help them explore, build solutions, and define connections to their own personal stories.

In this way, students' energies are directed into doing things in the community. They explore their individual and collective responsibility for the ecosystem. They design how they want to take action to grow their reciprocal relationship with their environment.

Starting in kindergarten, the adults acknowledge and grow the children's competence in taking responsibility. They say, "Okay, kindergarteners, what do you want to do about that? How do we give back to our land? What is our kuleana?" They then build a plan, implement it, and share with the community what they've learned and accomplished.

Denise Espania, the executive director of the school, explained, "We believe that by doing the work, they're actually going to learn. That by doing the work, they'll actually become advocates for the land and its people."

Learning is grounded in this community-based work, from which students build their individual, social, and cultural identities as well as their sense of purpose and well-being. Espania continued, "Every trimester from kindergarten to eighth grade, we help them ask, 'O wai wau'—'Who am I?' How do I build that confident cultural identity? How do I connect with my land and my people and my stories and who I am?"

These problems and locations are specific to Hawaii, but is there any reason you couldn't take the same approach in any other location, whether rural, urban, or suburban? Every place has a wealth of assets to explore and problems to be solved.

Project-Based Learning

At both Red Bridge and Mālama Honua, students develop progressive levels of proficiency in essential, enduring skills as well as an ongoing, self-motivated process of intellectual and emotional growth. They develop this mastery in large part through project-based learning.

Bad project-based learning—unfortunately, there's a lot of it—means doing worksheets about a problem and then making a diorama or poster board. If you're a parent, you've likely done emergency craft-store runs to help your child complete one of these meaningless projects, which they usually tell you about the day before they're due, because really your child isn't deeply invested in the work.

These so-called projects don't educate—from the Latin *educere*, to lead forth or bring out—your child's unique personality and curiosity. They don't help your child understand their values, passions, and purpose. They don't develop personal mastery or civic engagement or productive work skills. They add a little sugarcoating on the endless stretches of a 180-day year of knowledge input so that time passes and your child can be promoted to the next 180-day grade.

In contrast, well-designed project-based learning is built on what are called "essential questions," which are not unlike the types of big questions that philosophers, scientists, or historians pose. They're open-ended questions that don't have a right or wrong answer (which is where values come in). They provoke children to discuss, debate, and even disagree. Essential questions, in partnership with caring educators, hold maturing children's hands through the unknown;

they are the guideline that enables students to go deep into learning, along their own individual pathways of exploration and values-based action. An example of an essential question at Mālama Honua is, "How can I use my growth in Nā Mea Waiwai [Hawaiian values] to contribute to my community?"

This question is not unlike the open ocean; you can go in a lot of different directions. But if you're asked questions like this from kindergarten, slowly, over time, and with many rich experiences, you'll begin to refine your answer to it. You'll begin to understand who *you* are, what excites *you*, what *your* strengths are, what *you* want to grow in, and how *you* want to make a difference in the world. The questions may stay consistent, but your answers will shift and grow and change as you reach toward adulthood. You'll progressively develop your answers to it as you develop your skills, character, and, at Mālama Honua, kuleana.

In the fifth and eighth grades, students at Mālama Honua do an even longer project, called a capstone, which is another core element of true project-based learning. If all year you've done one-to-three-month-long investigations, and you've been steadily growing your personal and academic mastery, a longer capstone helps you stretch further. It brings together your personal and learning development and applies it to an even deeper exploration of a topic or to building something new.

Kamaliʻiokekai Akiona, a Mālama Honua graduate, published a blog post reflecting on her eighth-grade capstone. She did her final project at the school on an eighty-eight-acre fish farm, where she and other eighth graders were mentored by a local elder, Uncle Kanaloa. He taught them about the problems in the fishpond: invasive fish, overgrown mangroves, the need to build walls.

Like the roly-poly investigators at Red Bridge, the Mālama Honua middle schoolers began by acquiring a deep enough understanding of the problems they each were exploring. Then they had lots of choices about what they wanted to do to improve conditions. They decided to collaborate to make a *ki'o pua*, a small enclosure to raise fish, using the free material available: mud.

Kamali'iokekai wrote, "Our project can be seen as something small and insignificant as all we were doing is digging a pit to raise some fish. But I think that this mud pit of ours is a perfect display of mālama honua, because by simply doing our part in this seemingly huge—but actually small and connected—world we can make an impact. By increasing the population of native fish maybe it can start a chain reaction and change the world for the better."[11]

These fourteen-year-olds are doing meaningful work that helps them master themselves and build their path through the world, something a diorama will never accomplish.

Navigating: Making Sense of Who You're Becoming

In the busyness of our daily lives, adults often have a hard time remembering what they learned or accomplished. We may use daily journals or January reflection time to take stock of the year, to catch up with ourselves by making sense of our wins and failures, which help us set our future goals.

To develop character and personal mastery and a sense of self, children and especially teenagers need a similar space, though with more structure and support. The best project-based-learning schools intentionally design for this; reflection and identity construction are parts of developing personal mastery. Students consistently document their learning in portfolios they curate with the help of trusted adults (teachers, family, community experts) and sometimes even trusted peers. This happens at the end of every project, then again at the end of the semester or trimester, and then again at the end of the year. They write reflections, like Kamali'iokekai did, ideally for public consumption.

Like Red Bridge, Mālama Honua is a K–8 that prepares its young people for independence and agency from kindergarten on. It also recognizes that middle schoolers need a more public transition ritual that can lead them forth from childhood into the next, even more independent phase of their lives.

Most elementary and middle schools in the United States have some sort of culmination ceremony. However, they happen because the children have sat in their seats for enough 180-day chunks of time. In the Instagram age, these ceremonies have become ever more elaborate, external displays full of balloon arches and cakes and fancy outfits and makeup that make still-maturing medium-size people look like mini adults.

The focus is on external optics. There is little acknowledgment or celebration of what children, now growing into teenagedom, have internally become or what they can independently do.

At Mālama Honua, at the end of fifth grade, students do a portfolio defense, which is yet another component of good project-based learning.

To accomplish this successfully, they have to sort through the previous six years' worth of evidence and reflections to make sense of who they were, who they've become, and what they've accomplished in their community. They pick one or two mind-of-a-navigator skills and walk the community through the journey they've personally taken to arrive at mastery of that skill. They do this defense in a public forum, one by one. Their teachers, families, and the public can pose questions and offer comments. Unlike most elementary graduations, their fifth-grade ceremony really is a culmination, a public sharing of the years of growth and effort in achieving a goal.

If they're successful, they go on to sixth grade, the year when many children start to undergo physical and emotional changes. Sixth grade at Mālama Honua is where the school more deeply lives its heritage. All sixth graders get to take their growing mind-of-a-navigator skills to the next level: onto the open ocean, where they learn to sail on a traditional boat using the ancient methods.

Not every school can channel the energies and growing independence of its young people into sailing the open seas. But

Mālama Honua's mastery system—based on rich, community- and place-centered project-based learning—can readily be used in any locality, as can the emphasis on character, values, and responsibility.

Healthy, Happy, and Civic-Minded

A skeptic might ask: How might mastery-based learning work in a middle school (typically grades six to eight) where all children's cognitive and character development hasn't been nurtured since they were five (as is the case with Mālama Honua and Red Bridge)? We found a compelling example that answers that question.

Also on Oahu is a public charter middle school called SEEQS, the School for Examining Essential Questions of Sustainability. It's grounded in values and emphasizes the development of skills through real-world responsibility and work. It's project based and uses the island as its classrooms. It has capstones and public defenses and student-led conferences. In short, it's very much like Mālama Honua, though without the explicit Hawaiian-culture focus. However, SEEQS takes in sixth graders from every elementary school background to mold them into SEEQers in three quick years.

Since it only has grades six through eight, the school homes in on what may be hard to imagine: building a joyous path of personal and civic mastery through the difficult middle school years, when student engagement drops off a cliff and adolescence triggers complicated changes. As anyone who has one or has been one knows, there's no such thing as a standard middle schooler. Physically, they're in very different stages of development. Some are still children and have boundless morning energy. Others have entered puberty and can't wake up even if you yank off their covers and shake them like an earthquake. Emotionally, they're on high-speed roller coasters, in different states by the hour or even by the minute.

SEEQS recognizes and designs for these differences. It starts every morning either with Physical Activity or Advisory class, both spaces where young people can grow their personal and social well-being.

Together, the students build community and learn self-regulation techniques before entering academic explorations. Academic classes don't begin until 9:20 a.m.

Both Advisory and Physical Activity at SEEQS follow the same format: greet, share, and play. Everyone greets each other through some fun or silly activity, like making a favorite animal noise. Then they share something from their lives: how they're feeling, what they did over the weekend, what they're looking forward to. Teachers, by the way, follow the same greet-and-share prompts as the students. The bulk of the time is then spent playing, teachers and students, together as equals.

In Advisory, play might be Ping-Pong or kickball or untie the human knot. In Physical Activity, teachers and students fill out a Google Doc at the end of each quarter listing the activities they want to lead or engage in. They then choose their "class" based on the available offerings. It can be anything from gardening to yoga to running. Sometimes outside instructors teach the classes, which allows the school's teachers to learn and grow just like the students.

The greet-and-share portions of the morning create community: space for people, including teachers, to be vulnerable, to know each other and feel known.

Play creates space for middle schoolers to try out what the world of grown-ups is like, to explore their desire for independence and power. It also positions teachers in the role of learners, because there will be things in both Advisory and Physical Activity where the students know more than the teachers.

In most middle schools, the relation between adults and young people is command and control, with adults owning power and children obeying or rebelling against it. SEEQS, however, has designed a school based on strong, caring, collaborative relationships that allow young people to stretch and explore their personal power.

Something similar happens in another institution at SEEQS, town hall. Five to eight times a year, students can propose changes in the school. There's a Google Form that guides them through the process: What's the problem I've identified? Whom have I spoken to for input? What have I learned from them? What's the solution I'm proposing?

Then the entire school gathers for a town hall, which Buffy Cushman-Patz, the school's founder, likened to a gathering of the legislative branch. In the legislative session, there's procedure. Students and teachers can ask clarifying questions; they can speak in favor of the proposed motion or against it. There is discussion and debate. At some point, someone—student, teacher, administrator—calls for a vote. If the motion gets a two-thirds majority, it passes.

Students, teachers, and administrators have one vote each. The adults are always outnumbered; they can always be voted down. The school's two administrators, who are called the executive branch, do have veto power, but only if the proposed motion violates the school's charter or state or federal law.

You'd think this would be a recipe for mayhem. Instead, it's one of the best preparations for civic responsibility we've heard of. It teaches people how to self-govern and the deep responsibility involved with it. It enables students (and adults) to learn and practice, in contexts that matter in their daily lives, all the skills needed for self-government: forming positions, developing arguments, and learning to listen, weigh consequences, change your mind with reason, and compromise. It also teaches them how government in the United States is supposed to work. There is no judicial branch at SEEQS yet, but they're thinking about it.

Two recent proposals showcase democracy in action at a school level. Students at SEEQS wear bright-green uniforms (T-shirts, hoodies, sweatshirts) with the school logo. Cushman-Patz told us the uniforms serve two purposes: (1) they erase economic inequality so that some kids aren't showing up in $500 outfits while others are wearing Goodwill; and (2) given how often students are off campus and out in the field, the bright green makes it easier to keep sight of them.

A student proposed that the adults be required to wear uniforms as well.

You'd think that a bunch of middle schoolers would instantly vote to exert power over their teachers by forcing them to wear bright-green shirts. Instead, in the midst of thoughtful discussion in favor and against, a teacher stood up and argued that, as adults responsible for so many things, the teachers had earned the right to dress themselves as they choose. The motion failed to pass.

These issues may seem trivial, but they are the stuff of teenagers' daily lives. They are where young people learn to take care of themselves and, as budding adults, learn how to relate to their teachers as almost peers.

Another motion involved gum. Several years ago, some students had proposed that students should be allowed to chew gum in class. The motion had failed. Last year, a student and a teacher co-proposed the same thing again. Again, there was much discussion, thoughtful questioning, and serious debate. In the end, the motion was recrafted as a trial period for gum chewing so that everyone could see whether it was working. During the trial period, there were no hygiene and cleanliness issues, so, at the next town hall, the original motion passed. Gum chewing was now allowed.

However, this year, with a new crop of students—in a middle school, one-third of the students turn over each year—gum hygiene and cleanliness issues have begun popping up. There will likely be another motion to revisit the great gum issue.

In a traditional school driven by the relentless quest to put more and more knowledge into young people, there is no time for growing their capacity to self-govern. Adults work to maintain order over the surging, untapped energy of the students that can, at any moment, devolve into mayhem. Instead of growing self-regulation and self-governance—which, as the gum example shows, means constantly revisiting issues—schools build elaborate systems of consequences and penalties. Or they pile on more work so that students are exhausted.

SEEQS instead designs for meaningful self-governance, meaningful community, and meaningful work, as well as personal health and well-being.

We were curious about how SEEQS students felt about their unusual experience a few years after they graduated. Would they look back on SEEQS fondly? Would they feel it had prepared them for high school and life?

We interviewed a group of four alumni, eighth-grade graduates of the school, who were now in different high schools across the state, ranging from virtual school to a public high school to an elite private school. They were not particularly happy with their high schools and were eager to discuss SEEQS.

We asked them what they missed the most. All four said they missed the community: the strong relationships with peers and with the teachers and administrators. We asked them what was missing from the four very different high schools they now attended. Three out of four said community. The fourth said meaningful work. We asked them what their biggest takeaway from SEEQS was, and, you guessed it, they all said community.

Lainey, a thoughtful eleventh grader with a big smile, told us, "I am a member of a community, and I can actively choose to engage with that community and be meaningful, or I can be a bad community member and not be a part of it. I can make that choice. When you choose to engage with the community and be intentional about what you're doing, you learn and gain so much from that. It feels so much better. It's recognizing the systems that are at play, and that you are a part of that system. That's my biggest takeaway from SEEQS."

The writer, actor, and comedian Baratunde Thurston has a remarkably wide-ranging podcast called *How to Citizen*, which turns "citizen" from a noun into a verb. It explores how Americans from all walks of life engage civically in ways beyond voting. Both Mālama Honua and SEEQS teach their young people how to citizen, and how to make the responsibility and agency of citizening second nature. At a time when active, critical, and committed participation in democracy is sorely needed, these students are showing us how to develop a strong mastery of the mindset and skills necessary for taking up civic responsibility.

Report Cards

One major sticking point at SEEQS is report cards. Cushman-Patz was adamant about not using grades. She explained that grades take away from student agency, the key to personal mastery. "As soon as someone else gets the ownership of telling you how you did on something," she explained, "you no longer feel you have ownership over your choices."

Like at Red Bridge, the SEEQS teachers create long narratives about student development using four stages of growth toward mastery and competence: starting, striving, succeeding, and soaring.

We thought this was a wonderful way to build a relationship with your preteen and teen. These are the years when they stop sharing about their lives. Wouldn't it be great to get input from the school to make up for the grunts and shrugs at home?

Cushman-Patz laughed when we proposed this. She said many parents agree with us, but about 10 percent just want to know, "How did my kid do? Is it an A or a B or what?" Those same 10 percent want to bulldoze their way past the carefully constructed mastery system of student-led conferences and defenses and just talk to another adult, the teacher, to get the scoop on their teen's performance.

For eighth graders applying to high schools, the school does build a traditional report card, into which they translate their competencies and narratives. This is double work for the school, which, as at Red Bridge, puts a huge burden on the teachers.

We spoke with many schools across the country exploring the mastery paradigm, and almost all of them face some version of this problem: helping students, parents, teachers, other schools, state agencies, and accrediting agencies understand what they are doing. When that's not possible, the schools build duplicate systems that translate back into the old, standardized way of doing things. Translation always generates additional work for already overburdened teachers and administrators.

Conclusion: The Two-System Problem

All three schools we've showcased in this chapter are operating in two different systems simultaneously.

On the one hand, we have the standardized industrial education system that's been in place since the nineteenth century. It batch processes masses of young people along an assembly line of 180-day units called grade levels, through set subjects of study. It assesses via one-and-done tests and sorts people and schools based on the outcomes. In this system, test outcomes, as well as behavior expectations, lead to strict discipline; top-down, one-way accountability; and consequences. It envisions knowledge as an ever-growing but standardizable body of information that teachers are tasked with inputting into children, even if a whole lot of learning is lost along the way.

Then there's a new system being designed in many places around the world. This is a system that thinks of learning as part of human development, where a school's job is to grow humans who thrive in the changing, globalizing, polarizing world of today and tomorrow. For humans to thrive, they need the ability to make choices that support productive work, an active and informed civic life, and personal growth, health, and well-being. They need cognitive and character skills that enable them to keep learning as the world continues to change.

To accomplish this, mastery schools have needed to redesign most of their component parts from the ground up: from schedules to pedagogy to assessment to human relationships to schools' relationships to the communities in which they're located. Above all, it has meant that schools don't standardize their humans; they recognize individuality, including curiosity and interests, motivation, strengths, areas of need, pace of learning, and sociability. The schools also need to keep evolving. As the world changes and the young humans they serve change, the schools have to keep redesigning themselves to accomplish their missions.

In this chapter, we've explored three schools that work with learners before high school. We've seen them all grappling with designing a new, mastery-based system grounded in individual curiosity and agency that develops enduring, transferable cognitive and character skills, as well as essential academic skills and civic responsibility. They're designing and running these new-paradigm schools, and they're heavily chained to the demands and accountability structures of the old standardized system.

Until we create more flexibility and new mastery-based accountability systems, these schools—especially those that are public—are trapped with a foot in both worlds. This places an enormous, unsustainable burden on teachers and school leaders.

Denise Espania, the executive director of Mālama Honua, struggles with this tension daily. "We need to make sure that our children know how to play the game," she explained. "If we don't teach them how to jump through the hoops and take tests and know how to sit down and do what they're supposed to do when they're supposed to be doing it, we're actually not doing a service for our students."

Given the current state of education, ensuring that children can succeed in both systems is part of the school's kuleana to the young people in their care. Sadly, it's also a disservice to those students— and much more work for the innovative teachers and leaders helping nurture them. Such work is very difficult at scale. This is one of the reasons why innovative schools are often small; all three of the schools discussed in this chapter are under two hundred students.

And primary schools often have far fewer regulations and constraints than high schools. Attempting innovative mastery learning under the pressure of graduation and college requirements is an even more daunting undertaking. In the next chapter, though, we'll visit very different high schools braving the challenge.

CHAPTER 4

Growing Mastery in Secondary School

O N A SUNNY Tuesday morning in the greater Seattle area, Gibson Ek High School is as silent as a monastery. All its chattering, squealing, buzzing teenagers are not at school, and this is just fine.

Julia Bamba is the founding principal of Gibson Ek, a mastery-based alternative high school open to all Issaquah School District students. She greeted Sujata at the soaring brick-and-glass entryway and explained, "Students are only required to be on campus three days. This is one of the off days."

Issaquah, once a small, rural, coal-mining town, is now a leafy suburb of Seattle. It is home to powerhouse companies like Microsoft and Costco. Its residents work in the creative and technology economy. The average house price is $1 million.

Issaquah has three very traditional, highly ranked high schools offering a range of International Baccalaureate and Advanced Placement (AP) programs and courses, what the Committee of Ten, *A*

Nation at Risk, and many high-achieving parents define as the pathway to success.

These schools immerse teenagers in the world of great thinkers and traditional subjects. They measure student preparation for graduation and adulthood in terms of Carnegie units. At Issaquah High School, for example, you can move on after four credits of English; three of math, social studies, and science; and two of world languages, with a smattering of other subjects like health, PE, and electives. Each credit is one course, 120 hours of seat time, with grades and GPAs. The student experience is about studying what school tells you you're supposed to learn.

Despite these successful schools, the district leaders in 2014 decided to design a new alternative high school. Alternative schools in the United States are often where districts send the kids who aren't succeeding in a traditional school setting, especially students on the verge of dropping out.

Because they're for the almost dropouts, alternative schools are regulated a lot less by states and districts than traditional schools are. The education they offer has a reputation for being less valuable and less rigorous. It's not the sort of place high-achieving families consider sending their kids. But this wasn't the type of alternative school Issaquah's leaders had in mind when they funded Gibson Ek.

Bamba explained, "We really needed a choice school for students who may not be thriving in middle school and were looking for a different way of learning—and also for students who were just not being challenged."

Issaquah gave Bamba and her team a year and a half to develop an intentional, coherent school model different from the haphazard hodgepodge of often archaic courses and programs that is a traditional academic secondary school.

The team researched. They engaged with community stakeholders. They explored a variety of school models and visited local businesses and coworking spaces, all to make sense of what high school could be, if you could wave your magic wand and start from scratch in the second decade of the twenty-first century.

The school's community statement gives you a sense of the breadth of its ambition to transition young people into adulthood. "We are a community of creators, thinkers, makers, artists, engineers, thespians, writers, collaborators, friends, mentors, activists, programmers, builders, advocates, scientists, marketers, designers, learners creating a place where students find and develop their passions and use this discovery to make a difference in the world. We know this world is complex and dynamic and needs people who are critical thinkers who can engage with diverse people."

The school design they landed on was the Big Picture model. The Big Picture Learning network was established in 1995 to put students in charge of their own learning. The 275 schools in the global network follow ten design principles, many of which focus on nurturing each individual student; building a strong, supportive community; and resourcing students to learn what interests them out in the larger world they will soon join as young adults.

This is not possible in massive high schools of two to four thousand students, so most Big Picture schools stay under two hundred students. Their reasoning is grounded in Dunbar's number, based on the work of social anthropologist Robin Dunbar, who determined that the maximum number of people you can know at any given time is about 150. If relationships are important to the school model, then you have to stay small to build a stable, cohesive community where supportive, caring relationships can be built. Go larger, and you'll need much more management, control, compliance, and discipline to maintain stability and cohesion—a trap that traditional large high schools often fall into.

Big Picture schools also stress learning through interests and internships. Real-world experiences connect young people to "the big picture"—how their curiosities, their strengths and weaknesses, and their connections to their peers and community might help them accomplish something in the real, nonschool world. As they participate in more and more external work experiences, they come to understand how their current learning might link to a future career and life. They also design the steps they might take to navigate to where they want to go.

While more schools are encouraging students to do internships to explore their interests in real-world workplaces, the number of students who actually get to do them is still very small. As of 2020, only 2 percent of high school students completed internships, even though 70 percent of those who did received job offers.[1]

Usually, students do internships in their senior year when they've completed all other graduation requirements. At Gibson Ek, students can do external learning experiences for 40 percent of their high school careers: two full days a week for four years.

Today's World of Work

How can young people know what they want to do when they grow up if they aren't exposed to many options? How can they learn what they're curious about and, over time, develop that curiosity into a passion if they don't have the opportunity to apply learning to real-world contexts that matter to them? How can they grow grit, competence, creativity, and the ability to collaborate, as well as an understanding of their gaps and needs for deliberate practice if we have them spend the bulk of their time learning things from other centuries that most of them are largely indifferent to?

The answer is to flip the traditional script. Instead of high school being something you have to do—something you get through in order to go to college so that you can start your real life—what if high school became the place where you make choices that move you toward a life of your own design?

We live in a time of choice and inventiveness. To be able to seize new opportunities, you need the durable cognitive and character skills that let you add value by being analytical, creative, and deeply human. What if high school was designed to do this?

Secondary education is one of the key institutions that can help young people make these choices. It's where teenagers can practice becoming adults, ideally in a nurturing and challenging environment. It's where, with the support and coaching of knowledgeable teachers, young people can explore and develop their interests, as well as grow their sense of self and community. It's where they learn what learning means and what excellence means. Above all, it's where they can develop initial understandings of what work they want to do in the world.

In this chapter, we'll spend more time with Gibson Ek and then visit a variety of very different schools that are actively and iteratively designing what postprimary education could be.

Thriving in a Changing World

Given that Gibson Ek was created for those who don't thrive in traditional, compliance-based environments, we asked Bamba if there were young people who might not succeed at a school designed for the creative economy. She thought for a moment and answered, "Kids who want the easy way through high school."

By easy way, she didn't mean kids who don't want to do any work. She meant teens (and their parents) who want the well-trodden path to success: good grades, AP courses, high GPAs. That path is easy because it's familiar and clearly marked, even though the journey itself takes an enormous amount of effort: turning in every single assignment for four years, excelling at test after test, emerging with a very high GPA that lets you credibly apply to a selective college that sets you on your path to white-collar success.

Research shows that teens who follow this track are exhausted from the effort. Some suffer mental distress and depression. They pile on extracurriculars and strategize about letters of recommendation and take grueling SAT prep courses. They certainly don't sleep enough. They may cheat: a 2018 survey of sixteen thousand students in fifteen high-performing high schools found that 79 percent self-reported cheating in the previous month.[2] These students are very focused on grades because grades are their ticket to the next stop on the track. Learning is secondary.

When Bamba talked about not being a good fit for the kids who wanted the easy way, this is what she meant: Gibson Ek does not offer this beaten track. You must forge your own path forward. And that path is through learning that matters to you. This is hard for teens whose curiosity and capacity for reasonable risk-taking haven't been honored and nurtured, who've been told what they need to do to succeed, who may have been discouraged from taking risks, and who may be copying their parents' path to success.

We wondered if a school that focuses on learning that matters to the student only works for kids who already know their passion. Bamba put an end to that idea by explaining that Gibson Ek didn't screen kids for any sort of prequalifications; admission is by lottery. Anyone whose number is picked can enroll. She also explained that many incoming students are fairly typical ninth graders who have no idea what direction they want to go in.

All the school is hoping for, Bamba continued, is one of two things: "That you want to put in some effort. Or that you're okay with being curious about something. Even if it's a tiny, tiny bit of curiosity, we can take it from there."

Designing for Curiosity and Effort

Gibson Ek, like other mastery-based schools we researched, understands that its job is to develop humans who can do things in the world rather than humans who can take tests on theoretical content. Bamba told us she looked for curiosity and effort. Curiosity provides the spark to seek and apply knowledge, and effort is critical to growing competence. Gibson Ek actively structures the development of both.

In Chapter 1 we met Stefaan van Hooydonk of the Global Curiosity Institute. He looks at curiosity as both a trait and a state. It is a trait in that it's innate in us; curiosity is how babies and children learn. And a state, in that it's nourished—or destroyed—by the environment we find ourselves in.

Environment is critical. Families, friend groups, communities, schools, the workplace—all have the power to quash curiosity. "Curiosity," Van Hooydonk told us, "is tribal. Some tribes allow for curiosity or endorse curiosity, and some tribes kill curiosity." This is the state of many American high schools; they are curiosity killers.

We asked Van Hooydonk: What does the trait of curiosity, that ideal that gets lost as we spend more time in school, look like in action? He explained that those who are curious by trait "are asking the right questions. They're finding the right mentors, they're constantly reading and learning, and no one is asking them to do it." This seems like the perfect description of intrinsic motivation and the drive toward growth and mastery. This is what we think all high schools should be nurturing.

When Gibson Ek launched, Bamba and her team were trying to design an environment where curiosity by trait could flourish. But what they found was that many young people needed curiosity by state, because by the time teenagers reached high school, they'd already lost the trait. It had been drilled out of them through an endless track of assignments and grades where students had no choice except to perform (or not). The Gibson Ek team found they had to learn to become curiosity designers, as well as engineers of effort. Now, seven years into their journey, they are very intentional in how they do this.

Young people "don't just get released into the wild," Bamba told us. They need to be "unschooled," which means being encouraged to no longer be passive, compliant performers in the game of school. And then they're taught the skills to navigate their way through uncertainty and change.

The ninth-grade teaching team spends a lot of time nurturing the incoming class's curiosity by exploring the community and allowing kids to experience new or ambiguous situations. They walk into local businesses where they talk to strangers. They explore the neighborhood and, like the Red Bridge kids, take the time to observe with care. Bamba explained, "We help get kids comfortable talking to adults or seeing things and thinking, 'What if?' We build their curiosity."

This is reminiscent of what Van Hooydonk called conceptual mastery, a "general openness of mind" linked to problem finding. It's also how Red Bridge, Mālama Honua, and SEEQS operate: encourage young people to observe the world outside of school walls and have adults who can thoughtfully, supportively, and rigorously engage with their curiosities and questions.

From *What if?*, Gibson Ek ninth graders move to *What can I do?* This question is a controlled form of risk-taking: open-ended, no clear-cut path, the possibility of both success and failure with real stakes. Freshmen take level-one courses, which include design labs. In labs, they learn the design-thinking process—identifying a problem and designing a solution—and project management skills. They do this work in rapid sprints, rich with feedback. Multiple labs—sometimes six weeks long, other times much shorter crash courses—repeat this same process so that design thinking becomes second nature to the students. They begin to feel comfortable applying it to any area of personal curiosity at different time scales. Not unlike training at a gym, this design deliberately builds students' effort and problem-solving muscles.

Bamba continued, "We help them think about a project that's more than the sorts of usual simple activities like create a little short video or a poster. We help them understand what projects at Gibson Ek really mean—the depth involved." When the students work at something with the risk of success or failure, something with depth that can make an impact whether in school or outside, it helps them become more gritty, able to stick to something and pursue it.

When Sujata visited, she spoke with a team of teens working on the topic of water, a global problem that will only grow in importance in the coming years (it's one of the seventeen United Nations Sustainable Development Goals). The students had taken a design lab on water where they built foundational knowledge and skills that would help them define a problem and conduct field research:

- Designing empirical arguments or models: What modes of research should be used? What data should be collected and analyzed?
- Understanding critical issues and events: How do we ask the right questions to understand issues more deeply? How do current events inform decisions for our future?
- Considering geography and our environment: What are the biotic and abiotic factors affecting our environment? What is land use and community design, and how does this play a role in our city and future development?

To apply that learning, the students chose to analyze the water quality at various sources in their school: the kitchen sink, garden hoses, water fountains. As members of the school garden team, they were particularly interested in the characteristics of their garden water supply and what impact it might have on the plants that flourished or failed.

Along the way they were learning about concepts such as water supply and its function and importance. They were learning many skills: how to test pH, the normal and abnormal ranges, and what it means; data measurement and communicating findings; and collaboration, since they were working in teams. They were also learning about their own curiosity and interests: what was interesting to them about water, measurement, data design and analysis, sharing findings, collaborating, and gardening. They had months of data tables on water quality at different places in the school.

Sujata was surprised at how long the project had lasted. The students laughed and explained that the course was only one month long and had ended several months earlier. In a traditional school, on the beaten path to success, no kid would rationally continue working on a project after the class had ended and the grade had been entered into the computer system. What would be the point of that? When Sujata asked the students why they were still taking measurements, they explained that they wanted to know. They *wanted* to keep track of their school community's water quality over the long term. It was their community, and they were contributing to it.

How to Grow Mentally and Emotionally Healthy Teenagers

Almost 50 percent of students at Gibson Ek experience some type of mental health issue. They're anxious; they're afraid of being judged. This is common for many teenagers, particularly in our post-pandemic world. Gibson Ek just chooses not to sweep it under the rug.

Every student, in partnership with an adviser they stay with for four years, develops a personal, tailored mental health and wellness plan. In the plan, they commit to meeting with their adviser every week. The adviser brings observations to the meeting: *I see you walking around the outside area rather than participating. I see you hiding in an empty room knitting. Is this what you really want? What strategies can we come up with together to shift your behaviors? What strategies resonate with you?* Parents and family members are also invited to the support team.

Cognitive behavioral therapy is embedded in every school day for every young person, whether with their adviser or with school-based mental health counselors. Through conversations with their adviser and team, students commit to small steps: For example, this week, share what you're creating with a few trusted peers, your advisory group, or the larger community. You choose.

Lily entered Gibson Ek with a single interest, knitting. She spent all her time knitting. During exploration time, when students were trying new things, Lily would roam the halls or go out to the parking lot. She was positive, kind, and committed to being at Gibson Ek but also really uncertain about how to engage in such an unusual school. She was—like many fourteen-year-olds entering a new high school—afraid and anxious about failure as well as peer judgment.

The school developed a personal wellness plan with her. She agreed to meet with a counselor once a week. She also agreed to meet with her adviser regularly and, with the adviser's support, committed to incremental steps: *This week I will try standing up in front of my peers and sharing my opinion. Next week I'll talk about my work.* The adviser and counselor helped her debrief the steps she took and, in the process, got to know her so that they could support her through her anxiety.

They also connected learning to her existing interest. For Lily, the journey became all about yarn. *This is what I made. This is what I'm curious about: How does science connect to yarn? Can I dye my own yarn? Can I test the flammability of yarn? How? What about the history of knitting? What about the art of knitting?*

Kevin entered Gibson Ek brimming with purpose. Basketball was his passion. Making junior varsity right away was his goal. Academic learning was not that important or enticing.

Given his goals, Kevin's initial health and wellness plan focused on physical health. His adviser also wanted to spark him academically and connect him with projects to pursue during his independent work time. Together they came up with questions related to his personal goal: *What conditioning and strength-training exercises can I do to increase my vertical leaps and quickness? How can I use filming myself as a training method to help adjust my techniques? How can I use video to analyze and set goals for the future? How do I create a multi-week training program? How do I collect data to test, iterate, and adjust the plan I develop?*

Gibson Ek was not going to let Kevin just play basketball during his independent work time. Through the adviser relationship and the health and wellness plan, Kevin designed a meaningful project that connected his basketball goals to academic inquiry and real-world processes: planning, data measurement and collection, data analysis, self-direction, and a stronger sense of agency. Using the training program he designed, he made the junior varsity team. Next, he began to go deep into designing athletic shoes that could support his health and academic goals.

Personal health and wellness plans help Gibson Ek meet the needs of each individual student.

How Gibson Ek Grows Student Competence

At Gibson Ek, there are five overarching competencies that all students develop to varying individual degrees based on their interests:

1. Personal qualities: How do I contribute to my growth and the growth of my community?
2. Communications: How do I take in and express a variety of ideas?
3. Empirical reasoning: How do I prove it? How do I reason?
4. Quantitative reasoning: How do I numerically understand, measure, compare, and represent it?
5. Social reasoning: What are others' perspectives? How do actions influence outcomes?[3]

The school has taken care to clearly define what each of these five competencies mean. Personal qualities, for example, is broken down into four parts in plain language that students can understand: "Better the World," use "Creativity & Imagination," develop a "Productive Mindset," and attend to "Health & Wellness."

Each of these sub-competencies has an essential question that teens can keep using, not just in high school but throughout their lives. For example, productive mindset's is *How do I persist to meet responsibilities?* Under these essential questions are further sets of skills and guiding questions that become more complex as the teens mature from fourteen-year-olds to eighteen-year-olds.

That's how schools using mastery- or competency-based learning work. They take on the big, risky, open-ended questions that were once the realm of classical texts in a liberal arts education: *What is a good life? What are my responsibilities to myself and my community? What is happiness?* These schools then help kids ask the questions and discover their own personal answers to them. Students do this not just through reading texts but through designing, participating in, and reflecting on hands-on, real-world, real-stakes experiences. And most importantly, the schools make explicit the thinking, analyzing, and creating processes that underlie cognitive skills so students can master them. These skills—not remembering when the Napoleonic Wars happened—are what serve you in life. Through grappling with these big, essential questions and arriving at their personal answers to them, students begin to shape a vision for their futures.

In traditional schools, if a student develops a vision of their own personal future, they likely do this outside of school or despite school. At Gibson Ek, however, this is the purpose of school: to help young people develop their vision while they're in school, beginning in ninth grade.

Building a Community of Mastery

Bringing ninth graders into the school's culture and expectations is a whole-community effort. We know that teenagers have a deep drive to be social and learn from each other. Instead of trying to control or suppress this drive like most schools do, Gibson Ek harnesses it. The school channels the older teens' growing sense of independence and responsibility into community and culture building rather than disengagement and rebellion.

Teen peers and adults in the school all work together to give incoming students encouragement and feedback. They also mentor them in developing character skills. When school begins, advisers bring in juniors and seniors as models. The older students discuss what has and hasn't worked for them. They share their learning plans and help younger students design their own. They help them set weekly goals and make explicit choices about what they're working on. In short, they help onboard the younger students into a culture of curiosity, effort, grit, and responsible choice making—into an early version of adulthood. They also help them design the path to get there, building a culture of caring and sense of community in the process.

Teens at Gibson Ek learn how to become learners to increase their skills and mastery. The school defines four levels of achievement of mastery: emerging, exploring, engaged, empowered. Peers and adults all help new students understand that they will keep growing along that continuum, with successes and failures, both equally important, along the journey.

Bamba explained the progression. "They come into school. They're emerging. We're just beginning to understand what their strengths and skills and challenges are. We're okay with them delving into a few different things."

The adults' jobs are to help each student go deeper as they mature. Bamba continued, "We celebrate growth. You don't have to master each and every one of the competencies and sub-competencies. We're not standardized, where all students need to demonstrate all these skills for their competencies. Rather, it's personalized for each kid, what their interests are, and where they want to go in life."

When Sujata asked Bamba how the school encouraged excellence, she explained what "empowered" meant for Gibson Ek's four mastery levels: "When a student is doing incredible work out in the community. They're working with mentors. They're implementing design thinking. They're inspiring their peers. That's empowered."

Parental Expectations

Traditional schools often keep parents at bay. Gibson Ek has learned that, to design a new model of high school, parents and families have to be part of the process, or else teens will feel caught between two worlds: expectations at home versus expectations at school.

The school brings parents and caregivers into the community in a variety of ways: close connections to students' four-year advisers, parent groups, and conversations around the students' individualized learning plans. There are robust discussions among the adults on what their roles are in nurturing the transition to adulthood, particularly on when and how to push and when to allow a young person to experience failure as part of learning.

The school has found that parents, as much as young people, need unschooling. Last year, juniors and seniors ran a workshop for ninth-grade parents called "From Floundering to Flourishing" to help answer questions like, "Why aren't there three hours of homework in this school?"

The school's success in the college admissions process has been helpful in allaying parent concerns about this new design of learning. The type of learning that happens at Gibson Ek can't be conveyed in the traditional high school transcript, composed of a list of courses and letter grades with a cumulative GPA that summarizes each student into a single number. Instead, Gibson Ek became the first school in the country to send out a new kind of transcript that showcases each student's unique mastery of the competencies the school focuses on. In fact, Gibson Ek's mastery transcripts don't include grades or GPAs at all.

The transcripts are in part student curated; juniors and seniors work on building their transcripts and portfolios of their work as part of a base of supporting evidence. They use the transcript to tell colleges the story of the adults they are becoming, with a school-backed portfolio of evidence to support it.

The school has been sending this transcript and portfolio out for five years now. About 180 students have sent out the transcript (about 70 percent of the school's students apply to four- or two-year colleges directly out of high school). Shawn Mulanix, the lead counselor, told us that most of the students get into their first-choice school. Fifteen students have chosen to apply to highly selective universities, and there have been eight admissions to institutions such as Caltech, Harvey Mudd College, and UCLA (one student accounted for two of these admissions).

The University of Washington (UW), as the local flagship state university, was particularly critical for Gibson Ek. During the school's first year, the admissions team visited and told Bamba, "You could have a student who cures cancer, but if they don't have a GPA and they don't have these specific classes, we're probably not going to admit them." Now, a few years later, the university admits a number of Gibson Ek students each year.

Much of the success can be attributed to the behind-the-scenes translation work of the team at the Mastery Transcript Consortium (MTC), which led the design of the new transcript Gibson Ek students have been using. In 2022, MTC began working with the UW systems office as well as various Washington campuses to help them understand the rigor behind the competency-based learning records and how demonstrated mastery of disciplinary and cross-content competencies aligns with university criteria for admissions and success. MTC's team has been doing this translation work with every university or college that students apply to from Gibson Ek and other schools.

Despite its many successes with students and now college admissions, the Gibson Ek model is not spreading inside the district. Issaquah's three traditional high schools remain traditional. In a volatile and rapidly changing world, parents rationally will hold on to the traditional path to success like a life raft in a sea of turbulence. It doesn't matter how irrational the selective college admissions process is and how little that pathway is preparing teens to succeed.

If we really want to transform high schools to meet the needs of teens in the twenty-first century, we adults need to be willing to take a risk and back new models like Gibson Ek. But change is hard and uncomfortable for most people, in part because we haven't been educated as Gibson Ek students have been. We haven't deliberately practiced how to take reasonable risks to forge new paths.

Agora School: The Netherlands

Agora is a Dutch school that also takes a radically different approach to helping teenagers become successful in life. It has no courses, no classrooms, and no standardized curriculum. And yet its students take and pass the rigorous national Dutch exams, despite not having had four years of an academic curriculum.

We spoke with Rob Houben, a former math teacher who founded Agora in 2015 in partnership with five colleagues, sixty students, and government funding. The original school now has about three hundred students, and each student is treated as the individual he or she is.

Houben explained that the school's radically personalized approach to curiosity-based learning focuses on what kids want to learn rather than what teachers have to teach. Just as toddlers learn to walk and to tell time at different ages, so teenagers learn different things at their own pace.

"There is always a window in which kids are open to learning something," he told us. "At Agora we start teaching something very soon when the window opens, but that doesn't mean the window is open for all the students. We need to be looking at how close are we to the last day of the window for this child."

We asked him why the last day, and he explained that this generates motivation. When young people want to learn something and are motivated to learn it, "then you can do very short interactions with students, and they learn stuff very fast. But you have to wait longer than you expect with some students."

Agora also understands that its job is to expose young people to more than what they're currently interested in. The school does regular "wonder and inspiration sessions" that can be anything from woodworking workshops to "Let's talk about volcanoes." The school brings in community experts all the time. An archaeologist will notify the students, "I'm going to be available for questions next Monday at 11 a.m." Anyone at the school can choose to join.

Teenagers drive their own learning journey, but they still need structure. Houben called it "a daily rhythm." Students can arrive at school early or leave late, but every day at nine o'clock they meet in the same mixed-age group with the same adult mentor. Here they discuss current events, build relationships with each other, and share the challenges they've set for themselves that day. Toward the end of the day, the mentor will check in with students again, to see how they fared on their day's challenge journey.

Challenges can be anything from designing a new skateboard prototype to learning about the Great Barrier Reef to building furniture to starting a diving school. Adults (teachers, parents, outside experts) can guide academic knowledge and skills development through the projects young people want to pursue, and public daily sharing of the challenges allows teens to collaborate and share their expertise as well.

Challenges have multiple phases that guide students in going deep and achieving mastery. Phase one is playing around with a topic; Agora calls it "experiment and research." When teenagers have arrived at what they want to achieve, they move to the next phase, "go deep and achieve quality." Finally, they "shine and share," which Houben explained means "you have to build or create a product or an activity in which you can show off to other people."

The quality of that product demonstrates mastery of learning, which, Houben emphasized, is not graded. Instead, adults support teens on their challenges, asking probing questions, stimulating their interest in learning more and going deeper. Houben continued, "What you see is when they're really engaged with their own topic and you ask a question about it, when they don't know the answer they will immediately tell you, 'I'm going to get back to you tomorrow.' And so, we don't have to grade. We are stimulating them to a mastery level."

Through these curiosity-driven challenges, Agora supports young people in building a vision of their futures, what Houben calls "future orientation": what they like and don't like to do. He explained this is very important because, in the Dutch educational system, 35 percent of students make a university or career choice they later decide they don't want, leading to dropouts and debt.

Knowledge and skills development plus future orientation combine to help knowledge stick. Learning has a purpose for life, not just for an exam or test. Surprisingly, this makes students interested in the national exams all Dutch students who want a secondary degree have to take, because they've begun to know themselves and have a sense of the future they want. After two to three years of curiosity-driven challenges, Houben explained, "our students start to talk more and more about 'What do we need to know for the exams? I know which occupation I want to do in the future. I know which university I want to go to.'"

That's when Agora steps in to help them map what they've already learned and what they still need to learn. Together, they design a customized program for each teenager that helps them meet the requirements of the next stage of learning they want, be it entrance to a specific university or a particular job or personal endeavor.

We asked Houben about Agora's students and parents. He told us that in Agora's first year, he interviewed all the parents to ask why they'd take a risk on such an unconventional school. About 60 to 70 percent of the parents told him, "If we don't put our son or daughter in your school, we definitely know that our child will be at home within eight weeks." These were the kids who weren't thriving in traditional schools, and over time, as they succeeded, their friends and neighbors began coming to Agora. It has also become a haven for neurodivergent students, sometimes with multiple diagnoses;

35 percent of Agora's students were labeled as having special education needs in primary school.

Agora, which began as a single secondary school in the Netherlands, is now a loose global network of twenty-five schools spreading through Europe.

Academic Tracks and Vocational Tracks

Postprimary education, what Americans call high school, has many names and forms across the developed world. Most countries don't have a single high school model as the United States does; they have different types and different levels of secondary education, all of which have different expectations of when students should engage with practical knowledge and make decisions about their career paths.

In academically focused systems like those in the United States, career paths are usually decided on after secondary school. The comprehensive high school, a heavily academic institution where students study and take exams, focuses on the transmission of traditional knowledge. Students learn about life and personal growth not in school but rather through extracurriculars like hobbies, sports, and clubs. Japan, China, and South Korea have more extreme versions of this system. Academic performance on entrance exams determines admission to academic secondary schools, which are hierarchically ranked in terms of the career opportunities they make possible. To succeed, you have to absorb a massive amount of content knowledge. The school years are forty to sixty days longer than in most other countries, and students attend additional "cram schools" in the evenings and on their days off. There's little room for career exploration or developing durable character skills aside from grit.

In more practically oriented systems, like those in much of Europe, vocational education is a common element of secondary schools. Some countries, like Germany and Luxembourg, test students at about the age of twelve and assign them to a vocational or academic track, depending on their test scores. In many Scandinavian countries, students can choose which secondary school track they want to pursue and can even blend academic and vocational studies. The percentage of European secondary students who are enrolled in a vocational or technical track varies depending on the country, with the European Union average being 49 percent.[4] In the United States, most school districts offer at least a few vocationally oriented courses, but only 10 percent of American public high school students are enrolled in full-time career and technical education (CTE) programs.[5] States' investments in CTE courses total only about 1 percent of all state K–12 education funding.[6]

Both these approaches have their pros and cons. The European system can engage youth in meaningful, purpose-defining work and personal development, but it can also lock them into career choices made when they're still immature. The US system can create academic opportunities for all students, but it can also leave them disengaged and questioning what relevance school learning has to their longer-term growth and development.

The schools and programs we'll look at in the remainder of this chapter are blurring the boundaries between academic and vocational tracks in ways very different from the two high schools we've discussed above.

Center for Advanced Professional Studies

Jenna Felson, twenty-six, works as a client marketing associate at GCM Grosvenor, an asset management company in Chicago that oversees $75 billion worth of real estate investments. An alumna of both the University of Missouri, Kansas City, and the commercial banking division of JPMorgan Chase, Jenna is active in her community and church. When we spoke with her, she radiated joy, enthusiasm, and thoughtful engagement. She had clearly transitioned into a thriving adulthood.

She credits this not to high school generally but to a specific high school program available in her school district. It's called the Center for Advanced Professional Studies (CAPS), and Jenna believes in it so strongly that she founded its alumni network.

Jenna explained how the program nurtured her. "CAPS helps you decide what it is you won't want to do, or it helps you find what you do want to do. I joined the program thinking I wanted to be a graphic designer, but now I work in real estate finance. So, CAPS helped me realize that, too, and save myself time in the long run."

We asked her how she figured out her path. Real-world workplace experience in high school was the key. She told us, "I interned at a start-up in Kansas City that was a supply-chain finance company called C2FO. It's the largest fintech [software technology for the financial sector] start-up in Kansas now." She joined the company when they had about 150 employees; now they're at 800.

The world of finance sparked her curiosity, and she kept putting in the effort and going deeper. She's very grateful to CAPS for exposing her to supply-chain finance, something she, like most teenagers, didn't even know existed.

CAPS, like the Hawaiian schools and Big Picture, is a network. It began in 2009 in an affluent suburb of Kansas City as a program open to students across the Blue Valley school district's five high schools. These large, comprehensive high schools are all high performing: graduation rates are between 96 and 99 percent, they're chock-full of AP classes and have very high college enrollment rates.

CAPS didn't redesign traditional high school like Gibson Ek did. Instead, it created a replicable system for profession-based learning: real-world, curiosity-driven exploration and risk-taking opportunities for juniors and seniors who've mostly completed their core graduation requirements.

Usually, these juniors and seniors take random electives to fill the space in their Carnegie-unit-driven schedules. CAPS, however, enables them to explore a variety of industry-based pathways focused on client projects, where students have the responsibility of delivering real value to real clients. No theoretical projects or simulations—every project is sourced from an actual company or nonprofit whose needs the teenagers strive to meet.

This might be exciting and motivating for teenagers biologically primed to take risks, but it's scary for organizations that have actual customers, boards, investors, key performance indicators, obligations, and legal accountabilities. Corey Mohn, the president of the CAPS Network, told us how the group got businesses to buy in. "We said, 'Hey if you're a nonprofit or for-profit corporation, or even a start-up, what's the tenth thing on your to-do list? You know you'll never get to it. It's not mission critical for you. However, your growth might be stronger if it were done. Take a chance on our kids to get that done for you!'"

In this way, CAPS gathered a bunch of low-stakes, high-impact opportunities where high school students could sink their teeth into meaningful work. The CAPS leadership really didn't know what to expect that first year. Mohn explained, "It could have been a real win or a total disaster."

He told us a story about students in the first Global Business class. They were embedded every day at Freedom Bank in Overland Park, Kansas. On the first day, bank founder and CEO Kurt Knutson handed students the tenth thing on his to-do list: determine if there is a market in the community for debit cards branded for each of the local high schools. Would such a product bring new customers to the bank, and would this drive up the use of debit cards for existing customers?

Students were divided into project teams. They set off to design cards for each of the five Blue Valley high schools and perform due diligence to determine market demand. In the end, the students were successful in generating professional, marketable design concepts and were also able to provide Freedom Bank with qualitative data regarding the appeal of such a product.

Then they presented to the CEO. Knutson was underwhelmed. He didn't think they had done enough customer discovery and concept validation. Their efforts at gathering a sufficient list of people committed to such a card was, in his opinion, not adequate. He told them he would not proceed with creating the debit cards.

CAPS is a real-world experience, and students learned a valuable lesson in the importance of leveraging their network and providing proof of market viability prior to a product launch. They also learned they needed to work harder.

For Knutson, the project was not unlike other business experiments he had run to test viable projects. Some will proceed, others will not. In this instance, the product (high school branded debit cards) was not validated and did not move forward into production. However, the work the students performed during the project cycle provided Knutson and his leadership team with a way to test new ideas with very little investment of time or resources. They decided to continue with the CAPS program. In fact, they even hired a number of CAPS students over the next few years.

In the end, both the students and the business community saw enough value in the program to soldier on. In year two, CAPS went from 100 to 250 students and doubled their business partners. The year after, it doubled again. By 2023, CAPS had spread to more than one hundred schools: thirteen thousand students from 170 school districts across twenty-three states and four countries (the United States, Canada, Kenya, and Kuwait). CAPS leadership created detailed case studies and blueprints for how local ecosystems, both rural and urban, can bring together secondary schools and employers to give students professional learning opportunities where they grow their career awareness and adult competence. As communities follow these step-by-step directions, they can turn to the CAPS team and the CAPS Network for support and, eventually, membership.

Developmentally Appropriate

Antonio Linhart, now a software engineer on the network connectivity team at Google in Seattle, was on our call with Jenna. A Blue Valley CAPS alumnus as well as an alumni association board member, Antonio graduated recently from the University of Nebraska, Lincoln, after interning at both Microsoft and Google.

Like Jenna, he credits CAPS for his successful transition to adulthood. He entered the program interested in game design, then got exposed to a wide variety of computer-science-based projects that sparked his curiosity and helped him see other career paths. Each semester, his CAPS cohort did three different projects: one for a business client, one community outreach project like organizing a hackathon, and one tech-based personal passion project. These projects widened his vision of what he could do with his interest in computer science.

Perhaps even more important to his development as an adult was the autonomy he had as a CAPS student. Antonio explained, "The way that CAPS works is that a lot of the work is done on your own. The teacher is not like, 'You have to do this from 9 to 10 a.m., then you do this from 10 to 11 a.m.' It's a lot more self-structure."

Unlike the hyper-control of traditional high school classes (bell schedule, grades, behavior and attendance policies, bathroom policies, assignments, tests), CAPS students have choice and responsibility. They have freedom to develop personal mastery.

"Having those three project structures throughout the semester really let me learn time management skills," Antonio said. "I realized that there are some days where I really didn't want to work on my business project—and there were some days I really didn't want to work on my personal project. I learned about my work preferences, and how to go back and forth to be able to ensure I was completing what I thought I'd be able to complete while also doing what I wanted to do."

He continued, "It really helped me feel like a professional even though I was still in high school. In CAPS, you're treated like an adult. You're given the guidelines, and you're trusted that you'll make the right decision, and you'll get your work done."

Like Gibson Ek, CAPS scaffolds young people into adulthood. Adults make thousands of decisions per day; children make far fewer. All too often, school severely limits young people's decision-making domains and opportunities, leaving them few chances to make good and bad decisions and learn from their successes and failures.

We asked Jenna and Antonio who might not be successful at CAPS. Jenna replied, "CAPS is not a great place if you're someone who likes structure." Like Julia Bamba at Gibson Ek, Jenna was talking about a very specific kind of structure, one where the path and the destination are marked out for you.

On a separate call, Mohn, the CAPS president, confirmed this. "The kids that tend to struggle the most in CAPS are the highfliers because they want to 'play' school and it doesn't work here, because we present them with ambiguous situations and client projects that have no right answer. And they don't like that." Instead, these students are used to a clear-cut path with clear-cut content and questions on tests that have clear-cut answers. But none of that is helpful in navigating a rapidly changing world where ambiguity is the norm and creativity is often part of getting to the solution.

CAPS, again like Gibson Ek, is highly structured in its own way. It's intentionally designed to help teens get comfortable with ambiguity by developing their self-awareness and showing them processes for time management, problem-solving, engineering design, and so on. Instead of focusing on learning rote content, students learn methods and processes they can use to create their own structure in open-ended and uncertain terrain.

Mohn continued, "Most of the highfliers who enroll in CAPS get there once they realize that this is how you step through, how you iterate, how you not let a failure crush your spirit. There's a process you can go through to get there, and a culture that gets you there." The clarity of the process helps reengage those who are more comfortable with clearly defined paths.

On the other hand, he explained, "The kids from the alternative pathways thrive in it, because it's like, 'This is different. This is exciting. I can see how I can do something real!'"

Diverse Communities

Blue Valley is an affluent, mostly white school district where students enter with a lot of support and access. The district built CAPS its own building, a multimillion-dollar innovation center where students could explore subjects such as bioscience, engineering, and entrepreneurship in state-of-the-art labs and facilities. We asked about how well the program worked in more diverse and high-needs environments. Mohn introduced us to Mike Poore, then the superintendent of Little Rock School District in Arkansas.

Poore began his CAPS journey when he was superintendent of the Bentonville schools. Bentonville, where Walmart is headquartered, is an affluent community. Poore placed a group of young Bentonville high schoolers at Walmart corporate offices. The point of contact was the head of technology, and he was supporting five interns. "After the kids had been there a little bit, he called me and said, 'Mike, we have a problem.'"

Walmart's head of technology insisted that Poore come to corporate headquarters to meet in person. Poore was worried. He thought the program would collapse because the teens weren't up to the projects they'd been given. "We go up. We were terrified," he recalled. "And he says to us, 'Our problem is that what we gave these kids for their internship—they've done it in a week! They're outperforming our college interns.'"

The Walmart team had severely underestimated the high school students, and they had created a program that entailed some simple coding and some job shadowing. Once the professionals saw what the high schoolers were capable of, they were put in charge of developing, designing, running, and evaluating a hackathon inside Walmart corporate headquarters. Poore explained, "We didn't teach a coding language. They learned whatever language they needed for the time. They became adept at multiple coding languages, and they used the adults at Walmart in the profession to help guide them." After a few years of stories like this, Poore became a CAPS believer and began to think about how it might work in other circumstances.

In 2015, the state of Arkansas put Little Rock School District under state control for low standardized test scores. They brought Poore in to run the show, and he had his opportunity. State control, or receivership as it's also known, usually has a "turnaround" playbook, which often calls itself "innovative" but is far from that. Key moves include firing a certain percentage of teachers and administrators and doubling the amount of time spent on basic English and math classes, which entails eliminating the few classes, like the arts, that actually excite students. Test scores are the alpha and omega of turnaround success.[7]

Instead, Poore brought CAPS in to unite community stakeholders toward a different path to success, one that focused on reigniting teenagers' curiosity and launching them on journeys to mastery through a hands-on, real-world pedagogy connected to the job opportunities of today. He explained, "This whole concept of career education and project-based learning was something of a godsend because everybody could agree to it. The unions did, as did the business community. It became a rallying point for us as a part of working our way out of state control." It created an inspiring vision of what school could be, rather than a pathology report of how twenty-first-century students were failing to meet nineteenth-century expectations.

Corey Mohn also introduced us to Tim Murrell, principal of the Topeka Center for Advanced Learning and Careers in Kansas. Topeka—where 71 percent of students come from low-income families—took a different path to CAPS. In the early 2000s, vocational education began shifting nationwide to career and technical education. CTE, trying to undo the two-tiered system of the college-prep track and the manual-arts track, prepared students for college and career. CTE courses were designed to teach technical skills and include more classical academics. That way, students who wanted to learn hands-on skills could also have the option to go to college, if they wanted.[8]

Topeka had a robust CTE program, and CAPS was layered in as one of the ten pathways that offered skills-based certifications for post–high school careers. Here was real-world professional learning as icing on the CTE cake.

Murrell told us about the variety of business community partners that had joined the program to offer professional opportunities to CAPS students: "At Central Business Technologies, our students are working in marketing. At Advisors Excel, a firm here in Topeka, students are working in marketing and video production. The Topeka Zoo is bringing in our students in animal science. We have students working at Hill's Pet Nutrition, which created Science Diet. It's been an amazing experience."

We also interviewed John Burgess, president and cofounder of Mainstream Technologies, a seventy-person tech consulting firm that joined the Little Rock CAPS program as an employer.

Poore, Murrell, and Burgess all told us the same story about the value of the program. CAPS helped young people see what they were capable of when given responsibility for real-world projects that mattered to an existing organization. And, once the businesses and nonprofits saw the results of what young people could do, the businesspeople and educators in traditional classes changed their expectations of students. Learning was happening in two directions.

Murrell told us a story about how he won over high school academic teachers. A group of Topeka CAPS students in the web and digital communications strand were working with a seminary in Ethiopia that needed a catalog created. The students scheduled video conference meetings with their client, defined the project, developed the work, and created what the client needed.

Murrell then brought the high school English and math teachers to see what the students had produced. He explained what happened next. "The students actually sold the core subject teachers. The students said, 'Listen, we learned things in your English class. But here we can apply it, and it really makes a difference. We can grasp the concepts that you're talking about. We have to write, and we have to do it the right way, and we have to use the technology. So, it's the best of both worlds.'"

Burgess, the tech CEO, summed up what he learned from working with high schoolers. "CAPS showed us that by changing the traditional curriculum or the usual way that students are learning, what they're being exposed to, we could really accelerate their progress on the learning curve. Kids are sponges, and they're going to pick up what they're shown, especially if you can make it relevant to them, some context that really fuels their interest or their passions. Then it's also a window into us as future employers—a future they can envision because they've lived it. I think it's just a win-win situation."

For high school to be redesigned for mastery, to meet the needs of both teenagers and the communities in which they live and will work, we need many, many more stories like CAPS. Bit by bit, the various stakeholders in education—parents and families, employers, government, and especially teachers and administrators—will need to be won over to a vision of learning that grows the capacity and competence of young people to choose their individual paths to thriving in today's world.

Charlotte-Mecklenburg Schools, North Carolina

Nakesha "Kesha" Dawson is a revolutionary high school educator. She is the curriculum lead for the marketing CTE pathway for

Charlotte-Mecklenburg Schools (CMS). With over 147,000 students, the district is the eighteenth largest in the United States.

Dawson grew up seven miles outside of a one-stoplight town in rural North Carolina. The town had nothing. She got out and went to college, where she majored in economics. She lived in successively larger towns: Winston-Salem, then Greensboro, then Charlotte. These towns had amenities like malls and big businesses, things she hadn't been exposed to as a teenager. When she started teaching, she wanted to make sure her students understood the opportunities of the wider world they were lucky enough to have as part of their daily existence.

Before coming to Charlotte, she was teaching business and marketing to high schoolers in Greensboro. Other teachers said to her, "Dawson, you never keep your kids in school!" and she agreed. She wanted them to look at the world around them and develop their curiosity.

So, they'd hop a bus to the mall where she'd ask, "Who's the target customer of the Louis Vuitton store as opposed to the JCPenney?" They went to the circus in Greensboro, and she asked, "Can you predict how the circus will transform itself in ten to fifteen years? Think about PETA [People for the Ethical Treatment of Animals] and other vectors of change." Dawson was teaching her students how to observe, analyze, and predict—how to think, really.

We asked how she had the freedom to do these things at a time when test scores were the most important measure of success. She explained, "Our test scores were good because I also had students who, for the most part, knew how to 'play school.' And I'm not ashamed to get all southern mama and tell them, 'Y'all are not gonna embarrass me because we're gonna do all these field trips. You better do well on this test. It goes together.'" Dawson's students produced the test scores she needed to continue the sorts of learning experiences that kept them engaged.

Even though CTE is meant to be a pathway to both vocational careers and college, in many places it still carries a "less than" stigma—our centuries-old prejudice against those who work with their hands versus those who work primarily with abstraction. College prep is still seen as the preferred path to success. Dawson was having none of this. She sees CTE as a path to leadership.

CMS currently has twenty-two different pathways for their students, everything from advanced manufacturing and engineering to interior design to software development to firefighter technology to nursing fundamentals.[9]

Dawson told us her marketing pathway got started when the school district realized there was a gap between the skills its students were graduating with and the needs of the booming Charlotte economy. Hospitality is one of the major industries in the region, and the school district interviewed hotel managers to find out why they weren't hiring CMS students. The school administrators learned that customer relationship management (CRM) software skills, and Salesforce in particular, were nonnegotiable for the jobs they wanted their students to be able to access.

Today's businesses are organized by enterprise software, computer applications that manage inventory, supply chains, customer interactions, business intelligence, marketing, and more. Salesforce, the world's fourth largest enterprise software firm (behind Microsoft, Oracle, and SAP), is the largest global CRM platform. CRM is how organizations track, manage, and analyze all their interactions with their customers across communications methods (phone, in person, text, chatbot). Imagine a giant interactive database that holds the information about all the customers at the 8,700 Marriott properties in the world, so that when you check into the JW Marriott in downtown Charlotte, the receptionist knows from the Salesforce CRM that you have an allergy to feather pillows, which you made clear when you were at the Bangkok Marriott Marquis two years ago.

From these conversations with local businesses, Dawson and her team designed a marketing pathway for CMS students. They built it in close collaboration with the local businesses, and they designed it on top of mastery-based learning pathways developed by Salesforce itself.

Salesforce, like many tech companies, offers a robust catalog of online courses leading to certification in its very complex platform, tools, and applications. The courses are free, but the certification is not. Google also does this, as do Meta, Microsoft, and many other tech companies. Salesforce's learning platform is called Trailhead. It uses hiking and play metaphors to guide users through a self-directed online course. In digital "playgrounds," learners explore what aspects of Salesforce they want to get proficient in. Then they pick a "trail"—a specific sequence of learning—along which they complete skill-based modules and projects. There are thousands of trails, ranging from "Develop Loyalty Programs to Enhance Engagement" to "Build Apps," all of which, once mastered, earn learners badges and points. Learners can then show these to potential employers as evidence of real, validated learning. When all the badges along a specific trail are accumulated, learners qualify for a specific certification.

Companies, hungry for new talent, build these learning platforms and keep them updated. They're created for adults, though nothing prevents anyone of any age from using them—except for the educational system as it's currently designed. The existing school structure and regulations in the United States make it difficult to use corporate platforms. Dawson and her team figured out how to make them usable in high schools, solving many technical problems. They had to get the state to approve the courses. "The curriculum and the approval were the easy part," Dawson told us.

They then had to fit the courses, as well as internships, into existing school schedules. They needed to incorporate deep, extended projects into forty-five-minute classes. They needed to retrain teachers to think of their jobs not as delivering content via Power-Point lectures but instead as building relationships and giving effective feedback to self-directed learners. They had to figure out how teachers could be credentialed to teach the courses and how the state would approve those credentials.

Dawson wanted the students to get CTE credit for the courses. The state's CTE exam is one hundred multiple-choice questions, so Dawson and her team had to figure out how get the state to give credit without having to create such an arbitrary, teacher-made exam. They negotiated with the state to allow the proof of learning to be a series of simulated real-world experiences that showed mastery of Salesforce applications, as well as the actual official Salesforce test.

They then encountered another obstacle. Salesforce doesn't sell its credentialing opportunity to schools. Ever resourceful, Dawson and her team found a small tech company, Tech Talent South, that was willing to be the go-between that would buy the exam licenses from Salesforce and then sell them back to CMS. They then learned that the tests couldn't be administered at schools. The exams had to take place in a biometric testing facility, so Dawson created an officially sanctioned field trip to the testing center.

We were exhausted hearing about all the links in the regulatory chains that the United States puts on high school innovation, links that Dawson and her team had to dismantle one by one. But she is ever optimistic. Having succeeded with Salesforce, the Charlotte-Mecklenburg team has moved on to add Adobe and Google certifications for CMS students.

Growing Students' Self-Direction

In 2021, Dawson convened a panel of junior and senior marketing CTE students for us. Destiny, Nyala, Imani, and Ayanna attended a school where the student body had low test scores and high discipline issues. All four worked and had family responsibilities in addition to attending high school. All four planned to go to college after graduation.

We asked them to share what they appreciated about the program. They all agreed they liked the independence to learn without someone holding their hand or moving them through a rote sequence. They took pleasure in reaching a deeper understanding on their own.

Nyala explained, "I was a little discouraged on my first day when our teacher, Miss Mary, showed us the playgrounds [in the Salesforce online learning program]. I thought, 'I don't know how I'm going to be able to do this every day by myself.' But now I come to class, I get my computer, and I can easily log in and get through trails completely by myself with no help. I'm proud of myself for that."

They also remarked on how the program had taught them to be systematic in how they learned. Since everything built on the previous thing, they couldn't skip steps like they did in other classes. They had to master each piece of the puzzle. Destiny explained, "We have to get all the steps perfect in the playground in order to get the badge and finish it. This has also taught me patience. Because sometimes I get a step wrong, and then I have to go back and look at everything I've done."

The teens began to transfer this step-by-step approach to other aspects of their lives. Destiny continued, "I did tutoring at my nearby elementary school. And in order for me to explain a math problem to fifth graders, I would have to think about it for myself first and find a way to explain it to them step-by-step." Working in this systematic way with younger children also helped grow her patience. First, she learned thoroughness, patience, and systematic thinking for herself, then she transferred these skills into new situations dealing with others. In other words, she was developing what we call cognitive and character mastery.

The Salesforce pathway was also learning that mattered to the four teenagers we spoke with. Given their life circumstances, it mattered in a very practical way. Salesforce certification gave them life options. Imani wanted to go into the medical field, but she told us, "If something doesn't work out in college, I'll still have a certification." Ayanna felt the certification was the first step in her getting the qualifications she'd need to open her own business.

Nyala and Destiny were particularly worried about the high cost of college. Nyala summed up their concerns and how the certification helped them. "I've always wanted to go to college and get my degree. I want to go to a *good* college. But student loans are always a worry in the back of my head. After taking this class and getting the certification, I know I can take a part-time job during college doing something related to Salesforce. That means I don't have to worry about student loans, which has been a huge relief."

Teens in affluent communities who need to earn money in high school and college can supplement their income by lifeguarding, teaching yoga, coaching soccer or tennis, or tutoring—all of which can command lucrative hourly rates. None of these extracurriculars are part of the world of the CMS teenagers we spoke with. Salesforce certifications offer them ways to earn money at better hourly rates than fast food or other minimum-wage jobs.

We recently reached out to their teacher Mary Muckenfuss to find out what the students were up to. Miss Mary, as the students call her, emailed us back instantly. "They've all graduated," she wrote. "Destiny and Ayanna are interns with the Office of the Governor of North Carolina working in CRM for them. They both will be in college and possibly still interning. Nyala is pursuing medicine, and Imani changed her major to marketing technology."

Finally, we asked Dawson, the head of the program, whether there was still a perceived division between college track and CTE. She felt that it was more with parents, who grew up in a time where that distinction was strong. "Parents overall think that about CTE: 'Oh vocational ed, my kid doesn't need that. My kid's going to college.' Well, they *can* go to college. They can take AP Calculus and then come right over here and take this marketing class."

She continued, "I understand you don't have to go to college to be successful. But what we have are students who are thinking about going to college, and students who are thinking about not going to college. Our programs serve them both." She explained that for the kids who don't want to go to college, it creates a path to a lucrative career, not just a job. For those who do want to go to college, it's a path to an internship in university, given how many partner with Salesforce. It can also make a prospective applicant stand out. "You have something to talk about that makes you different."

She concluded, "We should *all* be in CTE pathways."

High School District 214, Illinois

One way to overcome the status and perception biases against the technical skills that CTE provides is to do away with the academic curriculum as its own distinct pathway.

David Schuler has done just that. When we spoke with him, he was superintendent of District 214, a high-school-only district in suburban Chicago, near O'Hare airport. There are over seven thousand supervisors of school districts in the United States, and in 2018 Schuler was named their superintendent of the year. District 214 has six comprehensive high schools and one specialized school, which together serve twelve thousand high school students.

All twelve thousand are in career pathways. They don't distinguish between CTE and academic pathways. Schuler explained, "We have forty-four career pathways in sixteen career clusters. . . . The reality is, we need academic pathways and programs of study. And that might be in business and finance. It might be in mathematics. It might be in welding and manufacturing. But when you talk about career and tech ed, in people's minds it's something separate from the core. And we've got to stop the separateness. Everything has to work together. Every kid, whether they want to be a doctor or a welder, has an external, work-based learning experience while they're with us. And so, we've just completely redesigned."

Instead of English, history, science, and CTE departments, the school is organized into forty-four career pathways in sixteen career clusters, and every student gets to choose theirs. Sample clusters include finance; IT; architecture and construction; agriculture, food, and natural resources; and health sciences. Within a cluster, a student chooses a pathway. For example, within the law, public safety, corrections, and security cluster, they can explore legal services or law enforcement.

When a student embarks on a pathway, they travel along a sequence of related courses and experiences (paid apprenticeships, internships, mentorships, industry certifications, dual college enrollments) that give them a strong sense of what careers in that pathway might be like. Through this variety of courses and experiences, they get to know themselves better and understand whether that cluster of work interests them. If they decide it doesn't, there are on-ramps and off-ramps and opportunities to change their mind and explore related paths.

This flexibility is critical so that a decision a student makes at fourteen doesn't trap them. Schuler emphasized this. "We want to make sure that we don't put a kid in a pathway and then they find out they don't love it and then that prevents them from having other experiences."

Getting Smart CEO Tom Vander Ark, who spoke so eloquently about learner agency in Chapter 1, developed the term "coauthoring" to describe the role young people need to transition into adulthood. Our current school system largely gives teenagers no real-world agency or decision-making responsibilities. How might school instead be designed so that young people can coauthor their lives, with the support of trusted adults, so that they become increasingly capable, confident, and competent on their own?

Schuler and his team have taken this to heart in their redesign of their district. He explained, "We've said we want student voice to be incorporated. But to me, coauthoring is just so much deeper. It means all our students identify a career area of interest by the end of their freshman year, and then we will guarantee them an external work-based learning experience in that pathway of choice before they graduate."

This is a massive shift in the work of a school. District 214 arranges for and runs almost three thousand external, work-based learning experiences every year for their students. A work-based learning experience is a minimum of thirty hours and can extend to acquiring registered apprenticeships. They also ensure that each student has a minimum of six college credits before they graduate from high school.

Since we interviewed him, Schuler has become the executive director of the American Association of School Administrators, an organization that represents more than ten thousand leaders of public school districts across the country. It's one of the most influential organizations in public education in the United States. In his position, he can spread the innovation he began in District 214 at a much larger scale.

Conclusion

The schools in this chapter are redesigning secondary education to break down the silos between academic and practical knowledge by giving young people choices in exploring the world of work and learning and giving them many opportunities to master themselves, master how they interact with others, and master key transferable skills—including creativity and critical thinking. These schools are building communities where curiosity is valued and nurtured and belonging matters, and they are partnering with people and resources in the broader communities in which the schools are located. They do not just cage young people in a self-contained building with teachers and other students.

There are many more schools and systems following these principles, both in the United States and abroad, but there are certainly not enough. We spoke with Chris Sturgis, a cofounder of

CompetencyWorks, the original online knowledge-building hub for all things regarding competency-based education. She told us we're still in the very early stages of what mastery-based schools will eventually look like.

"One of the reasons we're still early," she explained, "is that the state policy infrastructure is holding the traditional system in place. It undermines the more advanced mastery-based models where the focus is on learning, not grades." To really allow mastery-based school design to flourish, Sturgis told us we will need to modify or create flexibility in the policies that underpin the traditional system. Key among those policies are the standardized tests and dependence on GPA for college admissions and scholarships.

Sturgis asked, "How do we align state policy with the research on learning? For example, we know that executive function skills such as time management, planning, and metacognition make a huge difference in learning and in life outcomes. What might we need to change in terms of higher education, accreditation, and evaluation policies if we wanted to make sure every student was getting powerful coaching in building their skills to learn?"

We live in a world that demands lifelong learning. We now must design for it—at scale.

CHAPTER 5

Postsecondary Education

VIDYA KRISHNAN HAS a very demanding day job. She is chief learning officer of Ericsson, the giant Swedish telecom company, where she is responsible for learning and development for more than 110,000 global employees. But Krishnan's career was almost derailed before it even began by her experiences learning computer science at Princeton University. She told us the story of what happened to her when she was a sophomore in the early 1990s. Back then, she struggled in a programming class, trying to learn the computer language C++. Her grade, Krishnan said with a laugh, "was C minus minus." Assignment after assignment, Krishnan couldn't make any progress. "I never felt so lost in my life," she recalled.

Fortunately, that summer Krishnan landed her first professional internship with her top-choice company: AT&T. That dream quickly threatened to become a nightmare when she learned she was expected to code an algorithm in C++. "I was terrified. I felt I ought to disclose to them that I was an abject failure in this subject," she told us.

As she began working on her project, Krishnan was shocked to discover a very different kind of learning experience from what she'd experienced in her classes at Princeton. She didn't take a test, didn't receive a grade, and wasn't competing with colleagues. Instead, she received the "just-in-time" help she needed to do the work. She was expected to collaborate with and seek advice from peers, and she received regular coaching as a part of the learning process. By the end of the summer, she had not only completed the C++ coding project but also received an award for it. She was acquiring the skills to do things with C++.

Back at Princeton the next fall, Krishnan, buoyed by her summer success, took another computer science class. She failed again. A professor told her outright, "You don't have any aptitude for this."

Her internship experience, however, had shown her otherwise. She could code if she received help and guidance along the way, if she could move at her own speed and collaborate with others. "All I needed was to have the perseverance to not give up," she explained.

Krishnan continued, "The very thing that made me a terrible student, which was not understanding C++ quickly, made me a great developer, because I would comment on every bit of code and make it easy for another person to use. And I would be empathetic about how people who didn't know could find value. Looking back, everything that made me a bad student in that class made me a good employee during that internship."

The internship focused on building something that added value for AT&T, which involved collaboration as well as growing the capacity and competence of other employees, not pitting them against each other for As. It entailed learning C++ to be able to build something that mattered in the real world.

Krishnan went on to earn a bachelor of science in electrical engineering from Princeton and later a master's degree in the same field from Stanford University. But her college experience—especially in the programming classes—points to some major shortcomings in higher education. The emphasis continues to be on theoretical rather than applied knowledge. Experiential learning is scarce. Competition, particularly at elite schools, supersedes collaboration. And grading in STEM courses often uses the bell curve, where only a few people can earn an A. The idea of everyone being allowed to acquire the knowledge and skills they need is a foreign concept. No wonder higher education struggles to prove its worth.

As we spoke to young and once-young people across the country, we heard over and over that higher education rarely helped them discover what mattered to them. It rarely helped them build the knowledge and skills to accomplish something meaningful in the world, even though they were deeply interested in learning.

Young people today are more willing to try new things than at any time in human history, and they're in search of relevant applied skills. They're accessing new learning options—internships, pathways, work-based learning, out-of-school learning, boot camps, and company-sponsored learning platforms, as well as YouTube and other social media platforms—that enable them to follow their curiosity, explore, and achieve in mastery learning settings.[1]

College, however, is all too often a relic of a different time. Like high schools, colleges and universities adopted the Carnegie unit in the early twentieth century, though in higher education it's called the credit hour. Courses, usually organized in semester-long chunks and clocked at three credit hours of workload for students, are the backbone of this system. Courses live inside departments: English, history, physics, mathematics, electrical engineering. As knowledge divided and specialized in the nineteenth and twentieth centuries, these departments became siloed fiefdoms where clusters of experts, each with their own specialization, organized the body of knowledge into individual courses often based on their personal areas of interest. The expert professors usually imparted their knowledge in the form of lectures, during which students were to obediently take notes. Then students would learn the knowledge and take tests to prove they learned it. The system was tailored to support the research of the professors rather than the interests and needs of students.

This is the higher education model that developed in the aftermath of the industrial era and that is still the four-year research university of today. However, society has changed drastically. Today, it's not just professors who produce new knowledge. Many jobs and occupations involve creating new insights, designs, and products. The key skills society and the workforce need include creativity, critical thinking, and collaboration.

In these circumstances, what is the value proposition for college? How can higher education redesign itself to help students develop the cognitive and character skills needed to apply knowledge and accomplish something meaningful or valuable in the world?

Four Years, Twenty Projects

Olin College of Engineering, outside of Boston, is an elite nonprofit school serving about four hundred students. Pre–financial aid costs run around $80,000, though the average annual cost after financial aid is closer to $21,000. Across the student body, 17 percent of Olin students receive federal Pell Grants for low-income families, and 14 percent are Hispanic or African American—statistics Olin is working on improving, according to Gilda Barabino, the college's president.[2]

Its graduates are successful; they have an average starting salary of $93,510, and 67 percent report being happy in their jobs.[3] The largest number of its graduates work at Google. The next most common employers are Microsoft, Meta, and other large tech companies.

Olin is a project-based engineering college, a new model for engineering education. In their first semester, all students take Design Nature, an introductory mechanical design and prototyping course that includes three progressively complex projects. Second semester, they take Collaborative Design, which culminates in a group project designing a product or service for a specific client. In Products and Markets, their introductory entrepreneurship class, students work in teams to conceive and execute a series of entrepreneurial experiments that develop their skills in designing and testing value propositions, improving product-market fit, and creating sustainable business models.

Other courses, including those for majors, follow a similar design philosophy: learning by doing, designing and making physical or conceptual artifacts, and collaborating with peers as well as users and clients. In place of traditional exams, students present their projects to the community as part of their final assessment. Extracurriculars are similarly project based. The student beekeeping group, for example, tends to bees, produces honey, and has investors with whom they must engage. By the end of their four years, Olin students will have completed at least twenty projects, and likely many more than that.

We spoke extensively with Richard Miller, Olin College founding president (now president emeritus). Miller is a bit of an iconoclast, and he appreciates other iconoclasts, especially civic-minded ones. Remember Frances Haugen? She's the engineer whistleblower who in 2021 disclosed tens of thousands of internal Facebook documents revealing the tech company's misdeeds against children, elections, national security, and democracy in its breakneck pursuit of profit. Haugen is an Olin grad, Miller proudly told us.

The spirit of questioning is part of Olin's founding story. The folks who founded Olin were not education theorists. Miller explained, "We were largely engineers and a few nutty people who liked engineers." They weren't satisfied with how they'd been taught. "We wanted to teach people how to be engineers. It's not the same thing as thermodynamics or applied mathematics or physics, which is what we all studied." Although content is absolutely necessary for engineers, it isn't sufficient. Miller continued, "To become an engineer, you have to *do* stuff."

Olin looks to support its students in developing five competencies, which it calls mindsets. These will look rather familiar by now: interdisciplinary mindset, collaborative mindset, entrepreneurial mindset, ethical and empathetic mindset (which Frances Haugen clearly learned), and global mindset. You may be wondering: Where, in these competencies, are the basic disciplinary knowledge domains, content like physics or calculus or thermodynamics?

In response to this question, Miller told us a story about how the founding team came to design the college. In 2010, they pulled a bunch of engineers together and asked them what they remembered from their undergraduate programs. "It was a very humbling question," he said. Most people remembered very little. "I had a ton of physics, but don't ask me to do a quantum mechanics problem today. I have no idea where to start," admitted one engineering professor.

Almost all of them, however, remembered their senior projects. In fact, they could remember where they were or what they were eating when they had their breakthroughs on those projects. Sometimes the breakthroughs were about what worked; other times, they were about what didn't work. No matter, the engineers remembered the project and their aha moments.

Miller and his team were fascinated by the idea that all the engineers had a project that they remembered deeply, and they all did it in the last semester. The Olin team couldn't find anybody who had done a project before the last semester. They wondered why.

Miller said, "We couldn't find any literature. We speculated that it's because of the folklore that we've all grown up with that you can't possibly put all these ideas together and make something unless you first have had two years of calculus and physics and then a year of engineering science and gotten As in all these subjects, and then maybe you could do something." These are all assumptions baked into the design of higher engineering education.

Engineers, however, like to test assumptions. The Olin design team ran a series of experiments to see if the assumptions were valid.

Experiment number one: test the assumption that you need content prerequisites to do interesting engineering.

They brought students into the design process as test subjects. They picked thirty high school students, fifteen male and fifteen female, anointed them "the Olin Partners," and gave them a project: design, build, and demonstrate a pulse oximeter.

Pulse oximeters are pretty complicated devices in that they contain a transistor, which, according to Miller, relies on some knowledge of quantum mechanics. They also have tiny little chips that need to be manufactured in a very specific way. Laughing, Miller told us, "We're engineers, and we couldn't even explain to the high schoolers how the chips work! We also let them know that we couldn't help them build the pulse oximeter because we didn't know how to do it ourselves."

The Olin design team told the students what they, the adults, could do. They could serve as the students' guides and mentors. They could help them find the patent literature where the inventor of the pulse oximeter discloses how the device works. They could show them where the machine shop was located and which tools the high school students might want to use.

They also explained what the students could do. This was not an SAT test or an exam, so students were welcome to work together. They were welcome to reach out to their parents or any other adult who might have expertise the kids needed. They were welcome to visit hospitals or any location that might help them figure out what to do. None of this was considered cheating. The goal was to figure how to build the device, then actually do it. There was only one constraint: they had five weeks, after which they'd move on to the next challenge.

The engineering professors assumed the young people would get stuck, given that they didn't have the underlying math and physics knowledge. They planned to praise the kids for getting as far as they got and then do a postmortem on the process. Instead, the kids successfully built a pulse oximeter, ahead of schedule.

Olin ran several more project experiments with their high school test subjects who were, by now, becoming true design partners. Each time the adults wanted to oversupport the young people, and each time the young people rejected that support, they surprised the adults with what they could achieve. When given an interesting challenge, freedom to exercise their agency, and support when needed, the young people could learn to become engineers without content prerequisites. They learned the content they needed as they went.

Listening to and collaborating with young people fundamentally changed how the adults understood engineering and how they designed the engineering college. Miller described the most important thing the Olin design team learned. "Number one: No! Two years of math and physics are *not* necessary in order to be an engineer. The kids taught us this. They also taught us to look, for example, at the aircraft industry, at the Wright brothers—two bicycle mechanics from Ohio who kept jumping off a cliff with wings on their backs driven by a sense that there must be a better way, iterating as they went!"

From these insights, the Olin design team came to focus on the engineering process as the most important part of learning. In Miller's words, "Engineering is not a body of knowledge. It involves knowledge, but it's not the study of these knowledge facts. It's a process of envisioning something, trying to build something before you overthink it. Learning what immediately goes wrong. Correcting what immediately went wrong and trying it again—over and over again. That's the process of engineering."

This new blueprint for engineering education would not have been created without the faculty's willingness to question, explore their own curiosities, test assumptions, and collaborate with each other and with students—hallmarks of what we call mastery learning.

The Olin design team became convinced that, to enable students to achieve mastery of the five cognitive and character skills, they needed to hire faculty who also exhibited these mindsets, particularly collaboration. They looked for generalists with multiple intelligences who could offer opinions in a room with other faculty and students, rather than professors who needed to be "sages on the stage" and infallible masters in their own domain.

Designing for Mastery Learning

STEM faculty at traditional colleges are notorious for designing classes as weeder courses. These are intended to weed out students so that only a few, the supposed best at mastering knowledge, succeed. Olin doesn't have weeder courses. It activates student motivation by focusing on interdisciplinary experiential learning. Students do not spend four years learning all the theories of mechanical or electrical engineering, but rather they devote that time to twenty real projects solicited from real clients like Boston Scientific, Hewlett-Packard, Ford, and, in a twist that surprised us, local elementary school students.

It made for quite an array of projects. One for Boston Scientific was to "design a way to remove a gallbladder without making an incision." The fourth-grade clients requested animal-themed play experiences that abstracted the features, motion, or ecosystem of the animals. For example, the college students built a game to get joeys home safe into their kangaroo mother's pouch while dingoes tried to eat them, all constructed from PVC pipes, Ping-Pong balls, and other Home Depot materials. These real-world projects for real-world clients raise the stakes, interest, and relevance for students; they acquire the knowledge they need to effectively meet the client's request. Faculty are there to support the students along the way by giving guidance and suggestions and co-learning with them. The professors are not trying to find ways to fail them.

Olin students engage in twice-yearly public presentations of their learning to the community, including the fourth graders. Miller laughed when he described this to us. "We'd bring in the fourth graders to evaluate their work and, boy, did this put the fear of God in their heart! Kids either like it or they don't like it—period. And they don't give partial credit. They're really tough graders."

We spoke with a group of 2021 Olin graduates. One of them, Niyi Owolabi, who when we spoke to him was a mechanical design engineer at Tesla in the Bay Area, confirmed this: "There's nothing scarier than a fourth grader with a clipboard who's actually writing stuff down."

Olin has no grades in its first year so that students can get comfortable with this new way of learning that promotes collaboration over competition. After that, they do receive grades, but much more important are the project portfolios that demonstrate the mastery they have developed.

When Olin students graduate, Miller told us, "They have a three-ring binder with twenty tabs in it. In each tab there's a set of blueprints for the thing that they made in that project. There's often a testimonial letter from the client that says, 'This is how it changed my life.' There's a team assessment where students evaluate each other with comments like, 'I'll go anywhere for a job if I can work with John and Susie, my two collaborators on this project who are amazing! The three of us together can change the world.' This is what employers read. And of course, that's the language that corporations talk."

The Olin project-based model for higher education is innovative in so many ways, and yet, two of the three recent alumni we interviewed named an extracurricular project as the most meaningful for them. We came to understand that it's because that's where they had the most agency and community. The project, Formula SAE, is an annual car-building contest organized by SAE International (previously the Society of Automotive Engineers). College and graduate school teams from many countries participate.

Teams take the project very seriously. Rachel Won, who now is also a mechanical engineer at Tesla in the Bay Area, explained to us that, at universities with graduate programs, grad students will devote their entire master's thesis to designing the car.

Olin has no graduate program. Their Formula SAE team consists of fifty undergrads, roughly one-seventh of the college, and they work on the design in their spare time. They also take it very seriously. Olin Electric Motorsports, the student club devoted to the project, has its own LinkedIn page with videos, fundraisers, and updates. Rachel emphasized, "This is not a class. We get no credit or monetary sponsorship from the college. It is very, very much student run from the beginning to the end, and it's been running for seven years."

The Olin students have created their own self-organized team for a passion project. They divided up the work into sub-teams (cockpit, brakes and pedals, suspension and chassis) and created learning, mentorship, and project management structures for themselves—all to design and build an electric vehicle to win a challenge issued by SAE International.

Or so we thought. Rachel, who began on the team as a first-year student and rose into leadership by her senior year, clarified, "We want to win, but there is a classic debate we always have: Are we a teaching team or are we a competitive team? At a certain point you can't have both, and we wanted to be very clear to every one of our members, if we're here to be a teaching team, then we have to give up this very competitive mindset."

We asked Rachel to explain the trade-off. It came down to growing people's engineering capacity to build for the future. "Everyone when they're a freshman comes in knowing nothing. The seniors spend so much of their time not trying to make the engineering the best thing possible but trying to teach the younger teammates how to be an engineer." Rachel called this the "Olin culture of care."

She continued, "Once you've been mentored, when you become a senior you say, 'I want to do the same for the first years as what I got when I was a first year.' I think that's a very common feeling people have. We *are* doing better in the competition. We've gotten much, much better over the years with knowledge buildup, knowledge transfer, and different process improvements. But at the end of the day, I think people are most proud of the fact that they're able to give back to the people younger than them. I don't think I would be an engineer—the same engineer I am—without this team."

This culture of care—of finding meaning and purpose together—extends outside the bounds of Olin as well. Naomi Chiu, now a brake controls calibration engineer with Ford in Detroit, told us how Olin instills a sense of civic responsibility in its students. "Olin really encourages us to be engineers for the people—to think about the impacts of the work that we do and how that affects people."

Frances Haugen demonstrated that after she left Olin, and Niyi gave an example of a project he and Rachel participated in while they were in college. They worked with a Ghanaian company to design, build, and fabricate accessible food-processing machines for local women entrepreneurs. Niyi explained that this was particularly meaningful for him because he is Nigerian American, and Ghana is Nigeria's neighbor. He was delighted to be able to make an impact on the project stakeholders' lives: their sense of self, their businesses, and their families.

Meaningful, purposeful, impactful application of knowledge, according to Gilda Barabino, the current president of Olin, is the key to creating more diversity in engineering. Prior to becoming president in 2020, Barabino was the dean of engineering at the City College of New York, a public institution that serves a diverse student body. When we spoke with her, we asked her about what lay ahead for Olin.

She explained that, as innovative as Olin is, in the quarter century since it was founded, some things have gotten stale. The college was ready for a refresh. Barabino, the faculty, the students, and the staff were in the midst of designing the new vision and strategy.

The refresh is called Engineering for Everyone. It means making a global societal impact: How can Olin engineering impact human and planetary health? Equally, it means: How can everyone have access to becoming an engineer? Barabino thinks the former meaning of societal impact is the key to the latter meaning of equity.

"Social science literature is really clear that one way to attract women and people from historically excluded groups, particularly racially minoritized groups, is to help them better understand the relevance of the field to themselves and their communities," she explained. "Women and people from racially minoritized groups have a deep desire to make the world better in general but specifically to give back to their communities. So, if you can show and demonstrate the relevance of your field to what they care about, to what their communities care about, you're much more likely not only to attract them into the field but to retain them in the field."

Olin's approach to doing this is by integrating humanities, arts, social sciences, engineering, and entrepreneurship with real-world projects and a culture of care. Caring, of course, is a cornerstone of both civic engagement and personal health and well-being. Olin has clearly integrated the three education goals that we've described throughout the book.

Another Approach to Engineering for Everyone

Societal impact is something that's urgently needed in Harrisburg, a small central Pennsylvania city on the banks of the Susquehanna River. Despite being the capital of the state, Harrisburg has a 28 percent poverty rate.[4] It's known for a mayor who stayed in office for thirty years despite embezzling from the city, massive debt and bankruptcy, and being the first city ever charged by the federal government for securities fraud.[5] Like many declining communities in the nation and the world—communities being left behind by global economic forces—Harrisburg is looking to education as a solution.

In 2001, in the midst of this turmoil, a group of civic leaders came together to sponsor what Eric Darr, current president of Harrisburg University of Science and Technology (HU) called "a crazy idea": the idea to start a new nonprofit university.

Like Richard Miller, Darr follows his curiosity. It has taken him across many different work worlds. His undergrad degree, in mechanical engineering from Rensselaer Polytechnic Institute, led him to working for a defense contractor in Arizona, where they "blew stuff up in the desert." There, he told us, "I discovered I was more interested in the dysfunction of groups of people than the stresses and strains in the metals or composite materials we were working with."

He moved on to Carnegie Mellon, where he got an MBA as well as a PhD in organizational theory and strategy. That experience led him to an academic position at UCLA's business school, where he quickly became frustrated with "writing peer-reviewed journal articles for the sixteen other people on the planet who would read them." He used his research to found and lead Ernst & Young's knowledge management consulting services. Eventually, he raised $54 million in venture capital and started an educational technology company in Harrisburg.

For three years, HU was a passion project. Darr and five others worked to design and launch it. In 2004, he came onboard as a full-time employee. In 2005, they opened their doors to students.

Given the dire state of the city, HU's two-part mission was to increase access to higher education for previously excluded or marginalized students and to catalyze economic development in the community. The HU team zoomed in on giving students support to become entrepreneurial value creators in STEM.

Darr told us that HU graduates were working at Google, Microsoft, Meta, Cisco, and major pharmaceutical companies. He said, "2022 was our best year yet—95 percent of the graduating undergrad class of 2022 have a job or are in graduate school six months after graduation."

But only 37 percent of incoming first-year students actually graduate. When we asked Darr why, his explanation revealed the complexity of today's college student, particularly at places like HU.

Nontraditional Students

Traditionally, when people think of an undergraduate, they envision someone between seventeen and twenty-four who goes directly from high school to higher education, perhaps with a gap year in between. They envision students who, while in college, spend their time learning on grassy, tree-lined campuses with large libraries. In their spare time, these students participate in clubs, join fraternities and sororities, and socialize with their peers. They are full-timers. Even a radically different model like Olin largely serves this traditional student.

The actual picture of today's college student is much more complex. In 2023, according to the Lumina Foundation, 37 percent of college students are twenty-five or older. Almost a quarter have children or dependents; 84 percent work, and 40 percent work full-time while earning their degrees. Almost half are financially independent of their parents and paying their own way through college. In addition, 31 percent come from families at or below the federal poverty line.[6]

HU serves these nontraditional students. Of HU's 630 or so undergrads, seven in ten receive income-based federal Pell Grants. In comparison, at Olin, only 17 percent do. HU's population is very diverse: 32 percent African American, 17 percent Hispanic, and 5 percent Asian. Many students are the first in their families to attend college, and most have not had strong academic preparation for college, like Monique, whom you met in Chapter 2.

Darr told us, "The mission of our institution is to take students and give them an opportunity in science and technology when others don't give them that opportunity. We're more interested in curiosity than standardized test scores or GPAs. Give me somebody with curiosity who wants to know how the world works, or is curious about changing people's lives, and we'll give that person a chance."

The chance doesn't work out for many reasons. In a decade where other private, nonprofit colleges and universities increased tuition by about 40 percent, HU's tuition admirably has stayed at $23,900.[7] For most undergrads, HU discounts this tuition another 63 percent. The average expected family contribution is about $280 per year, according to Darr. Despite this, students drop out for financial reasons. They need to go to work to support their younger brothers and sisters or other family members. "These are very, very needy students and families," Darr told us.

Since 2013—long before COVID made Zoom a household experience—HU was a hybrid model. This means their classes are a mix of in-person learning and online. Hybrid learning creates more flexibility for students who need to work, because they don't have to show up in person all the time. But this hybrid model wasn't enough to meet the needs of HU's working students.

In response, during COVID, HU launched fully online degree programs. In these classes, all the learning is asynchronous, which means classes aren't set at fixed times, but rather students can access learning whenever their schedule permits. Darr and his team hope this added flexibility makes staying in college easier for students who have to work to support themselves and their families.

HU has also opened a campus in downtown Philadelphia, where there are many underserved students who may be interested in STEM as a path to a better future. Previously, those students would have to leave the sixth largest city in the United States to come to jobs-poor Harrisburg, about one and a half hours away by train or car. The HU team, noticing how many of their students came out of Philadelphia public schools, thought they could reduce dropout rates by bringing their campus to where the students were, rather than vice versa. They have also partnered with a well-respected, mastery-based

K–12 design nonprofit, Building21, to create dual-enrollment STEM courses for high school students. It's too early to tell whether this satellite campus is making an impact, but it does speak to the HU team's dedication to making STEM higher education available to everyone.

The Math Problem

Another reason students drop out of HU has to do with academics, particularly math. High school teachers, college professors, researchers, and policymakers all question the design and sequence of the standard math curriculum laid down over a century ago by the Committee of Ten.

Math reformers are tackling five big problems: (1) many K–12 students don't have access to advanced math courses, especially in high-poverty districts; (2) colleges use high school math courses as admission filters; (3) colleges use math as internal weeders, blocking students from STEM and economics majors and minors; (4) the way we teach math, both in K–12 and higher ed, is not effective for many students; and (5) the content being taught across the math pipeline, from high school through college, doesn't reflect the changing needs of the jobs of today and tomorrow, where, for example, data, estimation, probability, and statistics are much more likely to be useful than calculus or trigonometry.

A mastery learning approach to math can help solve many of these problems. Such an approach would mean shifting the focus of learning and evaluation from mere content knowledge acquisition to the development of the skills needed to apply math to the solution of real-world problems. It would mean measuring learning not through tests graded on a bell curve to weed students out but rather through experiences where learners show evidence of being able to use the skills and knowledge they have acquired. Finally, it would mean designing learning processes that develop individual interests, intrinsic motivation, and character skills.

No one doubts the need for math. In today's world, math is everywhere. Math and quantitative reasoning are important for many high-paying jobs and even lower-wage ones. It's needed to make decisions about personal finance and public policy. But the math we need is rarely the math we teach, and the ways we teach it limit rather than create opportunity.

In higher ed, the biggest blocker is calculus. This is very much the case at HU. Darr explained, "The reality of it is college calculus is college calculus. You've got to make it through calc or nonlinear algebra for some of our pathways. We try to make people as successful as possible. Sometimes, they make it, and sometimes they don't."

Amie Baisley, now an assistant professor in the college of engineering at the University of Florida, wrote her 2019 dissertation on "The Influences of Calculus I on Engineering Student Persistence." Her findings affirm what Richard Miller and his team discovered when they were first designing Olin. Insisting on calc as a prerequisite to engineering doesn't activate the curiosity or passion for solving real-world problems that leads people to consider becoming engineers in the first place. Calculus needs to be, in Baisley's words, "academically integrated" into engineering programs, rather than the gate you have to get through before you can start to become an engineer. She also recommends a different pedagogy: instructors who are invested in engaging students using active and collaborative learning methods, and who want to help students integrate into the engineering community.[8]

The past decade has seen a variety of efforts to redesign the math pipeline via such mastery learning approaches. In 2020, the Dana Center at the University of Texas, Austin, put forth an initiative, the Launch Years, which, in their words, "supports the scaling of mathematics pathways from high school through postsecondary education and into the workplace, aligned to students' goals and aspirations."

The initiative is grounded in a 112-page report detailing the problems we mentioned above, as well as possible solutions for "modernizing math pathways" out of the rut they've been stuck in for a century. In three short years, twenty states have signed on to the Launch Years Initiative.[9]

There are also working examples of change in colleges and universities, often led by faculty who have dual appointments or are in math-heavy fields but not mathematics itself. Over a decade ago, Lior Pachter—then with joint faculty appointments in math and biology at the University of California, Berkeley, and now at Caltech—designed a new math sequence in collaboration with his colleagues. Methods of Mathematics included key concepts from calculus, statistics, and combinatorics, and focused on how data and technology have transformed biology in the past few decades. This is now the math sequence that most life science majors at UC Berkeley take today.

Around the same time, UCLA's life sciences faculty did something similar. They created a math series that embedded calculus into the modeling of complex biological and physiological systems—the sorts of skills their students needed for productive work in life science fields.[10] In addition, they consistently taught growth mindset, moved into a team teaching model with different instructors bringing different strengths and experiences, and ensured that teaching assistants were paid for double the time of a traditional class so that students could get more support in mastering the skills. In a multiyear research study on the students participating in this course sequence compared to students taking the traditional calculus sequence, they found that students in the new sequence did better not only in their biology courses but also in subsequent chemistry and physics courses.[11]

Calc also serves as a gatekeeper in business, weeding students out of lucrative economics pathways. In 2023, the University of

Pennsylvania began piloting a new math sequence for economics majors. Unlike the traditional multivariate calc courses, this one focuses on applying calculus to financial predictions, growth rates, and modeling, as well as game theory and optimization. These courses also use mastery pedagogy, with an emphasis on collaborative problem-solving rather than lectures.[12]

HU's Mastery Learning Approach

HU is designed around high-demand technical STEM course sequences, including biotechnology, cybersecurity, advanced manufacturing, data analytics, forensics, nursing, and—perhaps most exciting to many young people who are gamers—esports management, production, and performance. Each of these degree pathways focuses on the application of knowledge in a jobs-rich area of the local and global economy, and they're all designed with input from industry. They're also taught by a mix of academic faculty and faculty who are currently working in these industries.

Even before a student enrolls, they can see what any particular degree entails. The HU website clearly shows the path forward: each degree's learning goals and outcomes, the courses, the external learning experiences (internships, etc.), and the academic faculty and "corporate faculty." Some pathway web pages even indicate the number of students enrolled in that degree program and the percentage who have successfully completed it.

Tom Vander Ark, the CEO of Getting Smart whom we met in previous chapters, explained the importance of this clarity in mastery learning design. "The most important and overlooked objective of mastery learning is to create an environment where learners are clear about what's important in the environment. They understand with a sense of priority what the learning goals are, and what their developmental priorities are."

Computer science at HU, for example, has the following learning outcomes:

1. Analyze a complex computing problem and apply principles of computing and other relevant disciplines to identify solutions.
2. Design, implement, and evaluate a computing-based solution to meet a given set of computing requirements in the context of the program's discipline.
3. Communicate effectively in a variety of professional contexts.
4. Recognize professional responsibilities and make informed judgments in computing practices based on legal and ethical principles.
5. Function effectively as a member or leader of a team engaged in activities appropriate to the program's discipline.
6. Apply computer science theory and software development fundamentals to produce computing-based solutions.

A student sees that this is what they need to learn to succeed in this major, which enables them to make informed choices. Vander Ark continued, "Clarity and transparency allows coauthoring of learning experiences and journeys."

You'll notice that the computer science pathway is a mix of disciplinary knowledge and durable character skills. HU focuses on eight competencies across all their pathways: civic engagement, written and oral communication, critical thinking, entrepreneurship, ethical awareness and reasoning, global awareness, information literacy, and teamwork and collaboration. Once again, we see that there's clear alignment between innovative higher ed, innovative K–12, and the durable skills employers are calling for.

Most importantly, HU wants its students to walk out with industry credentials that can lead to productive, sustaining work that improves their life outcomes. Where possible, the faculty have aligned the courses with external standards and certificates to prepare students to pass credentialing exams. For example, the cybersecurity program was designed to align with the National Security Agency (NSA) and Department of Homeland Security criteria for excellence, and in 2024 the program sought and received official designation as a National Center for Academic Excellence in Cyber Defense from the NSA. To achieve this, HU had to submit to rigorous NSA vetting and validation.[13] For students who can't bank on the social capital that an elite, name-brand school offers, such designations, based on alignment to industry credentials and access to real-world experiences, grow their value in the job market.

The student experience is hands-on and mastery based. To graduate, students must complete three internships, or two projects and one internship, each with learning objectives. Projects are assessed by faculty, and site supervisors evaluate internships. Students also have four one-credit seminars to grow their mastery of durable skills. Freshman year, they focus on study skills and time management; sophomore year, they jump to communication skills, including how to build a résumé and how to get a first job. Twelve of the credits needed to graduate (one-tenth of a 120-credit bachelor's degree) are associated with experiential competencies and skills.

Like Olin, HU looks for faculty with open mindsets who are not wedded to the traditional university model. Darr laughed as he explained to us, "We don't use 'D' words. There are no departments. There are no deans. There are program leads who are not directors—they don't direct their colleagues, they lead them. They provide guidance and organization and leadership in terms of ideas."

HU purposely mixes faculty member offices on the same floor, rather than having specific floors or buildings devoted to specific disciplines. Darr said, "We're interdisciplinary in that we build market-oriented programs that all mix disciplines." That's what today's economy and society need, for adults and young people.

Expanding HU's Reach

The HU leadership sees their work as a form of civic engagement. They have designed the institution and its learning experiences to make a difference in the civic life of the communities the university serves by growing the capacity of their students to do impactful work. We've seen how they do this by opening the doors to STEM for undergrads who, in traditional colleges, might not qualify for STEM majors—or might not have gone to college at all.

HU is reaching out to even more nontraditional learners through its entrepreneurship and graduate programs. Jay Jayamohan, a serial tech entrepreneur (two successful exits, one failure, about $22 million in venture capital raised), built and leads the university's incubator and accelerator, the Center for Innovation and Entrepreneurship. Jayamohan told us about how he reached out to the Harrisburg community and discovered that "there was a huge appetite for entrepreneurship in central Pennsylvania, mostly from the people that you wouldn't think of from a Silicon Valley or DC or Boston perspective." He found that women and minorities were doing side hustles, but they didn't attend the usual start-up events. They didn't feel they belonged.

Jayamohan explained, "They thought, unless it's a very specific technology, or building the next Google or Facebook, you're not considered a founder or entrepreneur. That was the misconception in a lot of their minds." They also weren't familiar with start-up vocabulary.

Instead of designing an incubator that molded these local side hustle founders to fit how entrepreneurship is usually taught, Jayamohan designed a personalized program to meet their needs. It was one and a half years long rather than the usual three to six months, given the complex life circumstances of the nontraditional entrepreneurs. He baked in explorations of failure and failing forward, pivoting, and learning about product-market fit. His goal was to enable them to deepen and extend their existing interests into entrepreneurial mastery that would give access to global business and capital networks—where you do need to have a full vocabulary of start-up terms. The center currently supports seven start-ups, four of which are led by African Americans. Four of the seven, including some led by Black founders, have gotten funding.

We spoke with Sharina Johnson, founder and CEO of Arcana Recovery, which had just raised a $200,000 seed round and was in beta testing. The app is an AI-supported platform that helps both people in recovery and their providers. It currently uses AI to record user moods and suggest coping skills. In the future, the team plans to use that data to predict relapses. It also helps various support providers manage their caseloads and track their clients.

Arcana is named for a feature of the video game *Mortal Kombat*. Johnson explained, "It's the superpower that comes from your pain. Those who go through these addictions—there's so much pain that brought them to where they're at that if they can connect with themselves and find that self-awareness, there's so much that could come from that."

Johnson told us she was a rebellious young person with learning disabilities who always had drive, resilience, and entrepreneurial energy. She wanted to make an impact. As a child, she participated in sock drives for homeless people; as a teenager, she started a summer program and then a community center to serve young people in Harrisburg.

Then she joined the army at seventeen and was deployed in Baghdad seven days after turning twenty. Coming back from Iraq, she struggled. Now she knows it was post-traumatic stress disorder, but at the time she had no name or support for what was wrong. She self-medicated with drugs until she was, in her own words, "just shattered."

A recovery center helped her through that time. As she grew stronger, she found that people came to her for advice on turning their own lives around. Gradually, she had the idea of developing an app that could reach many, many more people than she could have direct conversations with. HU's incubator has helped her build on her idea, passion, and personal experience by acquiring the skills and network she needs as a nontechnical founder to bring the idea to life.

Jayamohan and Darr know there are hundreds of Sharina Johnsons in their region: people with curiosity and passion who need the opportunity to develop the technical, cognitive, and character skills that can make their ideas a reality. They've launched an entrepreneurship program for high school students. They had also started designing a low-cost, competency-based bachelor of science in innovation, where students, working at their own pace on their own passion projects, would gain mastery of innovation skills while they develop their businesses. Unfortunately, they backed away from this plan due to the difficulties in getting traditionally minded accrediting organizations to understand what it was.

HU is expanding its model and reach quickly. Its 5,500 graduate students, seeking upskilling to improve their career prospects, come from and live in 102 countries. Darr told us they're working on setting up satellite campuses near where their learners are. They have a campus in Panama City, a Copa Airlines hub that's a quick one-and-a-half-hour direct flight from Bogotá, Medellín, and many other Central and South American cities. They're about to open a regional hub in Dubai to serve students from the Middle East, Africa, and South Asia. This expansion, the HU administrators feel, lets them live into their dual mission of expanding opportunity for those who don't have access and—by growing the technical, cognitive, and character skills of both young people and older learners—position them to seed and grow economic opportunity in their local communities.

Higher Education in Crisis

There are more than four thousand institutions of higher education in the United States, and they are closing at the rate of one per week.[14] Within six years of enrollment, only 62 percent of students have completed their degrees, a number that drops to 42 percent for students enrolled in public institutions. There are forty million people with partially completed degrees and no credentials, as of 2021. Underemployment for those who complete their degrees is, as we discussed in Chapter 2, a huge problem. Clearly, higher education as currently designed is not working.

In 2022, Gallup and the Lumina Foundation conducted a survey of over twelve thousand adults. Half were currently investing in a postsecondary degree, including bachelor's (four-year) degrees, associate's (two-year) degrees, and certificates (nondegree). They also surveyed over three thousand adults who had dropped out of college and three thousand who had never attended college. All groups were racially diverse and diverse by age (eighteen to fifty-nine years old), the full spectrum of traditional and nontraditional learners.

For all three groups, the most important reason for continuing education was "to obtain knowledge or skills." The next two reasons—their order varies for the three groups—were "personal fulfillment or achievement" and "it will help you get a higher paying job."[15]

Traditionally there have been two main recurring rationales for education beyond high school. One school of thought argues that college is the place for personal growth. It is the time for young people to explore the world of human knowledge, discover their personal passions, and become better leaders and citizens by growing their critical thinking, communication, and problem-solving. This idea emphasizes the global competencies we discussed in earlier chapters that we think should become part of learning from primary school onward.

Another school of thought pushes the practical: higher education is the place for acquiring the knowledge, skills, and experiences that advance economic opportunity and career prospects. We believe that this also should be part of primary and secondary school.

In these two schools of thought, you can see the history of higher education: the liberal arts argument to grow human beings to become leaders of themselves and their communities, and the technical argument that universities must grow individuals' capacity to meet the needs of changing economies. What people—of all ages, in an economy that calls for lifelong learning—want is both, not either-or. Mastery learning enables both.

Mastery Learning as a Solution to the Crisis: The University of Kansas

Barbara Bichelmeyer, the provost at the University of Kansas (KU), is a strong proponent of mastery-based learning. We talked to Bichelmeyer and asked her why. "When I was hired as provost, KU had a $50 million structural deficit," she explained. "The university had to get honest about its mission and revenue sources. With cuts in state appropriations, tuition increases, and a substantial decline in the numbers of college-age students, we were hitting this important inflection point."

The university leadership took a good, honest look at who they were and weren't serving. Bichelmeyer continued, "We knew we weren't going to build a future on a lot more first-time, full-time freshmen. Our growth is in what we would have called nontraditional students: traditionally underserved students, global majority students, Pell-eligible students, first-generation-going-to-college students. We have to let people into higher ed institutions that we haven't let in before. And we have to be successful in doing that."

Students nowadays are savvy consumers making intentional choices about whether to invest in higher education. Bichelmeyer and the KU leadership recognized this new reality. "Students vote with their feet and their tuition dollars," she told us matter-of-factly. "They go places where they can use technology to mediate their success, so they don't have to show up and listen to a lecture or pay for parking or for babysitting. We've got to engage them in a way that's meaningful. And that engagement must be much more focused on the outcomes that they need to be relevant in the world."

The answer, Bichelmeyer believes, is flexible, competency-based programs targeted at individuals who can't fit a sixteen-week semester into their lives, but who can work their way through a competency-based model. Under Bichelmeyer's leadership, the university created a Center for Certification and Competency-Based Education.

Designing for Lifelong Learning

We spoke with Julianna Stockton, the associate director of the center, to learn more about what they do. The center currently has competency-based projects and training related to IT, cybersecurity, law enforcement, fire and rescue, and teacher education.

Stockton talked about specific "use cases," a term that comes from software development and design thinking. A use case is a fictitious person who might represent hundreds or thousands of similar persons with similar life trajectories who would actually use the program being designed. Designers employ use cases to create meaningful, relevant experiences and products. It means you're designing for somebody rather than creating a theoretical, abstract thing.

Stockton explained, "Imagine a soldier from nearby Fort Leavenworth who's getting ready to separate from active duty into civilian life. They don't have a college degree in computer science. They don't necessarily have these technical skills, but they have a commitment to serve and protect. They have communication skills. They have attention to detail based on what their previous role had been. And they're getting ready to look for a job, look for a new direction in life." There are thousands of such soldiers in the United States. The use case was clear and real. We all want soldiers to be able to integrate into civilian life. But it's not so easy.

Stockton continued, "Cybersecurity has tens of thousands of unfilled jobs in the Kansas City metro area, in the state of Kansas alone. How do we get that person who doesn't think of themself for cybersecurity because of the cyber part of that word?" Soldiers think they're security, not cybersecurity.

What's new in the KU approach (and other competency-based approaches) is that it starts with the user. KU leaders have reimagined the role of the university as serving the needs of the person paying for the education rather than the student having to conform to the ways of doing things at the university—ways that may be hundreds of years old.

Stockton and her team were trying to figure out how higher education could help this archetypical soldier transfer their knowledge and skills into the civilian world, and what bridges they might need to make that transition. She continued, "They could do a ten-week boot camp and learn the technical skills and be a great fit for this role. But the jobs aren't finding them. They're not finding the jobs. We're trying to build that bridge. So, we're developing assessments for things like attention to detail, analytical thinking, growth mindset, curiosity, perseverance—in the cybersecurity context."

Stockton's team worked with industry experts to map these transferable skills to a range of high-demand, entry-level roles based on a national framework for cybersecurity. Students take these assessments on a regional cybersecurity talent exchange platform (still under construction), where employers will be able to indicate which transferable skills are most important for their open jobs and where candidates will be able to get personalized guidance toward cybersecurity job opportunities that are well aligned with their strengths.

What does it mean to be successful in cybersecurity? In a context where knowledge and skills are constantly changing, is it most important that you know specific firewall protocols? Or is it more valuable if you know some firewall protocols and how to learn new ways of doing things?

Stockton and her team are betting on the latter. The assessments, she told us, "are like holding up a mirror to help individuals see the strengths they already bring to the table that are incredibly in demand in a growing field but don't typically appear on transcripts." The platform then enables an increasingly diverse talent pool connect with specific work roles. It also helps graduates create their own personalized pathway in a field as expansive as cybersecurity.

Lifelong Learning in Traditional Programs

Beyond these new programs, Bichelmeyer thinks all college courses should emphasize teaching and assessing core competencies over subject matter. "My priority isn't that we teach chemistry a certain way or we teach biology a certain way or we teach biochemistry a certain way," she told us. "What I care about is making sure that in our courses we commit to teaching students how to think so that they are forever relevant. Let's just be clear that we're teaching students the scientific method, regardless of the title of the science course."

This perspective applies to the humanities as well. "When I talk to English faculty, I say, 'I don't care if you teach Introduction to Werewolves or if you teach *Jane Eyre* or whatever you teach. But if you teach students how to empathize, that's a skill everybody needs.'" Students often think of introductory English as simply a required course to get through. "But I say to them, 'Do you understand that in English 101 you learn how to develop an argument, how to refute an argument, how to think about the rationale behind the argument? That is a fundamental skill you use every day of your life no matter where you are.'"

Bichelmeyer is keenly aware of the obstacles to change, beyond accreditation. She explained, "It's a mission challenge, it's a student demographic challenge, it's an infrastructure challenge, and it's a financing and cash flow challenge. It is the very difficult work of fitting new wine into old wineskins or saying that the wineskin has to go away completely. The whole model is broken."

However, for Bichelmeyer there is a great deal at stake. "This isn't just about workforce development, and it's not even about competency-based education. It's about the way the world is changing, and the forces and powers that exist wrestling over who's going to be able to lead that change. It comes down to, Do we want to live in a democratic society? . . . But you can't have a democracy without an educated citizenry. And you won't have an educated citizenry if you don't teach them these skills. I never really thought in my wildest dreams that I would be an educational leader fighting for democracy."

Other Experiments

We have chosen to highlight Olin, HU, and KU because they're not on the radar of many people having education redesign conversations, and they provide three very different and yet fundamentally similar models of innovation. But they are far from the only experiments in disrupting the traditional model of the university.

Southern New Hampshire University began offering inexpensive online classes for nontraditional students in the mid-1990s and launched the College for America as a competency-based learning option for underserved students in 2013. In 2017, it expanded competency-based learning online and at scale globally, serving refugee students and displaced learners in partnership with local, on-the-ground organizations.[16]

Western Governors University was founded in 1997 as a nonprofit, low-cost, online, competency-based university by, as the name would suggest, a group of state governors in the West. It serves over 145,000 students in all fifty states and US military bases around the world.[17]

Minerva University—currently the most exclusive university in the world, with an acceptance rate of just 1 percent and tuition and fees of $36,000—was founded in 2012 to give young people from around the world a competency-based education that actually takes place around the world.[18] Students rotate their time at the university fully immersed in learning and work in seven different cities: San Francisco, Buenos Aires, Seoul, Taipei, Hyderabad, Berlin, and London.

There is even a call for change at one of the most prestigious of our existing universities. MIT professors recently released a white paper calling for a "new education institution" that redesigns higher ed for "cost, value, equity, and relevance."[19]

These are just a few of the many new models being designed and implemented. We are in a time of deep economic and social change, and we are seeing innovative institutions springing up to solve the problems of the old ones and create the learning that matters for a changing, global world.

Conclusion

The higher education institutions we've showcased in this chapter serve different populations and train their students in different content, but their approach to learning is quite similar. They all engage in mastery learning.

Except for the University of Kansas, all these universities and programs are relatively new, founded in the past quarter century. This newness has been their way of shaking free from the constraints of the industrial model. Even though they are new, they are continually reinventing themselves: Olin is refreshing itself under the leadership of Gilda Barabino; HU is developing new ways to serve nontraditional students in Pennsylvania and globally.

But innovation doesn't have to be limited to new institutions. The University of Kansas was established in 1866, and the focus on teaching core competencies is helping the university to renew itself. Barbara Bichelmeyer is optimistic about the possibility of KU creating a model for other universities. "When one highly successful, traditional research institution of higher education can show that you can do it, then you flip the switch and everybody else is going to come along."

She continued, "There are bumper stickers that say, 'Why do I need to send my kid to college? I have the Internet.' It begs the question of what is our true value-added. And the true value-added is not what you know. It's what you do with what you know. It's our cognitive skills and our ways of thinking."

CHAPTER 6

Adult Mastery Learning

I T SHOULD HAVE been a routine dive. Jarrod Jablonski, an experienced cave diver, wanted to show a friend a well-known and
well-explored cavern in "cave country," a popular diving spot in
northern Florida. "I had just wanted to show him what a cavern
looked like. But in retrospect I see that we both could have died—
maybe should have died. And it would have been all my fault,"
recalled Jablonski, who today is one of the leading cave-diving
educators and cave divers in the world.

Cave diving is an extreme sport in an extreme environment.
While caves are some of the most beautiful places on the planet,
they are also some of the most dangerous places to explore. There is
no natural light, no immediate exit, and no shortage of things that
can go wrong. Cave divers are required to have special certification
and go through extensive additional training, often after completing
hundreds or even thousands of regular scuba dives. It requires both
extensive knowledge and planning skills, as well as underwater skills
honed almost to the level of perfection.

The way many people dive in the open ocean is far less demanding. It is very safe and very few fatal accidents occur. The main

reason is that, in most instances, it is safe to ascend at any time when something fails.

Cave diving is the opposite: You can never merely ascend to the surface. You are inside an underwater rock formation, after all. Therefore, you must be prepared to deal with anything and everything while still submerged in the cave.

Jablonski's dive with his inexperienced friend, though, appeared to be low risk. A diver since his days at the University of Florida, Jablonski was both a dive instructor and an avid cave diver certified by several different diving organizations.

"We were going to pop in just a few meters, look around, and then come back out," Jablonski told us. The dive appeared to be so benign, in fact, that he had not brought a reel, an instrument divers use to lay down a thin line with directional markers attached, so they can follow it out of a cave. When visibility deteriorates, the cave line becomes a literal lifeline.

As they entered the cavern, Jablonski was focused on the environment, being careful not to disturb the silty bottom. He took his attention off his less-experienced friend, just long enough to trigger a potentially deadly situation, and all because this newer diver did not know what to do—or rather, what not to do.

The biggest danger in this situation is the silt that sits on the bottom of caves and caverns. Fins moving too close to the bottom can easily stir up the silt. When that happens, it can be a "silt out," like a whiteout in a snowstorm.

Jablonski's friend was not fully aware and had been kicking near the bottom while they entered the small passage. "I was busy appreciating the environment, maintaining my position. Then it hit me how stupid I was being. I turned to warn my friend and saw a huge cloud of silt behind him and blocking our exit," Jablonski recalled. As he grabbed his friend's arm, the divers were engulfed in a cloud of silt. "I couldn't even see my own hand," he added. If they lost their way in that cavern, Jablonski knew they would run out of air and die. His one thought was to grab hold of his friend and attempt to get them both to safety. Unable to see anything, he tried to remember the general direction of the cavern exit. He headed toward it, bringing the other diver with him. Repeatedly, they bumped into the cavern walls but kept moving forward along the path in Jablonski's mind.

"I am not a religious guy," he told us. "But in that moment, I made a promise. If I could get my friend, whom I had jeopardized carelessly, out alive, I would do my best to shift the balance in training and never do something like this again."

Slowly, Jablonski and his friend kept moving until, finally, they reached a patch of clear water where they could see the opening. Both divers exited and surfaced, grateful and extremely lucky to be alive.

That incident happened in 1993, but it continues to define Jablonski's sense of mission as a cave diver and world-class instructor. Today, he is one of the most accomplished cave divers on the planet, having set several world records for some of the longest and most complicated cave explorations.

The vow he made that day in the cavern also started him on a new trajectory. As the founder and president of Global Underwater Explorers (GUE), established in 1998, Jablonski is a leader in diving safety.

Over the years, Jablonski has known too many people—several of them close friends—who died while diving. Some fatalities were attributed to bad choices and others to weak or poorly considered procedures. Most involved some aspect of diving physiology—the science of what happens to a body while diving—particularly while diving to extended depths and for a longer time. Early diving procedures and training were insufficient to keep divers safe. As such, most of these fatalities can be attributed to human error.

When diving deep and long, it is necessary to manage the fact that humans are highly affected while breathing atmospheric air—that is, similar in composition to the air we breathe on land—under the pressure of deep water. The nitrogen in atmospheric air can cause illness and impairment at deeper depths. To increase safety in deep dives, you should use breathing gases that include helium and use lower concentrations of oxygen. The reduced nitrogen removes a narcotic impairment known as nitrogen narcosis. Meanwhile, less oxygen reduces the risk of oxygen toxicity. It gets even more complicated with deeper dives, and especially with deep cave dives.

Deep cave divers may have many switches between various cylinders. First, they must carry enough gas to manage the long penetration into and out of a cave, including a reserve for emergencies. Next, they may have to switch between different breathing gases across their multiple tanks during a dive. Unfortunately, one of the deadliest mistakes is switching to the wrong gas at a depth where that gas is not safe to use. In most cases, the fatalities could have been prevented either through more appropriate gas selection or with more meticulous procedures and more rigorous training.

That's why GUE takes a mastery learning approach in all its development programs, from entry-level divers to record-breaking experts. Its curriculum meticulously validates that each learner has mastered—and continues to master—crucial skills before continuing to the next level. Education must lead to an established level of performance. Casual, recreational dives do not have the same requirements as deep, technical ones, but all divers should be comfortable when something is not going exactly to plan. As divers progress through the training system, the number and type of challenges expand. More advanced divers must become comfortable managing several challenges at the same time.

GUE's diver training has evolved into a curriculum and learning progression that is the most well-developed system of true mastery learning for adults that we've seen. Its approach to mastery-based learning is radically different from the mainstream diver training, especially those organizations that dominate scuba diving and certify hundreds of thousands of divers every year. Those organizations teach basic skills such as taking your mask off and putting it back on while kneeling on the bottom in shallow water.

The problem, though, is a real emergency is not likely to happen in a nice stable situation while sitting on the bottom of anything. Instead, you would more likely be swimming in the water, some distance from either the surface or the bottom. Suddenly, you're unable to see anything without the mask that was accidentally knocked off your face. Stressed out and even panicked, you're wondering if you will be able to retrieve it.

These scenarios happen more frequently than you might think. That's why the general recommendation is never to dive alone. For one thing, a buddy can usually retrieve your mask and put it in your hand. But how prepared will you be for that moment if your only training and practice has been taking the mask off (often reluctantly) while kneeling on the bottom of a pool or in fifteen feet of water?

GUE prepares divers for such contingencies by having them practice mask removal and replacement dozens of times and to do it in mid-water while keeping both depth and location. Ironically, the building of this capacity is not particularly difficult. It just takes a bit more time. First, practicing the technique in the pool is common, but the proof of sufficient mastery is the ability to use the skill in a more challenging context. Mask removal and replacement are among the many skills and procedures that GUE integrates into diver training to achieve a high level of competency, where actions and reactions become second nature. In this way, fundamental skills are developed progressively and organically, almost without the diver noticing. This means they are prepared for the day when they really need to focus their entire attention on solving a complex or even life-threatening problem.

With GUE diver training, the objective is more than just a safe dive for an individual. While several of the mainstream diving agencies have promoted solo diving, one of GUE's standards is always to dive as a team. You may be able to do certain dives alone, but usually with increased risk—and preferably not as your default approach. At GUE, the educational approach includes a team focus, developing divers to be independently proficient and team oriented.

Being a strong team member requires a set of acquired skills and character traits, the same set that is key to all the mastery programs we have highlighted throughout the book. We find the roots of this approach in aerospace and aviation, which led the way in the late 1970s with the development of dedicated team training in the form of crew resource management.[1] Since the early 1990s, this approach has been translated into health care, maritime operations, nuclear power plant management, and other high-risk areas.

GUE has taken this approach to team performance a step further: When a diver in training performs underwater skills that are assessed by the instructor, the team is allowed to help that student. Actually, they are required to help. As Jablonski explained in a conversation about solo diving, "Some people wrongly interpret our team approach, imagining that we devalue the individual. Teaching people to be capable team members is actually more difficult, as there is more to learn. We start with a solid foundation, building individual capacity while expanding awareness and communication in a way that supports strong team performance. When you are comfortable and competent, with the awareness to be a good team member, everything you do becomes easier and more fun. We dive as a team so we also train as a team."

This is a prominent example of GUE's commitment to what it calls "beginning with the end in mind," and it reflects how the organization approaches mastery learning. The goal of the education system and the practice sessions is to ensure divers reach a level of comfort that exceeds that of a given scenario. The mastery level sought prepares them for the immediate challenge as well as challenges they could very well face at some point.

Over time, all team members move toward true mastery of not only diving skills but also team skills within complex scenarios. The "end" to which the training is geared considers that someone may reach diving environments in which quickly coming to the surface may not be an option. Early training programs focus on simply becoming comfortable and competent, slowly evolving across progressive programs, along with the type of diving pursued by the individual. With very complex technical dives, advanced skills are necessary to manage the high-risk situations that may occur on long and deep dives, where death or disability of one or more team members is a possibility. Such preparation is essential for team members who may later join some of GUE's more advanced diving expeditions, whether for research, exploration, or recreation.

Sardinia-based Andrea "Mara" Marassich, who is GUE's global cave program director and examiner for new cave instructors, explains, "The worst thing is a non–team player. One bad apple can easily destroy the whole atmosphere of collaboration in the team. It becomes dangerous to everybody as it takes focus away from safety and mutual support."

GUE may be a pocket of extreme human performance, but we believe that the future of humans in an increasingly technology-based world is determined exactly by this: our ability to bridge vast amounts of knowledge, skills, and dispositions as team players and citizens.

Mastery in the Workplace

Life-and-death, mission critical, no margin for error—such examples quicken the pulse, but can we really relate? In most industries, of course, the risks faced do not equate to an immediate matter of life and death. But there are still threats that will likely determine the fates of individual jobs, companies, and sometimes even the communities that surround those companies. The rapid pace of change in the workplace requires adults to continue learning well after they leave school.

The most visionary companies are seeking to introduce a mastery-based approach to workplace learning, not just to introduce a new skill or increase awareness of a new product or solution. Rather, the goal is to change behaviors and attitudes.

The harsh fact is the readers of this book probably have experienced little (if any) mastery learning in the workplace. There is a running joke in corporate learning circles these days, and it goes something like this: Given all the turnover among employees over the past few years, employers don't want to spend all that money to train people, because what happens if they just walk out the door with their new knowledge and skills? Then comes the punchline: But what if we don't educate them, and they stay?

What looks like a jest is actually today's reality. Many organizations, both for-profit and nonprofit, may express support for more training and education, yet workplace learning has not changed significantly.

As a percentage of total training hours, you'll often find the majority of the content to be compliance, procedural, or risk oriented. Cameron Hedrick, who heads learning and culture at Citi, called this "a necessary training event that can also serve as an artifact for auditors and legal, where, if needed, they can say, 'Look, [this employee] completed the training and you can see they completed it on this date, at this proficiency level.'" This way, should a problem occur—such as an allegation of sexual harassment or a deviation from a standard operational protocol—the company will be able to provide evidence that the employee was trained, and potentially limit its legal liability.

Our quest to discover more about the state of learning in the workplace took us to thought leaders on the front lines of an evolving landscape. Among them is Annmarie Neal, the former chief talent officer at Cisco. She currently holds that position at Hellman

& Friedman, a San Francisco–based private equity firm with about $95 billion in assets under management. Neal acts as the firm's corporate psychologist and works with a team of other psychologists on organizational performance and innovation at the companies in the firm's portfolio.

Neal told us that many companies have recognized the importance of developing certain competencies that are aligned with their business strategies. It makes sense. People in the company need the knowledge and skills to carry out the business strategy. But most of the skill building in corporate America today usually occurs as part of executive and leadership development. As Neal told us, "Good companies should be doing competency-based [training] at the top," because having a leadership team that lacks critical skills would be disastrous.

Forward-thinking companies take learning and development from the senior leadership level down to about as far as middle managers. And it stops there. Even though a significant portion of payroll dollars goes to the lower tier, mastery learning to build competencies below the manager level is rare. Many employers today believe it is generally easier and cheaper to "buy" desired skills than it is to "build" them. And so, hiring people with skills from the outside is their go-to strategy.

Senior managers complain that the alternative, building employees' skills, is too costly and time-consuming. It often takes tremendous effort to get entry-level workers trained to the point that they can be productive. Neal said most companies' view is that it is "extremely expensive" to engage in skill building at all levels. "And corporations may not . . . have the disposable income or feel responsible that they should do this."

While corporations have traditionally preferred to buy skilled talent rather than build it, this will not be a sustainable strategy in the future. Today, it often costs far more to recruit and onboard talent hired from the outside than it does to develop talent on the inside.[2] People with highly desirable skills are also in short supply. As we look ahead, the simple law of supply and demand will force companies to revisit their willingness to train and develop workers. If they want skilled people for the jobs of the future, they must make that investment as well as support the changes needed in K–12 and post-secondary education that we've discussed at length.

Korn Ferry, a global talent and organization strategy firm, looked at skill development in its *Talent Acquisition Trends Report 2024*. It found that companies are recognizing the "untapped potential" of programs to develop their workforce, starting at the earliest stages of people's careers. "Employers are investing more into early career hiring as a way to bring in fresh ideas, develop skills, build networks, and identify new hires with the potential for high performance. . . . We expect to see more talent leaders double down on their early career hiring strategies, using online assessments and training programs to develop the future workforce," the report stated.[3]

As we consider what that will look like, a move away from merely serving seat time and toward embracing mastery learning will be crucial. After all, it's not what employees know (or, more often, think they know). It's how they use that knowledge. Nothing less than the health of a company and the professional longevity of its employees is at stake.

Why Workplace Learning Must Change

Generative AI and large language models such as ChatGPT will change the workplace at an unprecedented pace. Lower-level work performed by millions of employees in industries such as banking, insurance, publishing, accounting, and many others can be delivered by AI models that crush human performance in terms of both comprehensiveness and speed. Given that reality, traditional knowledge-based education will become increasingly obsolete.

This challenge was widely acknowledged in the business world even before the emergence of generative AI at scale in 2023. In its

2021 *Future Skills Pilot Report,* consulting firm Accenture sounded a rallying cry to "continually refresh skills and stay relevant for the future of work," describing this as "top of mind for everyone from Fortune 500 CEOs to store clerks."

The report added, "This isn't simply because of rapid technology innovations and automation. The entire concept of work is evolving quickly. And the upheaval brought on by the COVID-19 pandemic further crystalized an urgent and complex global employment challenge: how to prepare people for the future of work in ways that serve individuals, businesses, and communities. Solving this challenge requires an in-depth look into what it takes to upskill at scale both within and between industries, to maintain business resilience as well as people's livelihoods."[4]

Predictions of the percentage of both blue- and white-collar jobs that will be lost to machines in the coming years range from 9 to 47 percent.[5] This landslide of job losses in the knowledge-based economy can happen even faster than many imagine. For example, within just six months in 2023, Ulrik's company developed technology that outperforms many human learning engineers (the people who build education programs for either their own companies or others) with several years of experience.

"Reskilling" and "upskilling" have been catchphrases among policymakers, politicians, and corporate leaders since the 1990s, but in recent years, a growing number of leaders have been advocating for training people to meet the evolving demands of a technology-driven workplace, and this was before the introduction of generative AI. Now, we are facing explosive changes.

Lifelong learning needs to change to a new, much more agile model where the skills are constantly acquired and reshaped. In this future world, reskilling and upskilling as we talk about them today will be history. You don't learn new skills to get a job. It *is* your job to continuously master new skills.

Despite the widely recognized talent imperative, a mastery approach is rare in most workplaces today. Our research and conversations with corporate leaders and chief learning officers revealed organizations that have a vision for mastery learning. However, actual examples of implementation in the workplace—and at scale—are few and far between.

Our findings were echoed in the Accenture report, which quoted Amy Goldfinger, senior vice president of global talent at Walmart: "No company today is equipped to operate upskilling efforts at full scale. That's the problem and the opportunity."[6]

This lack of mastery learning in the workplace might seem to undermine one of the main premises of this book. After all, one driver of mastery learning in K–12 and beyond is the need to keep up with a changing workplace. This includes not only ever-evolving technical skills but also those durable skills we've discussed, such as collaboration, critical thinking, communication, and character.

So, if this isn't happening in corporate America, does that mean mastery learning in schools is not, as we have argued in these pages, essential? No, not at all. Mastery learning can, should, and does make a difference from the youngest learners to the most experienced. It is the education world's equivalent of vaccines. It is a method that protects us against the changes and threats to our relevance and well-being.

What High-Stakes Occupations Still Need to Learn

As we look for examples of learning in the workplace, it makes sense that aviation would be a frontrunner, given the fact that the lives of hundreds of people—passengers as well as crew—are at stake each time a plane takes off.

Fortunately, emergencies are rare. Aviation has a long safety record and advanced technology to minimize human errors, all of which would seem to also minimize the risks involved. As counterintuitive as it may sound, though, those same safeguards can instill a false sense of invincibility, thus undermining the urgency to learn and, in particular, to pursue mastery. In other words, the risks no longer feel that risky.

That's why, even in aviation, there is a missed opportunity to embrace mastery learning. Lulled into complacency, some pilots fail to see the urgency in training meant to sharpen and refresh their skills. Until something goes wrong.

On the evening of June 1, 1999, Captain Richard Buschmann and First Officer Michael Origel were in charge of American Airlines Flight 1420 from Dallas–Fort Worth to Little Rock. Due to a late incoming aircraft, Flight 1420 was delayed two hours and twelve minutes. If only the flight had been delayed just thirty-six more minutes, then the pilots would have "timed out" and not been allowed to fly their last flight of the day. That would have averted disaster, but that is not what happened.

Shortly after the plane departed, air traffic controllers issued a weather advisory. Severe thunderstorms were in the vicinity of the Little Rock airport. Instead of diverting to their alternate airport in Nashville, Buschmann and Origel decided to expedite the plane's approach. But as they got closer to the airport, the wind direction changed, and the weather conditions worsened.

Right before landing, Origel told the tower that the pilots had lost sight of the runway. The air traffic controller gave the crew permission to do an instrument landing, and Buschmann decided to rush to land as soon as possible before the weather deteriorated further.[7] The decision would be Buschmann's last.

Tired after a very long day and under significant stress from the severe weather and changing conditions, the pilots made several errors when configuring the aircraft for landing. The plane managed to touch down but then began to slide. The auto spoilers on the wings (which control lift and drag) were not armed, and the auto brakes were not configured. Buschmann tried to mitigate these factors by applying reverse thrust of the engines, but it was too much. The pilots were no longer in control of the plane, which continued past the runway and crashed.

Buschmann and eight passengers died on the scene, and two more died in the hospital. Origel, three of the flight attendants, and forty-one passengers were seriously injured.[8]

Today, nearly twenty-five years later, Origel is a flight officer on 787 aircraft for American Airlines and an advocate for better training. In our conversation about what happened that fateful day of the plane crash, we asked him to reflect on our assumption that pilots are intrinsically motivated to keep learning because mistakes could be the difference between life and death. His reply was eye-opening: "We don't think of dying every day. [We think] we're invincible."

Flight simulation and team training are integral parts of both pilot education and continuing certification. Pilots must demonstrate mastery in a wide range of critical situations using simulators. But that was also the case before the disastrous Flight 1420 in 1999.

Origel has devoted his career to improving pilot education to make flying safer. He has built his education program on four elements: clear and concise procedures, being familiar with the unfamiliar, continual learning, and sharing. Importantly, he advocates for education that goes beyond the mandated training and is critical about the increased use of check-the-box, computer-based approaches that pervade aviation training.

"You've heard this material over and over and over again. And at some point, you basically believe that you already understand the material. So, you think there's no reason for you to be in a refresher class," Origel told us. "I have a colleague who pays his teenage daughter to take his computer-based training for him." That attitude—*I know the material and don't need to learn or review anymore*—can lead pilots to a false sense of confidence. It happens when people believe they know something, but they really don't.

The problem, as Origel sees it, is rooted in the commercial aviation industry's approach to continuous training: First, many pilots don't believe there is even a need for this training. The common perception is that "airplanes are really safe because of the layers of technology," he explained. Second, the nature of training is unengaging and repetitive. And third, no one is really held accountable for whether the learning results in mastery of the material.

Improving aviation training starts with changing the thinking. That's why Origel believes it is crucial to make pilots realize that just because they can fly from point A to point B several times, "that doesn't mean you can do it every time."

He also highlights a more recent problem. Aviation has become so safe that pilots have developed the equivalent of speed blindness. In other words, they have gotten so used to things going okay that they ignore the hidden risks. We believe this is an example of a high-stakes environment that still needs to learn, including from its mistakes.

Not Just Training, but Lifelong Learning

With a mastery learning approach, education is not episodic. Rather, mastery learning encourages lifelong learning, and it can and should be a goal for everyone, not just young people in school. To explore what that might look like, we reached out to experts and thought leaders in education.

Brandon Busteed, CEO of BrandEd and a former executive of Kaplan, has worked closely with colleges and universities to respond to changing demands for learning. "My thesis about the future is that we're going to see a lot more work-integrated learning in schools or colleges and a lot more learning-integrated work in places of employment. Ultimately, I think we're looking at what I call a merger of learning and work. Those two things are just going to increasingly blend together."

Busteed added, "If I'm being provocative, twenty-ish years from now, I think it'll be really hard for somebody to walk into a physical place and say, 'Is this a school or is this a place of employment?' Or a virtual place and say, 'Is this a school or college or is this a company or an employer?' Because I think what you're going to see is there will be so much learning and training needed to be relevant in a workplace."

The need for lifelong learning has also captured the attention of the OECD, the organization responsible for the Programme for International Student Assessment (PISA). As part of its research, PISA regularly tests the skills and knowledge of fifteen-year-old students in mathematics, reading, and science, as well as their financial literacy, creative thinking, and capacity for lifelong learning.

An important driver toward the need for lifelong learning is the concept of "skills inflation," introduced to us by Andreas Schleicher, the director for education and skills at the OECD who oversees PISA.[9] Anybody who has bought food, gasoline, or other goods in the past couple of years has experienced inflation. Things cost more. Another way to say that is that our money buys less.

The same decline in the value of our money at the cash register also applies to many workplace and technology-based skills. What was cutting-edge twenty years ago simply is not as valuable today. For example, coding was once a highly sought-after skill, but the ability to work with AI is now the skill in highest demand. By the same token, the skills employees possess today will be worth far less going forward because the ability to contribute in a meaningful way continues to be elevated.

"Skills are very much a currency in our lives," Schleicher told us. "So, skills inflation can push us forward." After all, preparing for the future is not just about learning how to do the next task. It is about learning how to identify what those next tasks are and how to accomplish them. Organizations must offer workers more opportunities to build skills, demonstrate competence, and pursue mastery. The lives and livelihoods of hundreds of millions of people will depend on it.

Skills gaps can be challenging to address. Often, learners must make significant investments in terms of time and energy. And new skills that will become increasingly relevant and valuable will be even harder to master. This will require resiliency and a general passion for learning new skills, both of which are important character traits.

A New Curriculum for the Modern World

Ideally, the workplace picks up where secondary and postsecondary education leaves off. Learning is ongoing as people enter the workplace and advance. Charles Fadel, who has been doing research in multidimensional and lifelong learning for decades, described the future as he sees it: "So, you continue learning on your own as your life requires it, but you're not starting from scratch. You're like a Swiss Army knife. You have a good blade, but you do not have the perfect blade."

Learners come in all types, abilities, and experiences. This is true in elementary and high schools, where there is a wide range of aptitudes and natural abilities. And it's also true among adults, for whom learning can be motivating for some but drudgery for others.

To appeal to the greatest number of people, we have found that learning for all adults, as well as students, must be tailored to each person. With personalized learning, people's backgrounds, experiences, aptitudes, and skill levels are all considered. The overarching belief is that every learner can become competent and achieve mastery. All they need is enough time and ample support.

With a personalized approach, learning is not viewed as only being for some employees—the highest performers or the most ambitious. Lifelong learning can be introduced to every person at every level. As people learn, they move from unskilled to skilled and from skilled to highly skilled.

An illustrative example we found is VEJ-EU, the Danish road-safety certification organization that trains workers on public roads. These workers encompass a wide variety of learners, from civil engineers with advanced degrees to laborers who did not complete high school. Yet all must pass the same, proficiency-based certification exam. To carry out their jobs, they need to demonstrate mastery of safety regulations, best practices, and problem-solving skills.

For years, certification was earned with a passing grade on a multiple-choice test given at the end of a two-day, in-person class. This approach was problematic for several reasons: not only the different skill levels and schooling among the workers but also the fact that much of the content was presented in slideshows. This was static material that bored those who already knew it and confounded those who had difficulty understanding.

The Danish road authority recognized it needed to change the approach to make learning more relevant and engaging. Yes, this involved an investment of time, effort, and, of course, money. What the Danish safety organization achieved by transforming training with a mastery approach offers a stunning and compelling argument for making that investment.

First, the slideshows were converted to computer-based learning that allowed each person to progress at their own pace. This enabled a personalized approach so that those who knew the material could advance, while those who needed extra help and more resources could receive that support.

After learning the material online, workers attended a one-day, in-person session. Rather than sitting for eight hours while someone talked at them from the front of the room, every learner engaged in exercises. Group-based problem-solving brought together workers with varied backgrounds and skill levels to engage with each other and put their knowledge into practice. At the end of the training, all learners (99.5 percent) gained the required knowledge, and they knew how to apply it.

Of course, some workers took longer than others. But why should that matter? Learning shouldn't be a race or a contest, where the winners are rewarded with As just because they got to the finish line first. It is a process of developing competence and confidence that should leave no one behind.

Although there is an order of magnitude difference between the fastest and the slowest learners, the point is that all can achieve mastery given sufficient time and coaching. That's the aspiration, and the challenge. How many learning environments and education systems today can handle a wide range of learners? Can they cater to those who grasp content the fastest and those who learn at one-tenth that pace? Making it even more difficult, given the demands of today's workplace, the time for learning is extremely limited.

In K–12 and higher education, it's understood that few learners are familiar with a subject before they are taught. Corporate education, however, takes the opposite view. The assumption is that learners have a foundational understanding of the material. But what if that's not the case? When people's lack of understanding or misconceptions are not addressed, many are left behind. And that can lead to errors and even safety risks.

Another example can be found in an entirely different corporate environment: a large international auditing firm. The challenge was digital transformation, which is all about implementing digital technology to improve efficiency and results. For employees at the firm, digital transformation wasn't something that happened "out there" amid the company's various departments and processes. They needed to rethink their own daily business practices, including how they collaborated with others.

Through a combination of individualized, computer-based learning and person-to-person coaching sessions—known as a blended learning environment—employees gained knowledge and applied it by working together on projects to encourage digital innovation within the business. This was not just a onetime initiative but part of a broader shift toward lifelong learning to continuously build skills, practice creativity and critical thinking, and improve collaboration.

Celebrating Failure

As competence grows, the natural inclination is to celebrate success. In fact, much of corporate culture is built on doing just that: the winners win, and those who don't . . . For mastery learning to take root in any environment, from K–12 to the workplace, so-called failure must be embraced as an opportunity to obtain feedback, correct mistakes, and adjust strategies and approaches, just as in the deliberate practice we discussed in Chapter 1.

The truth, however, is that for all the claims that "feedback is a gift" in certain circles of the workplace (such as in HR, where training typically resides), most people—and even many leaders—avoid hearing it. Seeking out that critique is almost unheard of.

We had this discussion with Cameron Hedrick of Citi. He recalled his days as a musician, practicing the trumpet with the best teachers he could find and literally paying someone to critique him. "But in the corporate world, critique is often not welcome," he told us. "People don't want anyone to tell them their flat sides, because, to them, that means 'I'm a failure.' It is often taken personally. So culturally, critique is unnatural and not well received."

The problem is that only celebrating success is "upside down," Hedrick added. "People need to be motivated by resolving and improving, whatever the failure is. And that comes with humility and personal retooling. You get up and you do it again, and you do it again. But not a lot of people are wired that way."

Ulrik gave the example of a challenge within his own company when a minor data breach occurred because of a software glitch, which needed to be addressed right away. Otherwise, it could grow from a minor breach to potentially a serious one. For much of the global operations team at Ulrik's company, this occurred in the middle of the night. The protocols spelled out the response: who would get contacted, no matter the hour. The challenge is that if the fullest response is called for every single time, not only will it become cost prohibitive but also people will burn out.

Ulrik was the most senior executive in the appropriate time zone (i.e., awake and still available). He decided on a somewhat moderate level of activation protocol. Within just a couple of hours, a temporary fix was put in place, followed up by a permanent solution a few hours later.

Data breaches, no matter how quickly they are contained, are among the most serious challenges tech companies deal with. They are certainly not the kind of episodes that are typically celebrated. But that's exactly the attitude Ulrik brought to his team the next day. "This was a smashing success. I am so proud of you," he told them.

When debriefing to learn from the incident, Ulrik asked the team for feedback on his call in terms of escalation level. It had been years since he'd been in charge of the first phase of a crisis like this. The feedback was that the team would have welcomed one level higher escalation. In other words, more team members were willing to be awakened earlier in the process.

Although the team responded with swiftness and urgency and took immediate action, they realized that next time it could be worse. Because here's the thing when it comes to technology: there *will* be a next time.

Learning from the Best

One final story from the workplace where change—not only technology but also the skills to use it—requires continuous learning. Here we find learning in the flow of work, combining training, feedback, and mentorship. To illustrate, we turned to one of the most familiar locations for most people, whether as customers or employees: a restaurant.

Tyrone Redic Jr., a restaurateur in Chicago, was the first African American general manager to receive two Michelin stars. He has helped Chicago-area restaurants achieve a total of seventeen Michelin stars. How he got to this level is a testament to learning from the best in the flow of work.

A self-starter, Redic found college was not well suited for him. Instead, he learned more on the job, starting in the hotel industry. But the most valuable training, with built-in performance-based evaluations, was at a prestigious restaurant in Chicago that bore the name of a renowned chef, Charlie Trotter. Trotter received multiple James Beard Awards and other accolades, including "Outstanding Restaurant" and "Best Chef Midwest." In fact, many hospitality professionals attribute the modern service concept in top restaurants to Trotter.

Joining the staff at Charlie Trotter's, Redic became a service professional, meaning he was trained in doing multiple jobs needed to make the restaurant operate as seamlessly as possible. He began as a food runner, bringing plates from the kitchen into the dining room for the waitstaff. From there, he moved up.

It was a demanding job that often lasted until two or three in the morning, Tuesday through Saturday. Plus, Redic received regular, ongoing training at Trotter's: Tuesdays for service training, Fridays for beverage training. "It was classroom-like, where the entire team would sit down, pick up some material, and go through it," Redic recalled.

It was real-world training with evaluations that occurred in real time. What he learned in these sessions informed how to do his job better that very evening. "It was sort of mind-blowing. I, who literally never carried a tray of glasses before, [was] surrounded by these high-level sommeliers and wait professionals who had been doing this for years," Redic said. "And I was getting fantastic training materials, but then also required to participate."

He remembered being assigned food and drink challenges related to anything that might be served at Trotter's. "Go home, research it, come back, and do a full-fledged presentation in front of the entire team—in front of Charlie Trotter himself," Redic told us. "It was just a fantastic experience."

What made Redic's training at Charlie Trotter's so unique was he wasn't simply thrown into a kitchen where chefs and sous-chefs barked out orders. There was a curriculum in place. Evaluation and feedback occurred in training and on the job—truly, learning in the flow of work.

Employers everywhere take note: it's not enough to hire someone for a job and expect that they'll pick up skills by osmosis. Too often, people are left to sink or swim in their jobs, without enough guidance or training, let alone assessment. If employers want to win the war on talent—hiring and retaining the people they need to be competitive— more time, effort, and money needs to be invested in learning in the flow of work. And that learning needs to continuously build both competence and confidence. Just like Redic's presentations, employees need to demonstrate and discuss what they've learned and how they are applying that knowledge in their jobs every day.

Mastery on the Playing Fields

Given the dearth of mastery learning in the workplace, one place where it may be more commonly experienced by adults is sports. It happens on the golf course, soccer field, tennis court, ice-skating rink, and dozens of other arenas. Whether someone is a professional athlete or a weekend enthusiast, skill building looks and feels the same: learn it, apply it, practice it, keep learning.

In professional sports such as soccer, team performance is paramount. When these players practice or play, they are building collective skills, because that, frankly, is their job. We learned of an exceptional example from Kasper Hjulmand, who took over as head coach of the Danish national men's soccer team in 2020.

Just from the sheer numbers involved, it's logical that a large, populous country would be more likely to field a championship team than a much smaller one. There are simply more talented people to draw from and more opportunities for these talented people to practice and play together, becoming a championship team. But certain small countries—Denmark, Belgium, and Portugal—have been successful at fielding world-class teams in soccer for years.

This is not a fluke. Rather, it's an example of what a mastery approach can achieve with individuals and teams. The secret sauce is in the way the players are educated and coached, particularly in those durable skills we've referenced throughout the book, such as collaboration and critical thinking.

Soccer—or football, as it is called in much of the world—is an interesting case study for mastery learning because of the team aspect. Yes, this sport has its superstars, and some teams may have stellar performers who rise above the rest. But one player alone cannot win a soccer match; the team must come together and play as a unit.

"It's a complex sport. It's a fluid game," Hjulmand told us. "And it's a low-scoring game. Because of that complexity, you can absolutely be the worst team on the pitch and still win it—and be the best team and lose it. . . . You need to work a long time . . . to reach excellence."

In taking a mastery approach, we might expect a coach like Hjulmand to drill tactics, playbooks, and technical skills. Surprisingly, he puts a laser focus on what he calls "identity"—a reflection of the values of each player and the team as a whole. Identity determines both individual behaviors and what it means to be a team player who respects collective performance above individual achievement.

Ulrik first discussed this concept of identity with Hjulmand in 2021, just as Denmark was preparing for the Euro 2020 championship (delayed because of COVID). As Hjulmand said at that time, "Identity is the yardstick by which you know the right thing to do."[10] Within shared identity, there is respect for individuality and diversity. Differences in experiences, viewpoints, and thinking can come together to strengthen the team around the foundation of common values. This is a leadership approach that speaks to what organizations everywhere need to create to encourage the pursuit of personal and organizational mastery.

In their most recent conversation in mid-2024, when Hjulmand was still coach of the Danish men's team, he and Ulrik returned to the topic of identity and its importance to performance. In fact, Hjulmand estimated that identity determines 90 percent of what the team achieves in any given game. "So tactics matter only 10 percent," he added.

"It's trying to create learning environments or learning hubs through football," Hjulmand said. "And that starts with identity [to support] a style of behavior. That's what we are trying to do."

Being able to establish a common identity on a team is also a crucial leadership skill, to coalesce individual efforts into team performance. "I cannot say that the way we play is the right way [for every team], but it is the right way for us," Hjulmand said. "We have to fit our identity and our values into a style of play."

In instilling a sense of identity and the cohesion that comes with it, national soccer team coaches face an interesting leadership challenge: The players all have full-time jobs in top clubs around the world. If they are selected to play for a national team, they only meet for a few weeks a year. The players are already top performers, but they are used to performing on completely different teams. As the national team coach, Hjulmand has very limited time to establish a coherent team performance. Therefore, he needs to quickly instill both the attitudes and the aptitudes that would bring these athletes together, not only as a team but as a national team.

To address this challenge, when Hjulmand became head coach for Denmark, he studied successful national teams in Germany and the United Kingdom, among others, and how they define themselves in five key areas. The result is a framework he used to build a team identity.

1. **Who we are:** How does the team or organization define itself?
2. **How we play:** What is the style of interaction and collaboration? How do we innovate and win?
3. **The player:** Given what we know about the first two elements, what traits and competencies must people possess? (This speaks directly to a mastery learning approach.)

4. **How we lead:** What leadership style brings out the best in our players?

5. **What we are doing:** What mission, vision, and sense of purpose drive the team?

In Denmark, instilling this sense of identity—what it means to be part of a team—starts early with the three hundred thousand or so youngsters in the country who learn how to play soccer. As players mature and progress through the club system, coaches of all the teams, influenced by Hjulmand's thinking, stress the concept of team identity. Importantly, this speaks not only to what these young athletes learn about soccer skills but also to how they learn about teamwork.

This framework also supports the kind of innovation that every organization would value and can only come with a mastery approach to learning that puts an emphasis on how people think and perform in teams. It is not enough for people to learn about the organization's mission. They need to apply that understanding to everything they do as part of a culture of continuous improvement.

A shared sense of identity also reinforces individual and collective values—as Hjulmand described it, "the core things in one's life"—that apply not only on the playing field but also when faced with more grave challenges. One such incident occurred during the opening game of Euro 2020. Christian Eriksen of the Danish national men's team suffered a cardiac arrest during the game and was medically dead before being resuscitated by defibrillation on the field.

Amid this life-and-death drama unfolding before fans and televised to a global audience, the Danish team instantly clustered around Eriksen. It was a show of support for their teammate, while also shielding him from the cameras that kept rolling.[11] The European sports media later praised Hjulmand as the coach for how he handled Eriksen's medical crisis. As *The Independent* observed, Hjulmand offered "a human touch to his players" and managed to "marry empathy with football intelligence."[12]

Recalling that difficult day (Eriksen fully recovered and continues to play soccer), Hjulmand gave full credit to his team—not only their cohesion but also their devotion to their fallen teammate. Three days after Eriksen's medical crisis, while he was still in critical condition, the Danish national team was scheduled to play another match. At least five players from the starting lineup told Hjulmand they were not sure they could play that day. With no pressure, he gave them permission to make their own decision. In the end, the team came together and played as an expression of their unity.

Most importantly, the fans surrounded the team with what can only be described as unconditional support. Incredibly, the team won the game without Eriksen on the field. The players felt "totally safe . . . totally loved. We could have lost ten-zero and still walked out of there feeling celebrated," Hjulmand said.

Just a year later, the Danish team had the exact opposite experience at the World Cup championship in Qatar in 2022. It started when the Danish team announced it would wear jerseys in support of human rights for migrant workers and to honor workers who had died doing construction work for the tournament.[13] The Danish soccer federation had promised to wear critical messages to highlight the plight of migrant workers, which created a media frenzy. Suddenly, the team was plunged into an "impossible environment" with a hostile audience, Hjulmand recalled, in which it was extremely difficult to play at their best.

Further, most of the players on the Danish team decided not to have their families attend the World Cup, for fear they would be hounded by the press for comments. That meant the players had to be in an unwelcoming environment without their personal support systems.

Two championships, two very different outcomes due to incidents not directly tied to the game. In the former, victory came out of cohesion and feeling supported. In the latter, frustration and feelings of rejection undermined any chance of performing well. Despite high expectations for the World Cup due to their strong showing in previous championships and their impressive qualifying campaign, Denmark failed to advance past the group stage.

"There is a lesson here: If we want the best out of people, they must feel absolutely safe," Hjulmand said.

It's an important takeaway for all of adult learning. When people feel safe, they are more apt to engage in the trial and error that is foundational to mastery learning, with its emphasis on feedback loops and deliberate practice. However, if people are afraid of failing—if the punitive consequences keep them from even trying—then they are already lost, even before their first attempt.

"If people know they are safe, that whatever happens they are still loved or respected, there is no limit to what they are able to do. In the right environment, there is no limit," Hjulmand said. "So I think at every level, every individual can do more, can learn more than they think."

Mastery Learning for Personal Satisfaction

For most of us, pursuits in sports and other leisure activities are for pleasure and a sense of accomplishment. Expressing one's passion is its own reward. We often find examples in our own lives or among the people we know. For many people, singing, dancing, sculpting, photography, poetry, or any number of other activities are an outlet for their passion. Whether they recognize it or not, it's also a way to pursue mastery. These endeavors have nothing to do with their day jobs. The purpose is solely enrichment.

By broadening our lens, we can find numerous examples where adults experience hands-on learning, from art studios to music classes, from writing workshops to golf courses. We pick up a musical instrument and learn to play a few notes, then a simple song, then a more challenging composition. We take classes in sketching, painting, or writing, learning from the instructor as well as from feedback from peers. In the cycle of coaching, playing, and practicing on the guitar or on the basketball court, we continue to improve.

Growth and Grit

To become a lifelong learner, both in our jobs and in our vocations, we need a growth mindset. Author, researcher, and psychologist Carol Dweck of Stanford University defines people with a growth mindset as those who grasp that "abilities can be developed." This attitude, put into practice, can help increase "the brain's capacity to learn and to solve problems."[14] Rather than being frightened by change or frustrated by obstacles, learners with a growth mindset embrace the process of building their skills and developing their competence in pursuit of mastery.

We see this in the workplace, where workers can motivate themselves to develop the skills that will keep them relevant. The reward will be both intrinsic, with the satisfaction of self-improvement, and extrinsic, as workers become equipped to take on the jobs of the future.

Hand in hand with a growth mindset is the importance of grit, which researcher Angela Duckworth of the University of Pennsylvania describes as persistence applied toward long-term achievement.[15] As adults, in particular, look for examples of where they've experienced both a growth mindset and grit, it's likely that they'll find them in their passion pursuits. From piano to pickleball, learning something challenging builds a host of skills, aptitudes, and attitudes.

The most dramatic examples are when people overcome odds that seem stacked against them or the norms that would eliminate them out of the gate. Only with grit and a growth mindset can they rise above and achieve. In some instances, they exceed all expectations to become champions.

At six foot four, Viktor Axelsen was considered too tall to do well in badminton. He has, however, struck down that assumption, becoming a two-time Olympic champion, including at the 2024 games in Paris; a two-time world champion; and a four-time European champion. This is the result of developing grit at a young age, when growth spurts could have become a detriment to his ambitions. Instead, he was determined to become the best he could be despite not fitting the mold of a typical player.

"What I realized from a young age is I have given my soul to this sport," Axelsen told Ulrik.[16]

While badminton is almost nonexistent in the United States, it is one of the most popular sports globally. A recent survey ranks badminton the most popular sport in China, which historically has produced the most champions over time.[17] So how did Axelsen, who is Danish, become widely recognized as being one of the greatest—and perhaps *the* greatest—badminton players of all time?

Grit certainly plays a big part, with passion that ignited early and has been kept alive for decades. This is crucial for the athlete who faces the inevitable losses and injuries, as well as the entrepreneur who must persevere through the rejection of early ideas and the corporate leader who must revamp business models and strategies in the face of disruptive competitors.

But determination alone is not enough. Axelsen credits how he trained—with intensity, not sheer volume of hours. He calls this the "Danish system," in reference to his home country. Typically, he practices twice a day for a couple of hours each session. This is a sharp contrast to the typical practice sessions for Chinese competitors, which last five to seven hours a day or longer.

To be sure, he is an admirer of his Chinese, Indian, and Indonesian counterparts, who are among some of the best players in the sport. Axelsen is also fluent in Mandarin and has been given a Chinese name by his teacher: An Sai Long, meaning calm competitive dragon.

However, Axelsen acknowledged that he would not have fared as well in the Chinese system of training badminton players. Those long practice sessions would be too grueling and, in his mind, less effective for him than shorter, "higher quality" sessions, as he called them, in which he incorporates the coach's feedback in real time. Axelsen practices hard, but he always tries to have fun. For example, he devotes time to develop his trick shots. "They're fun and make me feel inspired," he said. "But I also know that at some point during a match, I might be able to pull a trick shot."

Fun is another word for engagement, fueling the intrinsic drive to learn, practice, accept feedback, and improve. In this way, Axelsen's training might also be seen as an "innovation lab" for finding creative solutions and pursuing positive outcomes.

In some professions, fun at work may seem to be a paradox. Yet, from the C-suite to the factory floor, the laboratory to the library, performance can be enhanced by finding joy. This is what enables grit and expands a growth mindset.

Where Mastery Learning for Adults Needs to Go

As you know from this chapter discussion—and, no doubt, from reflecting on your own experiences—mastery learning in the workplace at all levels is rare.

Education for adult learners will have to go deeper. For organizations to adapt more quickly, employee training and other education should not be limited to senior and middle management. People at all levels of organizations will need education and skill building to help them do their jobs today and prepare to take on new jobs tomorrow.

In a fast-changing world, the people on the front lines need to be equipped for what they are facing. Companies are moving in this direction, slowly but surely. And those that get there first will have the competitive advantage.

To experience what's possible, adult learners need to connect the dots from their avocations and leisure activities to their jobs. The more they see the connections, the better they will be able to advocate for, seek out, and embrace opportunities for mastery learning.

CHAPTER 7

Assessing Mastery

I

T's a late fall evening in Allen County, Kentucky, a place so rural they have more cows than people. There are over forty-five thousand cows and only 20,797 people, and a little more than three thousand students in their four public schools. It's not the sort of place you'd expect something revolutionary to be taking place.

This evening, there's a line of people over two hundred yards long in the Allen County Intermediate Center (middle school) parking lot. They're not here as spectators to cheer the school's Patriots football team defending their home turf. Instead, they're here to listen to middle schoolers defending their mastery of learning. In Allen County, there's no hard wall between school and the rest of the community. This evening, that means a middle school full of nervous, motivated students proving they're becoming competent to enter the next stage of their development, and adults invested in young people as the future of their community coming to support and question them. This is what assessment looks like in Allen County, and it's both exciting and engaging for all involved.

Kentucky has a long history of top-down educational reforms—reforms that in the past have not resulted in substantive improvements in all students' learning. Jason Glass, when he was appointed state education commissioner at the height of COVID in 2020, decided to try a different approach. Soon after taking office, he began a nine-month listening tour, including thirteen virtual town halls attended by around one thousand Kentuckians.[1] He asked citizens what was working and what wasn't in their public schools, and what kind of learning experiences the adults in the room remembered that had excited them. "We then asked, 'What should school be to have more learning experiences like that?'" Glass told us. The answer was the same everywhere: make learning inspiring, fulfilling, and personal.

His department also convened a coalition of fifty-three stakeholders called Kentucky United We Learn. It was one-third appointees, one-third open applicants, and one-third a random selection of citizens from across the state. The coalition included educators, business leaders, nonprofit leaders, and parents. It was also 17 percent students and recent graduates.

"The coalition conducted even more interviews in their own communities," Glass said. "So, we just had reams of data around perceptions of where Kentucky's education system was now and where people would like it to go."

With support from Glass's office and the data gathered during his listening tour and the United We Learn interviews, districts around the state began developing what is called a profile or portrait of a graduate. The idea was to sponsor discussions with local parents, students, community members, and business owners that would result in consensus about the most important skills and dispositions that every high school graduate should possess in their community. It was a bottom-up effort to complement the statewide initiative.

Carmen Coleman told us what it looked like in Danville public schools when she was superintendent. It all began in a district meeting with one simple question. "Someone at the table asked, 'What does our diploma mean?'" Coleman said. "So, we started trying to answer that question. And the best we could come up with were things like: It means they've served their time. It means they've met a set of very minimal requirements—with a D-minus at least, I mean. That was the best we could do. And so, we said, 'All right, here's a place to start. What do we want it to mean, to our kids, to our community?' It's a promise, right?"

Allen County, under the leadership of Superintendent Travis Hamby, who had been part of the United We Learn effort, developed its own graduate portrait, which they called "Profile of a Patriot." The profile lists five essential education outcomes—in effect, the promise that Coleman referred to, along with descriptors for each.[2]

The Allen County district's promise is very similar to ones that have been created in many communities and states, and there are a couple things to note. First, it is a list of skills, not academic content knowledge. Parents and community members around the country intuitively understand that these are the qualities that matter far more than mere knowledge. They are the skills that enable students to do something in the world with what they know. Second, these competencies are essential to meet the three goals of education that we have identified: preparation for work, citizenship, and personal health and well-being. The outcomes are the following:

- resilient learner
- effective communicator
- creative problem solver
- engaged global citizen
- accountable collaborator

Students' progress toward these education goals is regularly assessed according to clearly defined performance objectives. One key assessment tool that was introduced was what the district calls "defenses of learning." Students in elementary, middle, and high school are periodically asked to show their work and explain to an audience where they are in their journeys toward proficiency in the five outcomes above. Allen County middle schoolers' defenses of learning were what the community had turned out to see in droves.

Defenses of learning are critical for two reasons. Students are far more motivated to do their best when they have a real audience for their work. Such defenses also create a kind of face-to-face account-ability. The community can clearly see what its students can do with what they know. The defenses are a performance, much like ones in the arts or on the athletic field, and the results are transparent to everyone.

Louisville's Jefferson County Public Schools (JCPS), an urban school district that is the thirtieth largest in the United States, has their public defenses at a much larger scale. In 2018–2019, their first year of defenses, more than twenty-one thousand fifth, eighth, and twelfth graders stood up in public forums to describe their learning in relation to the district's profile of a graduate.

Like CEOs presenting earnings reports or researchers giving TED Talks, the students craft stories of their academic achievements as well as how they participate in their school community and the com-munity at large. Complete with visuals and performances as well as a probing question-and-answer session, the presentations showcase what the students have learned from successes as well as failures, both in school and in the many out-of-classroom events and activi-ties they engage in. They share how they're developing as young peo-ple ever more able to innovate, collaborate, and take on challenges. They peer into their futures, envisioning how these competencies will help them in the next stage of their life journey, beginning at the age of nine or ten.

In her presentation—a YouTube video available for anyone to see—Amari, a serious fifth grader from Bloom Elementary, highlights two personal strengths aligned to the JCPS success profile: innovation and citizenship. As evidence of innovation, she shares her fashion designs. For citizenship, she talks about raising money for a local nonprofit.

She also identifies a personal problem and the steps she took to overcome it: "A growth I have is confidence, because when I present, my legs shake a lot and I, um, stutter. To work with that, I tried out for rock band and made it. I tried out for cheer and I did the fifth-grade talent show. It will help me in middle school because I need confidence to raise my hand in class with projects, and I'll need it to make new friends."[3]

Like Monique, whom we met in Chapter 2, Amari has engaged in a variety of extracurriculars. But where Monique, as a high schooler, experienced these as discrete, disconnected (though enjoyable) activities, Amari's elementary school is teaching her to connect what she learns in these activities back to her growing sense of self and purpose. She is learning to identify both her strengths and her areas of weakness, take ownership of them, and make intentional choices to direct her growth. She is also learning to tell the story of her own development. Her family, teachers, peers, the local community, and beyond all witness her becoming a prepared and resilient learner.

Along with Allen, Danville, and Jefferson Counties, more than one-third of the Kentucky school districts have undertaken dialogues where parents, employers, the community, and students talk about the learning that matters most. Many districts are deeply involved in designing new approaches to learning and assessment that will implement their graduate profiles.

More than twenty states have developed some version of a profile of a graduate, and the work is ongoing. Many states are also exploring different kinds of performance assessments, like the Kentucky defenses of learning. However, this work is held back by the current outdated federal testing requirements.

The Problems with Standardized Tests

Developing new curricula where students do projects to acquire skills, finding better ways to continually assess students and give feedback, and planning community defenses of learning all require an enormous amount of time and effort. In addition to all this work, educators must also prepare their students for periodic statewide standardized tests that the federal government has mandated since the passage of the No Child Left Behind Act in 2002. States are required to test all students in reading and language arts and mathematics annually in grades three through eight and once in high school. In addition, students are tested in science once during grades three to five, once during grades six to nine, and once during grades ten to twelve. Test results feature prominently in each school's annual report card that the federal government requires states to make public, which causes enormous stress for educators. No one wants their school to be labeled "failing." And so, teachers must spend huge amounts of class time doing test prep, even though they know that projects and defenses of learning are what truly engage students and best prepare them for the future.

For the past seventy-five years, multiple-choice, machine-scored standardized tests have increasingly been used to determine what academic tracks students would be placed on for elementary and high school, what sorts of learning they will do in their classes, whether they will pass a course and earn a credit, and whether they will be admitted to higher education. The two essential elements of all assessments are validity and reliability. Validity in this context refers to the nature of the test: Are you testing the knowledge and skills that truly matter? Reliability refers to the ability to replicate comparable results repeatedly. Standardized tests are widely used because they are considered reliable—being computer-scored versus being scored by individuals—and they are given to large testing populations instead of just a sample of that population. They also offer the advantage of being comparatively inexpensive. It costs far more to have individuals or groups score an essay, for example, than it does to have a computer score a multiple-choice test.

In recent years, however, opposition to widespread standardized testing in education has continued to grow and has come from many quarters. Parents and teachers complain that the emphasis on high-stakes standardized tests reduces the curriculum to test prep, and courses that are not tested, such as social studies and the arts, get short shrift. What gets tested is what gets taught. And even in those courses that are tested—math, language arts, and, less frequently, science—teachers are told to focus only on the content knowledge and basic skills students need to get a higher score, not necessarily what helps them achieve deeper understanding or true proficiency.

Educators also complain that they do not get test score results in time to improve instruction for the students they are teaching. The tests are a postmortem rather than a diagnosis of education needs. Finally, many teachers are concerned about high-stakes tests' emotional toll on students, especially on those who are not good test takers.

A growing number of people who are troubled by inequities in our society also point out that standardized tests are easily gamed, allowing admission to elite public schools or name-brand universities. Kids whose families can afford to hire a tutor and provide their children with other social and cultural advantages outperform young people with similar abilities who do not have those advantages. Recent research has revealed that students whose families are in the top 20 percent of the income bracket are seven times more likely to get a high SAT or ACT score than those in the bottom 20 percent.[4]

While virtually all colleges suspended standardized testing requirements during COVID, in the spring of 2024 a few Ivy League colleges reinstated the requirement that students take either the SAT or ACT for college admissions. They cite controversial research that shows that test scores are a more accurate predictor of how well students will do in the first year of college than grades (though we argue that such tests do not measure the skills that matter most for future success). Even though students from disadvantaged backgrounds often have lower test scores, these college admissions officers say they take students' backgrounds into consideration, which can work in favor of moderately high scoring disadvantaged students.[5]

Many colleges and university admissions officers remain concerned that the SAT and ACT test requirements continue to keep talented minority students from getting into college. More than 80 percent of BA-degree-granting colleges and universities remain test optional, meaning that they no longer require students to submit any standardized test scores for admissions, according to the National Center for Fair and Open Testing.[6] A recent study has found that colleges that went test optional increased their percentage of minority applicants without any decline in graduation rates.[7]

Another concern with the increase in standardized testing is the cost in both time and money. In a study of the largest urban school districts, students took an average of 112 tests from pre-K through twelfth grade.[8] Preparing for these tests took many additional hours of class time. And the cost of such extensive testing continues to rise. A 2012 study conducted by the Brown Center on Education Policy at the Brookings Institution estimated that states were then spending $1.7 billion a year on federally mandated standardized tests.[9] That's about $2.35 billion in today's dollars.

So what are we getting for all this time and money spent on testing? We learned in Chapter 2 that reading and math scores have barely moved, and inequities persist after decades of high-stakes testing. Employers complain that they see no real improvements in job applicants' skills. There have been many reports outlining employers' dissatisfaction with applicants' basic writing (grammar, spelling, etc.) and computer skills. Many employers say new hires lack critical thinking skills, as well as durable skills, such as leadership, character, creativity, and collaboration.[10] These are qualities that cannot be assessed by means of conventional standardized tests.

Multiple-choice tests simply do not assess the skills that matter most in today's world. The central challenge of innovations in performance assessments has been to create ways to assess durable skills that are both valid and reliable and that do not add significant additional cost. Two tools are increasingly used in public and private elementary, middle, and high schools to assess the competencies that educators and community members have determined to be most important for students' futures: digital portfolios or collections of student work completed over time and presentations of learning, like those described in the opening of this chapter.

Performance Assessments: Portfolios and Presentations of Learning

The use of portfolios and presentations as assessment tools in schools has a little-known history. In 1980, Theodore R. Sizer, who was previously a dean of the Harvard Graduate School of Education and head of the prestigious Phillips Academy, launched a study of high schools. In a series of popular books, he described the low quality of learning in most American high schools, where he observed that teachers and students had a tacit agreement: teachers agreed to ask very little of students in return for their quiet compliance. This research led to the launch in 1984 of an organization called the Coalition of Essential Schools (CES), whose mission was to pioneer new approaches to bolstering learning and teaching in American high schools.

CES was organized around what were called the "ten common principles." Sizer and members of CES believed that a key to improving learning was to strengthen intrinsic student motivation. They advocated for smaller learning communities, where students were known by their teachers; greater student choice and voice in the learning process; a commitment to equity and diversity; and classes organized around intellectually rigorous projects and inquiry.[11]

The goal of learning in CES schools was much more than merely acquiring academic content knowledge. It was to instill in students what Deborah Meier, founder and principal of Central Park East Secondary School, and others called "habits of mind." These are ways of considering what is being learned from the perspectives of significance (Why is it important?), perspective (What is the point of view?), evidence (How do you know?), connection (How does it apply?), and supposition (What if it were different?).[12] In a number of CES schools, some variation of these five questions was posted on the wall of every classroom, and teachers often asked their students to stop and reflect on their progress toward proficiency in habits of mind.

Another key principle of CES—and crucial to this discussion—was a commitment to "authentic assessment." Rather than relying on traditional standardized tests, CES members advocated for the use of more open-ended assessments such as projects, essays, portfolios, and what CES schools referred to as "demonstrations of mastery," where students were regularly required to present their projects, defend their papers, and demonstrate the habits of mind in front of an audience. The audiences variously consisted of peers and other teachers, parents, and outside reviewers. To support these efforts, CES developed resources and tools to help schools implement performance-based assessments, including guidelines for creating rubrics, sample assessments, and professional development programs for teachers.

CES claimed nearly six hundred high schools as members at its height in the mid-1990s. However, beginning in the late 1990s, the push for more high-stakes testing came to undermine the work that these schools were doing to transform learning. Under ever increasing pressures to improve standardized test scores, teachers felt they could no longer afford to spend time on the educational innovations that CES advocated.

CES formally ceased operations in 2017. But the work of some of its best-known member schools—notably High Tech High in San

Diego, Central Park East Secondary School in Harlem, and Thayer High School in New Hampshire—has greatly influenced the innovations in many schools today. All three schools pioneered the use of student projects, portfolios, and public demonstrations of mastery as key instruments for assessing the quality of student learning and progress toward proficiency.

Established in 1998, the New York Performance Standards Consortium (usually just called the Consortium) was an outgrowth of CES. In the early 1990s, New York State education commissioner Dr. Thomas Sobol launched an initiative where highly effective public schools were asked to work with underperforming schools. One of the common practices of the mentoring schools was their use of a system of performance assessment.

Since 1999, all New York State high school students have had to pass a series of three-hour Regents Exams to earn a high school diploma: one each in English language arts, history, science, math, and an elective. (Prior to 1999, not all students were required to take Regents Exams to graduate; there were alternative diploma options, such as the local diploma.) Sobol granted a waiver that allowed a few schools to use their performance assessment system as an alternative to the Regents Exam.

Sobol's waiver allowed the thirty-eight Consortium high schools to replace all but the English Regents Exam with their performance assessments. The state Board of Regents has renewed these waivers, allowing the participating schools to continue to develop their assessment model. All but two of the Consortium schools are in New York City. Collectively, they enroll twelve thousand students who are racially and ethnically diverse and include a high percentage of multilingual learners and students with disabilities.

To graduate from a Consortium high school, in addition to passing the English Regents Exam, twelfth graders must complete written performance-based assessment tasks (PBATs) and present their work orally to a panel of adults. For both papers and presentations, external evaluators use guidelines that have been collaboratively developed by Consortium teachers. The required PBATs include an analytic literary essay, a social studies research paper, an original or extended science experiment or engineering design, and a narrative describing the mathematical thinking used to solve a challenging math problem. Participating schools often require additional performance tasks in the creative arts, a second language, and internships. While such rubrics used to assess the quality of student work are standardized across all schools, students choose their own topics or questions for each of their PBATs.[13]

Ann Cook, cofounder and executive director of the Consortium, emphasized that the PBATs represent much more than just a onetime summative assessment. They reflect a wholly different approach to classroom work that spans students' four years of high school. "It's about how you organize curriculum in such a way that you get kids engaged. We're interested in student voice. We're interested in choice. We're interested in analysis, not summary. We're interested in expectations. We're interested in revision," Cook told us. "And those are things that require practice. It's not something you can just wait until the senior year and do. So these things have to grow out of the day-to-day instruction."

We asked her about the high school completion and college-going rates for Consortium students. While their high school graduation rates are higher than other New York City schools with comparable student profiles, admission to the City University of New York (CUNY) colleges—which are the preferred options for many of their students—was initially quite challenging. The students consistently had low SAT scores, and the CUNYs were continuously raising minimum scores for admissions to improve their selectivity and resulting college ranking.

Research revealed that, because of this admissions standard, the percentage of minority students enrolled in the CUNYs was steadily declining. When this information became public, a new CUNY admissions director was hired, and Cook went to her with a proposal to try a pilot. Cook suggested that CUNY admit the students the Consortium recommended, based on their PBATs and GPAs, without requiring SATs. "So for the last seven or eight years, we've sent eight hundred to nine hundred kids into the four-year CUNYs, who never would have otherwise gotten in," she told us.

CUNY professor Michelle Fine and her colleague Karyna Pryiomka analyzed the results of the pilot and determined that it was a huge success. The professors report quantitative evidence demonstrating "that students in Consortium schools begin high school more educationally and economically disadvantaged than their peers and yet are more likely to graduate from high school, attend college, and persist in college than demographically similar peers. Those who go on to attend CUNY are more likely to be Black and Hispanic." The report goes on to note that "early evidence suggests Black males, in particular, appeared to benefit from a Consortium education when compared to Black males educated in traditional high school settings: They were notably more likely to persist in college and to receive higher grades."

The Consortium students not only went to college but were more likely to succeed there. "The results also indicate positive outcomes for students admitted to CUNY through the Consortium–CUNY pilot: On average, they achieve higher first-semester college GPAs, earn more initial credits, and persist in college after the first year at higher rates than peers from other New York City schools, who, on average, have higher SAT scores," the researchers found.[14]

New Approaches to Documenting Learning

While Consortium students only take one Regents Exam and no longer must submit their SAT scores for college admissions, the schools are still required to report students' GPAs. And they must translate student work into credit hours or Carnegie units for transcripts. We spoke with Alan Cheng, who is the superintendent overseeing the work of fifty alternative high schools in New York City—including all the Consortium schools located there— about the challenges of these near-universal college admissions requirements.

"As a district, we have the highest percentage of students that are in temporary housing and English language learners of any district here in New York City," Cheng told us. "And we can point to really successful models of implementing mastery-based learning. But we have these artificial constraints—semester deadlines for students to demonstrate what they know, for example. Also, our teachers spend four years or seven years with our students, and then when they apply to college, they have to convert everything to a traditional numerical grade for transcripts to send out to colleges because that's the only thing that they take. Admissions at two-year and four-year colleges still remain a pretty significant barrier."

Public alternative school leaders are far from the only ones who are now questioning the value of GPAs and the Carnegie unit as measures of learning. Educators from private schools and wealthy suburban public schools have long been concerned about how competition for admission to elite colleges has led many students to care far more about their grades than what they've learned as well as greatly increasing students' stress. These same educators observe that many students seem to learn more—and care more about their learning—when participating in extracurricular activities, internships, and noncredit seminars, which do not earn them a grade or a Carnegie unit.

And now the Carnegie Foundation for the Advancement of Teaching, the organization that pushed for the widespread adoption of the Carnegie unit as a measure of learning 120 years ago, is leading the charge to create an alternative. We spoke with Carnegie president Timothy Knowles about the current work of the foundation.

"The Carnegie unit or the credit hour was a very rational approach to a very particular problem at the time, but since then, neuroscience scientists and cognitive psychologists all say, 'Learning happens in these ways when it's at its most robust.' And really that has nothing to do with the conflation of time and learning, which is what the Carnegie unit ultimately is," he told us.

In April 2023, the foundation announced a partnership with the Educational Testing Service (ETS), the world's largest nonprofit educational testing company, "to create a set of tools designed to assess the qualitative skills that many of today's employers consider most important—such as creative thinking, work ethic and ability to collaborate. . . . Such tools could potentially be better indicators of a student's future success than the traditional Carnegie unit, or credit hour. . . . The new tools would also allow students to account for learning completed outside of the classroom, such as at a job or internship."[15] The two organizations followed this announcement later in 2023 with the publication of *A New Vision for Skills-Based Assessment*, which offers a comprehensive analysis of the ways assessment and testing must be transformed and the role AI will play in the process.[16]

Founded in 2017, the Mastery Transcript Consortium (MTC) is another nonprofit that's pioneering alternatives to GPAs and Carnegie units. (All three of us have served on the board of MTC.) The MTC approach has been to create an entirely new kind of mastery-based high school transcript. While initially founded by a consortium of independent schools, MTC's membership now includes more than four hundred high schools, a majority of which are public. Many of Cheng's fifty alternative schools, including the Consortium schools, have recently become members.

The concept for MTC was the vision of Scott Looney, head of Hawken School in Cleveland and MTC's past board chair. "I was convinced that if we're going to design our ideal high school, then the current assessment and grading system had to go," he told us.

The mastery transcript has evolved and currently offers a graphical snapshot of student work based on what we like to think of as a collection of merit badges developed by individual schools. The snapshot indicates both the badges the students have worked on and the extent of their work for each one. The mastery transcript includes a list of the courses taken with links to the work students have to produce to justify their credit.[17]

In 2023, the MTC began piloting the mastery learning record, a new product to document interdisciplinary and out-of-class learning—such as projects, field trips, and internships—that increasing numbers of traditional schools now offer their students, which can be incorporated into traditional high school transcripts. Mike Flanagan, MTC CEO, explained the rationale: "In the early days of MTC it was independent schools, lab schools, charter start-ups—schools that had kind of been purpose-built not to do traditional learning and assessment. Now the question is, how do you work with existing systems and help them transform at scale to make mastery learning available to the kids they're serving?"

Susie Bell, MTC chief program officer, told us about a recent breakthrough in Utah, a state that has developed a profile of a graduate. With support from the Utah State Board of Education and a grant from the Walton Family Foundation, MTC is currently assisting more than ninety schools that are implementing the mastery learning record. "What's really also unique about Utah is everybody wants to learn from what they're doing because it is more of a state-level approach," Bell explained. MTC is also now partnering with America Succeeds to find ways to adapt the transcript for employers seeking evidence of job applicants' durable skills.

These new approaches to transcripts and learning records clearly are helping students get noticed. Since the new transcript became operational in 2019, more than one hundred schools have piloted MTC's products and have received acceptances from nearly five hundred colleges and universities, including Harvard, Stanford, the University of California system, and numerous other state schools.[18]

Now MTC is poised for a dramatic increase in its impact. On May 15, 2024, MTC and ETS announced that MTC would become a wholly owned subsidiary of ETS. MTC will join ETS and the Carnegie Foundation in the Skills for the Future Initiative, which aims to "radically transform education from a time-based to a competency-based system undergirded by measures that capture evidence of what's most important for success in high school, postsecondary education, jobs in today's economy, and, jobs of the future."[19]

A Better Approach to Systems Accountability

The increased use of performance assessments, such as digital portfolios and defenses of learning, and the development of a new kind of mastery transcript are all promising efforts to create better assessments. These assessments result in improved local school- and community-based accountability, what we think of as face-to-face accountability. The validity of these assessments comes from their ability to represent students' proficiency in the skills that matter most, unlike most standardized tests. But they are locally developed and do not assess how groups of students do over time. They are not reliable as tools for what we call systems accountability. The question remains: How do we hold school districts and states accountable for ensuring that no child is left behind?

The state tests mandated by the federal government have only served to reinforce a culture of compliance and fear among educators, which discourages innovations in teaching and learning. They also do not measure the skills and dispositions that matter most, as we've seen.

What might better standardized tests look like? In our research, we have found two outstanding examples of standardized tests that measure what matters most: skills such as critical thinking, problem-solving, and writing. To score well on these tests, teaching and learning must happen at the highest levels.

Origins of the Collegiate Learning Assessment

Some years ago, Dr. Richard Hersh found that he had a serious problem as a liberal arts college president. "I would greet parents or contributors during events, and we'd all agree about the value of a liberal arts education," Hersh told Tony in an interview for his book *The Global Achievement Gap*. "But once in a while, someone would ask, 'Dr. Hersh, just what *exactly* is the value of a liberal arts education, and how do you know your college is delivering it?' I always had a smooth answer ready, but I'd go home and be thinking, 'I wish I had a better answer.'"

So Hersh worked with Stephen Klein and Roger Benjamin, both at the RAND Corporation at the time, to see if it was possible to measure the "value-added" of a college—that is, how much students learned between their freshman and senior years. Hersh said that college professors "couldn't even agree on the important academic content within their own departments, let alone across the campus or between colleges. But they all did agree on a core set of competencies that a college should teach all its students: critical thinking, analytic reasoning, written communication, and problem-solving. This consensus allowed us to design a content-neutral, skills-based assessment that we could give a sample of students in freshman and senior year and then measure growth in the four areas."[20] Out of this finding came the Collegiate Learning Assessment (CLA).

In the sample test that Tony took, he was given what is called in testing parlance a "performance task," where he had to advise someone running for mayor in a fictitious town with a high crime rate about which of two options for reducing the rate might be most effective. First, he had to evaluate eight documents that were posted online. They ranged from newspaper stories about crime patterns, to studies on the value of adding additional police, to a report on a drug treatment program. All were based on real examples.

Having read them, Tony then had to write two memos: one comparing the pros and cons of adding more police versus bringing in a specific drug treatment program, and another that was a position paper for the candidate. The test had no right or wrong answers. Instead, it assessed the ability to weigh evidence, distinguish fact from opinion, and construct a coherent argument. High school students who took the assessment and were interviewed afterward said they found the test both challenging and engaging, unlike the SAT and AP tests they'd taken. Tony had to agree. It was a test worth taking.[21]

The Council for Aid to Education, which has administered the CLA since 2002, went on to develop a middle and high school version of the test, now called the College and Career Readiness Assessment (CCRA). More than three hundred colleges and universities give the CLA to sample populations of their freshman and senior classes to determine to what extent students' skills in critical thinking, analytic reasoning, written communication, and problem-solving have improved over four years. A similar number of high schools and school districts use the CCRA for the same purpose. While these numbers are small in relation to the total high school and college population, we see the use of these tests as a bold experiment in institutional accountability.

Dr. Doris Zahner was hired in 2011 as the Council for Aid to Education's chief academic officer to greatly expand its offerings based on these assessments. The council now offers assessments that measure individual students' degree of proficiency, strengths, and areas that need improvement in critical thinking, problem-solving, and written communication.[22]

"Traditional transcripts—whether they're high school transcripts or university college transcripts—don't actually show any indication of critical thinking proficiency," Zahner explained. "So hiring managers are getting students who don't necessarily have critical thinking skills. They can't put together an email to a client or a colleague. We wanted to look at levels of proficiency. We have five: emerging, developing, proficient, accomplished, and advanced. At the top three levels, we are able to issue digital credentials to students should they want to have this information to showcase on LinkedIn, etc."

The Council for Aid to Education has also partnered with schools that use their tools diagnostically to identify areas where teaching needs to be improved. Zahner told us about an exciting collaboration with the Texas A&M business school, where the goal is to use assessments "formatively"—that is, as a tool to inform and improve instruction of critical thinking and writing.

Dr. Shannon Deer, associate dean for undergraduate programs at Texas A&M's Mays Business School, told us that the school's leadership wanted to know how their students were doing from a learning outcomes perspective. "We had done a couple of different types of assessment for critical thinking, as well as just evaluating student papers," she said. "But it was hard to really measure across different disciplines and different student groups, and scoring the assessments ourselves was also labor-intensive. We were looking for a tool that we could use that would give us an objective assessment, that we wouldn't have to grade ourselves. And we found CLA, which did that for us."

The results were illuminating. "We have very high-performing students, many of whom were in the top 10 percent of their high school classes," Deer continued. "When we got the results back in 2019, what we learned was that our students were doing great at writing mechanics, but they were not good at writing effectiveness or critical thinking."

Deer described how, in a meeting about the results, one of the department heads said, "I know our faculty think that they teach critical thinking. But I don't even know how to teach critical thinking myself." Deer went on to explain, "It broke the ice, and everyone was willing to admit they didn't really know how to teach critical thinking. Just because you asked an essay question on an exam doesn't mean it was a good question that made students think critically. So we went back to the council and said, 'What can you do to help us train our faculty?'"

Deer decided that a key intervention opportunity was the introductory course that's required of all first-year students, Business 101. She oversees the course and is one of the faculty who teach it. Some professors who teach the very last course students take—a capstone course—were also willing to get involved. Deer asked the Council for Aid to Education's staff to help develop an instructional framework and course materials centered around case studies. The case studies for both courses are built on examples of different business problems, and students must think critically about the challenges and trade-offs and then write an essay where they argue for a solution to the problem in the case. Unlike the Harvard Business School's case studies, which are based on something that has happened in a company, the Council for Aid to Education's case studies have no right or wrong answer. You are assessed on how well you reason out a solution to the problem.

New Approaches to International Assessments

Standardized assessments that compare the results of different countries' education systems have been around since the 1960s. But with the intensified global economic competitiveness of the last quarter century, the results of these tests have increasingly drawn the attention of politicians and the media. Today, the leaders of most countries understand that the economic health of their country is intimately linked to the quality of their education systems and so want to know how their schools stack up against schools in other countries.

Since 2000, two assessments have been used by growing numbers of countries to assess their education systems: the Trends in International Mathematics and Science Study (TIMSS), administered by the International Association for the Evaluation of Educational Achievement (IEA), and the Programme for International Student Assessment, an OECD project. Sixty-four countries participated in the most recent TIMSS assessment, while seventy-nine countries administered the latest PISA tests.[23]

The results of both assessments are widely reported in the media when they are administered every three or four years and are often used to buttress arguments for education reforms in the participating countries. However, they are quite different in both design and intention. TIMSS is a conventional standardized test that focuses specifically on the content knowledge students have acquired in mathematics and science in grades four and eight, using machine-scored, multiple-choice questions. PISA, which was first administered in 2000, assesses how fifteen-year-olds can use their reading, mathematics, and science knowledge and skills to meet real-life challenges through open-ended responses scored by people. It has also pioneered new approaches to assessing so-called twenty-first-century skills.

It turns out that the difference between measuring what students have learned versus assessing their skills for using their knowledge is profound, as Andreas Schleicher of the OECD explained to us. Prior to joining OECD, Schleicher was director for analysis at IEA, the organization that administers TIMMS. He has been the architect of the PISA tests since the beginning and is globally recognized for his many contributions to the science of assessment. We spoke with him at length about what makes PISA assessments unique.

"The transformational idea behind PISA," Schleicher explained, "lay in testing not whether students can reproduce what they have learned but whether they can extrapolate from what they know and apply their understanding of key concepts and ideas creatively in novel situations. To do well on PISA tasks, students also have to be able to think across the boundaries of subject-matter disciplines, design an experiment rather than reproduce its results, or solve a problem collaboratively rather than individually."

Another difference between PISA versus conventional exams is how they are developed. Most standardized tests are designed and administered by a single entity. By contrast, Schleicher told us, PISA assessments are, in essence, "crowdsourced."

"The challenge for PISA was that in the early years we had very little money," he explained. "But that turned out to be probably the greatest strength of PISA." Because they couldn't afford to hire an individual company's engineers to test and build new assessments that cost millions of dollars, the PISA developers attracted the world's best thinkers and mobilized hundreds of educators and scientists from the participating countries to explore new possibilities for testing.

This approach has enabled Schleicher and his colleagues to create some of the world's most innovative performance assessments. New computer-based technologies such as simulations and real-time online student collaboration enable test designers to go beyond paper-and-pencil tests. Since 2000, with every testing cycle, they have added one new assessment. In 2003, it was problem-solving. In 2006, it was how students used technology. In 2009, it was digital literacy. In 2012, it was creative problem-solving. They added collaborative problem-solving in 2015 and global competencies in 2018, with creative thinking up next. "In the last PISA assessment, we intentionally asked students questions where they had to distinguish fact from opinion," Schleicher said. "In the year 2000, we didn't ask those kinds of questions."

The contrast between the US citizenship exam and PISA's approach to determining students' readiness for global citizenship— or, in their words, "global competence"—illustrates the difference between a content knowledge test versus an assessment of students' abilities to apply knowledge. You'll recall from Chapter 2 that the

US exam is a multiple-choice test that asks factual questions about US history and government—such as naming the three branches of government—and is entirely based on memorized content.

PISA's assessment, on the other hand, "requires a combination of knowledge, skills, attitudes, and values successfully applied to global issues or intercultural situations," as Schleicher explained. In other words, it tests your ability to use your knowledge and skills to perform a task. It presents students with real-world scenarios related to global issues (such as climate change, migration, and international conflicts) and asks questions that measure their understanding and analytical skills. A typical task might present students with a news article, video clip, or infographic about a global issue. Students might then be asked to:

- identify the main idea or point of view,
- compare perspectives from different sources,
- analyze how local situations can be influenced by global events or policies, and
- suggest potential solutions to the presented challenges.

You can learn more about this assessment on the OECD website. Elsewhere on the website, you will find a wealth of information about their other assessments, as well as how countries have scored on these since 2000.[24]

The assessments described in this chapter point the way toward the development of wholly different ways to assess learning from kindergarten to college, and there is a growing investment in new approaches. In 2022, the US Department of Education gave $29 million in grants to ten states, including Kentucky, to develop next-generation assessments, and the ETS and Carnegie Foundation for the Advancement of Teaching, together with MTC, plan to raise and spend more than $20 million on new approaches to competency-based assessment to replace the current content knowledge tests.

Assessment in the Workplace: Informing Continuous Learning

Beyond individual teacher assessments of student work, much of the assessment of students in elementary and high schools is focused on systems accountability or college admissions. In college, almost all assessment happens in the classroom, and the purpose is to determine to what extent students have mastered the academic course content.

But what happens when adults enter the workforce, whether after high school, with some college, or as college graduates? To be sure, workers are evaluated, such as with annual performance reviews, which usually amount to little more than a perfunctory exercise for managers and their direct reports. Otherwise, assessment—like workplace learning itself—still lags behind the demands of the twenty-first-century, technology-enabled world.

In the last half of the twentieth century, as the United States shifted from an industrial economy to a so-called knowledge economy, new approaches emerged for assessing and improving white-collar workers' proficiency. One of the most well-known was a system created by Jack Welch, who was CEO of General Electric (GE) from 1981 to 2001. He implemented a performance evaluation plan at GE called "rank and yank," which aimed to sort employees based on their performance and potential contribution to the company.

Welch believed that it was crucial to differentiate employees into three categories: the top 20 percent, the "vital" 70 percent, and the bottom 10 percent. This categorization was based on managers' annual performance reviews, which were often subjective. Welch advocated firing the bottom 10 percent of employees, referred to as the "C players."

While the practice was widely admired and replicated in many companies during Welch's reign and is still used by some companies today, GE's internal HR leaders eventually found that "the practice failed to capture future potential, hurt morale, and did not boost performance." It also created a cutthroat work culture that discouraged collaboration and teamwork. Other researchers have since learned that rating-based performance reviews "often fail to change how people work, and dissatisfaction with the appraisal process has been associated with general job dissatisfaction, lower organization commitment, and increased intentions to quit."[25] Finally, the system placed a significant emphasis on short-term, quantifiable performance metrics, and it did not consider the now essential qualities such as innovation, creativity, character, and adaptability. In other words, assessing workers on a bell curve has all the same deficiencies as the summative standardized tests in education.

In the twentieth century, it was assumed that almost everyone in the workforce would get most of their education before they turned thirty. Once hired, the employee's challenge was to compete with peers on performance metrics to keep one's job or to advance. Continuous learning was not a significant factor in evaluations, and so Welch's sorting model appeared to work, at least in the short term. The reason? During most of the twentieth century, there was either sufficient unemployment (meaning a steady supply of workers) or the jobs didn't really need a lot of qualifications, or both. Neither are true today.

What is the solution? The simple answer is that employers of both blue- and white-collar workers will only be successful if they take responsibility for shaping—and sharpening—the skill sets of their employees. And this means fundamentally changing what is valued in the workplace and how contributions are measured. Assessments that merely rank employees are simplistic, as we've seen, and increasingly obsolete. They must be replaced with assessments that are formative, to support continuous learning and encourage skill building. Recruitment metrics must focus on the passion and perseverance to learn rather than paper credentials. The result will be not only greater motivation among workers to develop their skills but also habits that support lifelong learning.

This is the aspiration but, unfortunately, not yet the reality. Several attempts have been made to establish more reliable methodologies to assess the learning itself. Assessment in the traditional education system, including in the workplace, has had the primary goal of determining whether learning has happened. In the workplace, however, the best assessments now attempt to measure what employees do with what they have learned: How are they using knowledge to improve products and service quality or enhance customer satisfaction? In short, what are all the ways that employees hopefully increase profit or accomplish the goals of the organization?

One would think that this goal would make workplace evaluations the poster child for mastery learning assessment, but in most cases, instruments for measuring workplace learning and competencies cannot assess even snippets of mastery. There are simply too many other things that influence the performance of an employee. As a result, it is difficult to determine which workplace learning experiences make a difference or to quantify that difference.

Cameron Hedrick, who heads learning and culture at Citi, is one of the most respected leaders and most forward-thinking learning officers we've met anywhere. He has spent more than twenty years at Citi, an $80 billion global financial services company.

He agreed that in a high-stakes environment, where mistakes can mean the difference between life and death, the importance of learning is clear. But he went on to explain that in ordinary circumstances, "it's very difficult to quantify the value of workplace education." For one thing, it's hard to attribute improvements in performance in most jobs to any specific training because of what

Hedrick called "the number of confounding variables." He gave an example of sales training. "If someone says that, because of this sales training program, we generated 5 percent more revenue, I would laugh. Just think of the number of variables involved in that 5 percent." In addition, organizational outcomes cannot be tied back to individuals, let alone be used to guide further learning.

To solve this problem, chief learning officers in many forward-thinking organizations have attempted to adopt a model developed by Donald Kirkpatrick in the 1950s that advocated for evaluation of training at four different levels.[26] The most basic level is measuring the person's reaction to learning. Are they motivated by having an opportunity to learn more and build their skills? The second level measures whether knowledge and objectives of the learning itself were met. Did a particular training or other learning experience increase the person's knowledge and skills? This level is close to the kind of assessment we see in schools. The third level is measuring changes in the person's behavior. For example, are they asking questions to gain clarification, helping colleagues, or following up with customers beyond addressing a complaint? The fourth level is supposed to measure the ultimate goal for most companies and corporations: impact on product quality, customer satisfaction, and so on.

The Kirkpatrick model makes a lot of sense and is compatible with mastery learning approaches. However, the actual assessment methods used in the workplace have often fallen short. In many cases, companies have either stopped at level one (which essentially asks, *Do you think that you learned something?*) or have tried to go straight to the fourth level of business impact measurements. Both approaches miss the core objective for mastery learning assessments: guiding continuous individual learning and skill development. The only way to accomplish mastery is by facilitating a cycle of learning, deliberate practice, and additional learning. Such a cycle must be supported by regular feedback and coaching. It must be conducted in environments where it is safe to fail during the learning and where the end goal is true mastery.

Assessment for the Innovation Economy

Imagine assessing workers' knowledge and skills on a continuous basis—think movie, rather than snapshot. This approach informs a process of continuous learning and improvement. With this approach, mastery is not an end point but rather continual progress along a trajectory of steady growth. Importantly, the purpose is not to "rank and yank" employees, as Welch did. Rather, the objective is to systematize personal development and career paths. In this way, workplace assessments become a key component of a continuous feedback loop, showing what employees do well and where they need to improve and build new skills.

The good news is that we have found some true mastery learning environments for adult learners. These environments have leapfrogged beyond the past decades of experiments in schools and colleges and inadequate assessment methods in the workplace. Tellingly, they appear to have a common characteristic: if people do not achieve true mastery, lives are lost. In other words, where the stakes for performance are the highest, we found the best examples of assessments that truly foster greater competence, continuous skill building, and support for lifelong learning.

Think of an airplane pilot who makes a critical error that results in the deaths of everyone on board (including the pilot). Or a physician who makes an error during treatment or surgery and the patient dies. There are other examples too. These include nuclear power plant operators, astronauts, emergency responders, and military service people, especially those in special forces.

To explore what assessment looks like in the high-stakes environment of medicine, we reached out to Dr. Marc Berg, a clinical professor of pediatrics and critical care at Stanford Medicine Children's Health in California. He is a noted expert in cardiopulmonary resuscitation, better known as CPR. He specializes in designing and conducting pediatric resuscitation education using simulation.

It is important to emphasize again that mastery is not about perfection. Rather, the goal is continuous improvement. This is a stark contrast to the summative standardized tests, including medical licensure exams, which are being used (and, we would argue, *mis*-used) to rank people based on a few peripheral percentage points. Scoring 96 percent will land you a residency over someone with a 95 percent. That is not the mastery that Berg is looking for. Rather, it's about developing competence with any medical procedure. As he explained, "It's not that we have the hubris to believe it's going to be perfect every time we do it. But we absolutely expect that there will be a review of how it went with the expectation that mastery is the goal. [Achieving] as close as we can to perfect is the goal worth striving for."

But even when lives are on the line, time-pressed professionals do not always recognize the need for assessment. As a result, there's no guarantee of getting their cooperation to assess skills. Ulrik observed this a few years ago at a large East Coast teaching hospital. A physician by training, with more than two decades of work in medical education, Ulrik was visiting the hospital's surgery department. Suddenly, a code red was triggered, signaling a patient had suffered a cardiac arrest.

He watched as the entire team went into action. Each member assumed their assigned roles, ready to begin the treatment protocols. The team started chest compressions and ventilations immediately. IV lines were inserted, and they attached the defibrillator. When the attending physician arrived, however, she did not find a patient, but rather a full-scale patient simulator. "I'm too busy for this," the physician complained and immediately left the room.

Reading this, you might be inclined to sympathize with the physician. Why spend time working on a simulator when there are real patients in a hospital who need medical attention? Is it right to interrupt physicians and nurses from their rounds for what amounts to a fire drill? The answer lies in the consequences of not doing training and assessment.

According to the *Journal of the American Medical Association*, more than 290,000 adults in hospitals each year in the United States go into cardiac arrest.[27] For these patients, having a well-trained medical team that knows how to act—and fast—is the difference between life and death. To avoid the consequence of deadly errors, it makes sense to practice using simulators so each team member can be assessed, given feedback, and supported in developing the skills they need.

Given the stakes involved, why not go all the way, with drills that simulate medical emergencies, such as cardiac events? Why not treat a simulator as if it were a real patient in distress to assess the team's skills and, in the process, see where the system can be improved? The answer lies in the findings that Berg summarized for us from the last twenty years of research in the field: "In order to instill mastery across large-scale systems, we have to weigh the risks of training against the benefit."

Fortunately, there is an alternative to unexpected fire-drill-type simulations, as Berg explained. "We have found that we can identify many of the system errors during *planned* simulations. A lot of true mastery can be practiced out of the context of the in situ simulations. We should relentlessly pursue building of mastery of the skills to handle these frequent and acute conditions, but we should do it with the least costly and [the fewest] potentially harmful means."

What Berg described is a research field in its infancy that could be named "edunomics," education and economics. It balances what people must know and demonstrate in their jobs through formative assessments with a cost-benefit analysis of getting them to mastery.

To explain, Berg used the example of someone taking a Ferrari to a racetrack to teach a teenager how to drive. "You could teach a fourteen-year-old how to parallel park using a Ferrari at a racetrack, and it would be very expensive," he said. Clearly, there are less expensive ways to learn the basics of driving. In clinical medicine and in health-care education more broadly, simulations have become crucial for pursuing mastery in safe environments. For example, lifelike patient simulators can be used to simulate medical crises with almost endless possibilities to shape both individual and team skills.

You can learn a simple skill like doing chest compressions within a few minutes if you have a manikin and receive immediate feedback on the placement of your hands, the frequency of compressions, and the depth of your compressions on the manikin's chest. Most things in health care, however, are far more complicated than that and require more complex—and expensive—simulations.

Even more challenging, simulations are only as useful as the coaching that accompanies them. To make their use truly impactful, simulations must be combined with debriefing or "after-action review," as it is called in the military. "Ten minutes of simulation can cover numerous learning objectives," Berg told us. "I could probably debrief for two or three hours based on fifteen minutes of simulation."

A simulation can be a procedure in which a surgeon is trained on a simulated joint to learn how to insert a new type of hip screw used in hip replacement surgery. Or a video recording of a medical simulation could capture an entire team in action with a detailed debriefing to follow.

"It's not an assessment with the purpose of telling them whether they passed or failed," Berg said. "It's self-assessment, peer assessment, mentor assessment." The true value comes from the reflection that occurs after practicing something in a simulated environment. This reflection develops and shapes the ability to learn and change.

We've made the point that simulation should be reserved for those high-impact areas where time is of the essence, where applying skills in real-life scenarios is highly complex, or where team practice is critical. But there are still lessons to be learned and applied to training and assessment in general. Task analysis and skills engineering, which are required to develop effective simulations, as well as the practice of regular debriefing, can be applied to all levels of mastery-based learning. One way, for example, is breaking tasks and skills into smaller components and building the best possible environment to practice them with feedback. The result is a giant step forward in assessment for the twenty-first century, humanized to meet the needs of the individual.

Additionally, while using simulators under various scenarios is a great way to test skills and gather feedback, it is not the only way. An alternative is learning from the flow of work as it is happening. We also see this in medicine, using in situ assessments and cognitive task analysis. The goal is both to understand system errors (poorly designed or flawed systems, safety hazards, or other risks) and to establish a culture where health professionals constantly improve.

Across the workplace, assessments need to be put in place that capture how people perform their jobs. In other words, do they know what to do, and can they do it competently? Even informal assessments—being observed by a more experienced peer or a supervisor—can make a huge difference. Without such formative assessments—formal and informal—people run the very real risk of thinking they know how to do something when, in fact, they don't.

Unconscious Incompetence: The Great Killer

Unconscious incompetence results from thinking you know how to do something when you actually don't. Research in this area was conducted by Ulrik and his team at his company, Area9 Lyceum, and at McGraw Hill, based on millions of learners from second graders to specialist physicians. Results frequently showed that people are unconsciously incompetent in about 20 to 30 percent of what they think they know.

This is the most dangerous state of learning because you are not likely to change anything or reflect on what should be improved. The reason? You don't even realize that there is a problem.

We can see this in K–12, where 70 percent (or even 60 percent) is considered a passing grade, even though that obviously means misunderstandings and errors on 30 to 40 percent of the material. A C student, who on the bell curve would be considered "average," is going to progress to the next grade or level with a 30 percent deficit in knowledge and understanding. Those knowledge gaps don't get filled later on; they only become more ingrained.

Many human errors can be attributed to this pattern. We should not mistake this for knowingly going beyond one's training. In some emergency situations, that is fully acceptable; think of the novice student pilot who has to take the controls when the instructor has a heart attack. Rather, uncovering and reversing unconscious incompetence is a key factor in learning more generally. Let's take a look.

Identifying Gaps

Not knowing what you don't know—being unconsciously incompetent—is the most counterproductive and sometimes even dangerous place to be. This is where deliberate practice comes in, by focusing your learning effects on your weakest sides or where you will benefit most from improving.

That's why the first step to moving beyond unconscious in competence is to realize where the gaps are in your knowledge or performance. This moves you to conscious incompetence. You know what you don't know. You are in what could also be called the learning zone. With continued learning, the progression toward competence and mastery can happen.

The goal is to become consciously competent, which is key to achieving mastery. When you become consciously competent, you are confident that you know or can do something. For some things, you want to master them well enough to be able to do them without any cognitive effort at all—what's known as automaticity.

In high-stakes environments, certain knowledge and skills need to be raised to the level of automaticity. These skills become part of the arsenal, to be drawn on for complex problem-solving or when there's no time to think too much about what must be done, let alone look it up on Google or ask an AI chatbot.

Examples of automaticity can be found in all dimensions of learning. They include doing basic arithmetic (knowledge), changing gears of a manual transmission car with a stick shift (psychomotor skill), speaking a language (communication), or acting ethically (character).

Current evaluation systems in adult learning and practice environments rarely assess these metacognitive aspects of learning. However, if the role of humans in the future is as integrators—the quarterbacks of knowledge, skills, and performance, who can bridge all these dimensions quickly and fluidly—then learning environments and measurement instruments must be engineered to evaluate how learners are progressing toward mastery.

Adaptive learning systems, such as the ones Ulrik and his companies have been building since 2008, use a detailed approach to measure and understand learning progress to guide the learner to knowledge mastery. The research and development that led to these systems was the product of a journey that started almost twenty years before the first adaptive systems saw the light of day.

Adaptive learning systems not only assess what learners—whether K–12 students or corporate employees—know but also how confident they are in their answers. This is crucial in helping people uncover their own unconscious incompetence. As part of a formative assessment, determining competence and confidence together creates a holistic learning approach to identifying gaps and misperceptions and giving learners what they need to succeed.

Ulrik explained how he started this practice with his two daughters when they were young and studying their spelling words. With every answer, they had to rate their confidence: three fingers up if they were sure, two fingers up if they were only partly sure, and thumbs down if they gave it a shot. This gave them not only another chance to review their answers but an opportunity to self-identify when they were guessing. Similarly, in corporate learning, employees should be given the opportunity without judgment or negative consequences to admit when they, too, are guessing. Rating the confidence of one's answers should be built into all formative assessments. Otherwise, when people make a lucky guess and get the answer right, they assume they know the material when, in fact, they do not.

Adaptive learning systems are not an end goal in and of themselves. However, as high-precision instruments, they can help learners navigate the massive amounts of knowledge that must be mastered in the future in order to perform the tasks that humans will still be superior at: critical thinking, creative problem-solving, communication, and collaboration.

Certifications and Certificates

To round out this discussion, we turn to another area that professionals use—and companies rely on—to supposedly acquire, assess, and attest to expertise. This includes certifications and certificates. They may sound similar, but they are not the same.

Certifications are professional credentials that require testing to achieve. Certificates are meant to show a person has attained a particular skill. For example, they have learned how to do basic coding in a specific computer language, such as C++ or Python.

Of the two, certifications are far more rigorous. A well-known example is the certified public accountant (CPA) credential from the American Institute of Certified Public Accountants. The institute and its predecessor organizations date back to 1887. To attest to their accounting knowledge and skills in such areas as auditing, finance, and tax preparation, accountants may pursue the CPA certification. In the eyes of a consumer, hiring a CPA provides assurance that their tax returns will likely be accurate and so will the advice they receive.

There are also certified life planners, certified case managers, and certified associates in project management credentials—just to name a few. And of course, in medicine, there are multiple board certifications that verify the knowledge and skills of a physician. An example is the American Board of Internal Medicine and its rigorous board certification examination in internal medicine.

Then, there are certificates. These are not academic degrees. Rather, they are sometimes only acknowledgment of participation in a course, seminar, or other experience. Some employers, however, strive to offer certificate programs that seek to build skills and provide pathways to becoming more proficient by demonstrating them.

A longtime leader in this area is IBM, which claims a legacy in employee training back to founder Thomas J. Watson Sr. In 1916, Watson appointed the company's first "manager of education," the same year it graduated its first sales training class of twenty. As IBM notes on its website, "Over the years, this emphasis on education would expand into sprawling customer training courses, a global education system for employees and their families, partnerships with universities, virtual classrooms and beyond."[28]

Today, the company offers a variety of "IBM Credentials" with skills-related certificates and badging. It also partners with other organizations to offer skills training. As Jean Matthews, a learning lead for business transformation services, AI, and cognitive sciences at IBM, and Madhusmita Patil, an associate partner and cognitive solutions architect at the company, wrote for *Chief Learning Officer*, "In an increasingly automated and evolving job market, there's significant pressure on employees to learn the right skills. Identifying which skills are right and what skills will make our workforce competitive now and in the future is the need of the hour."[29]

Google also offers credentials in what it calls "high-growth fields," including digital marketing, cybersecurity, data analytics, IT support, and project management. These credentials then scale up into more advanced programs such as automation and advanced data analytics. Such training is part of the company's Grow with Google initiative, which is described as helping people "realize their full economic potential." In 2017, Google committed $1 billion to Grow with Google and a year later launched its Google Career Certificates. As of late 2022, more than three hundred thousand people had completed Google's Career Certificates program, with 75 percent of them reportedly achieving higher pay, a new job, or a promotion within six months.[30]

In addition, there is industry-specific and company-specific training and assessment in particular skills. Mechanics who work on high-performance cars are required to have specialized skills that match the unique engineering of each machine. Companies such as Porsche and Ferrari have programs designed to educate, train, and assess the competence of mechanics before working on customers' cars.

What about the other, nontechnical skills that are important to the future of work? As discussed earlier in this chapter and throughout the book, these skills include collaboration, critical thinking, communication, and creativity. Very few certifications outside high-risk areas are even remotely mastery based, and the vast majority test only for knowledge and facts. The modern assessments and transcripts mentioned earlier in this chapter should be considered a model for adult learning as well. As we look ahead, ensuring that employees at all levels have the durable skills that will help them perform in an ever-changing workplace will be the new frontier for workplace assessment.

Assessing for the Durable Skills

Throughout this book, we've discussed certain skills that are crucial to one's professional growth and development today: durable skills of leadership, character, creativity, and collaboration, as America Succeeds defines them. They are sometimes referred to as soft skills. Although they differ from technical skills, durable skills are far from soft. These skills help people perform their jobs better today and become lifelong learners who can move into new jobs tomorrow.

So, let's take a look at the development and assessment of durable skills as part of a job. We use the example of TJ, the UPS driver.

On any given morning, TJ shows up at Ulrik's home. TJ's job is to deliver packages safely and on time. As UPS describes the role of a package delivery driver, "You'll start your day at a UPS facility and then drive one of our famous, brown trucks on a pre-determined route. You will be in and out of your truck, interacting with customers and the community as you deliver packages. You may also pick up packages at the end of your shift."[31]

To that we would add, "And so much more."

TJ possesses the physical strength to haul packages. He also is a skilled driver who can navigate the traffic-clogged streets in and around Boston. In addition, he needs technology skills to use GPS and the handheld scanners that track packages. Beyond that, TJ possesses great interpersonal skills. He is warm and friendly and even carries treats for Ulrik's two dogs.

Does UPS know what an outstanding employee TJ is? No doubt there are some statistics captured for his performance, such as on-time delivery, absence of accidents, and other technical aspects of his job. But the interpersonal skills that make TJ truly memorable are probably not part of the UPS performance equation, just as they weren't a part of Monique's performance reviews in call centers, as we saw in Chapter 2.

We believe that focusing on interpersonal aspects would put more value on what humans bring to a job. As the package delivery industry considers how and where to use drones, the value of someone like TJ going to the door should not be overlooked.

The same holds true for other occupations, especially in the service industry. With more than three-fourths of all Americans now employed by the service sector, the future of the workplace demands that we look beyond technical skills and consider the interpersonal skills that elevate performance.

Yes, some of these skills we likely learn early in life and carry with us. But they can still be encouraged and developed later in life. In future workplace assessments of mastery, we need to move beyond evaluating only high-stakes jobs and focus on human interactions, such as between colleagues and with customers, especially given the fact that our economy is increasingly based on service rather than manufacturing. It's not enough for companies to rely on the customer satisfaction surveys in which employees have to get a five-star or ten-out-of-ten rating or else face a reprimand.

Assessing and appreciating a host of diverse skills—technical and durable—would help make the world a better place, with more interactions occurring in a human way.

Conclusion: Time for Better Assessments

As this discussion shows, from K–12 to postsecondary to the workplace, better approaches to assessments are not merely a nice-to-have. They have become essential. Checking the box will not suffice. Assessment must become truly formative. In other words, it must be a tool that informs learning rather than merely evaluating it after the fact.

With better assessments come insights into who people are and what they know, like to do, and want to become. The picture becomes complete, with feedback around what people do well and where they need to grow, as well as acknowledgment of what motivates them.

Assessment, like learning, is not about ranking and sorting along a bell curve. It is not one-size-fits-all, nor is it one-and-done. Rather, it is a vital part of a process of continuous improvement that promotes lifelong learning, individual growth and well-being, personal fulfill-ment, and organizational effectiveness.

There's a societal benefit here, too, by building knowledge, expanding skills, and creating greater competency and capacity in humans who must succeed in the age of AI. Here, we can borrow from a concept in Danish culture known as *samfundssind*. It trans-lates into being "society minded," even to the point of putting others ahead of oneself.

In education, a spirit of samfundssind and a mindset of the greater good impacts not only *what* students are taught but also *how* they learn. Samfundssind seeks to build proficiency across the entire population of learners. It is not enough for only a few individuals to excel (the far right of the bell curve). With individualized learning and formative assessments, learners receive the support and resources they need to become competent, which benefits the individual, the organization, and society as a whole.

CHAPTER 8

A Mastery Approach to Teacher Preparation

M OST TEACHERS TODAY teach in the same ways that they were taught because it is all they know. Often, that means a lecture-based approach that requires the memorization and regurgitation of copious amounts of academic information.

Teachers in mastery learning schools, however, need to be differently prepared. Beyond learning how to effectively engage and help a diverse range of students, they need to experience learning in the new ways that they will be using to teach their students, and they need effective coaching over time to hone the critical competencies required to support the development of the five Cs in their students.

That's why a core element in the transition from a time-based education system to one that is mastery based is the transformation of teacher preparation. Our discussion here starts with K–12 teachers, but this kind of transformation is also relevant to those who work with adults.

Tony's experience at the Harvard Graduate School of Education—reputed to be one of the best ed schools in the country—shows just how problematic the preparation of K–12 teachers has been and remains today.

In his early twenties, Tony decided he wanted to become a high school teacher. He applied and was accepted to the Harvard Graduate School of Education's master of arts in teaching degree program, where he expected to learn his trade and earn the necessary certification. He took the required lecture-based courses in education history, curriculum, and learning theory and passed the necessary final exams, but there was no course for how to become a good teacher. Instead, he was assigned to work with a so-called master teacher. It was supposed to be a kind of guild training, the apprentice working with the master.

After observing the master teacher daily for several months, Tony finally had his turn to teach. He spent sleepless nights creating lesson plans for his week of solo teaching. He was ready to demonstrate what he could do and open to seeing where he still needed more coaching.

While Tony was teaching, the master teacher was out of the classroom most of the time, only popping in occasionally to observe. No surprise, then, that the feedback Tony later received, along with his months of supposed apprenticeship, proved largely useless. This master teacher did not know how to supervise and wasn't even (from Tony's point of view) a very effective teacher. In his yearlong program at Harvard, Tony had learned nothing about how to become a good teacher.

Nevertheless, he graduated and was now duly licensed and certified. Three years later, having served the required time teaching in a large suburban public school system, he was given tenure—a job for life. But he still felt he was not as effective in the classroom as he could or should be. In his three years of teaching, Tony had received no feedback on his teaching and did not know what he could do to improve.

It wasn't until he had been teaching full-time for five years that Tony began to feel somewhat proficient. He had learned his trade in isolation through trial and error. He often jokes that he would like to send a "recall notice" out to the students from his first few years.

Two decades after Tony graduated with a master's degree from Harvard, he returned for a doctorate, determined to help would-be teachers become better prepared than he was. He applied to be a university supervisor in the teacher education program, which had improved somewhat since Tony had first gone through it. Students were still assigned master teachers in area schools, whose teaching was still lacking in Tony's view. But now Tony was assigned to be one of the university supervisors of the teachers in training.

The standard plan for supervisors, at Harvard and almost everywhere else where novice teachers were in training, was to conference with student teachers to discuss their lesson plans, then observe them teaching the lesson, and finally give feedback in another conference. The challenges of scheduling meant that several weeks often passed between when Tony observed a lesson and the follow-up review session. Tony did this a total of six times with each student teacher. However, over the course of the semester, he saw no real improvement in their proficiency. Most new teachers struggled to master even basic skills related to classroom management. He was deeply frustrated with this system of teacher preparation, but he had no idea what the alternative might be.

After he received his doctorate, Tony was hired as an assistant professor of education at a leading state university, where, in addition to teaching courses, he was asked to supervise student teachers. In his first year there, he tried using the approach of "conference, observe, conference" that was used at Harvard and was common practice in virtually all teacher education programs. Again, though, he saw little real improvement in his student teachers' performance, and he found it extremely difficult to find effective master teachers from whom his students could learn. So, in year two, he tried something very different.

A brand-new high school had been built in a southern New Hampshire town that was striving to implement the principles of the CES, whose work you learned about in the last chapter. Impressed with the quality of teaching he saw there, Tony persuaded the faculty to take all six of his interns as student teachers for the year. Having all his student teachers in one school enabled Tony to visit their classes more frequently and give more regular feedback. And his students finally had mentoring teachers who really were very effective.

Even in this new venue, Tony still wasn't satisfied with the slow pace of teachers' progress. So, he tried another innovation. For his supervision seminar with them, Tony asked his students to take turns bringing in a video of a portion of a class they had recently taught. As they introduced their video to the others in the seminar, the student teachers identified a "problem of practice"—a concept first developed by educator Étienne Wenger in the 1990s—that they were working on.[1]

In effect, the student teachers observed one another. That also meant they could engage in very different kinds of conversations. They could all talk together about the challenge of starting a classroom discussion, for example, or ways to connect with a learner who seemed disengaged. With protocols in place, the student teachers learned to give and receive constructive feedback. They became a "community of practice," working collaboratively to understand and solve their problems of practice.

Improving learning and teaching became a shared effort. In a relatively short period of time using this new approach, Tony began to see remarkable improvements in his student teachers' classroom practices. From this experience, Tony came to understand that in education, as in almost all professions, "isolation is the enemy of improvement," as a wise superintendent once told him. He also realized that this approach to teacher preparation, with an emphasis on understanding and analyzing the actual performance of teachers in real time, was far more likely to create educators who more quickly and effectively became true masters of their profession.

However, in virtually every graduate school of education in the United States and in most other countries, the old approach of "conference, observe, conference" remained the norm until an educator by the name of Arthur Levine decided to create a better way.

The High Meadows Graduate School of Teaching and Learning

Arthur Levine knows schools—from K–12 to graduate schools of education—from the inside out. He is a product of New York City public schools. And after graduating from Brandeis University, he taught in the Boston public schools. He then went on to earn his PhD in sociology and education and has published a wide range of articles, books, and reports about many aspects of our education system. Nearly twenty years after completing high school, he once even moved into a housing project in Lawrence, Massachusetts, and posed as a high school student for a research project he'd undertaken.[2]

But what Levine is best known for are his many efforts to transform the preparation of teachers. After a seven-year stint as a college president, he joined the Harvard Graduate School of Education faculty, where he taught for five years until he was named president of the Teachers College at Columbia University in 1994. In 2005, during his last year at Teachers College, Levine published a series of scathing reports that criticized the way schools of education prepared school leaders, teachers, and researchers.[3]

His critique of teacher-prep programs was especially sharp. He wrote that they were "unruly and disordered" and merely served as "cash cows" for many universities. He declared that most new teachers were not adequately prepared for the challenges of teaching and said there was a "serious" risk that ed schools "will fade away or even be declared a failure."[4]

Levine went on to head the Woodrow Wilson National Fellowship Foundation (now known as the Institute for Citizens and Scholars), where he spearheaded a major effort to reform schools of education. One of his goals was to raise the standards for ed school admissions, and so he established well-financed fellowships to attract the most highly qualified students to become STEM teachers for inner-city schools. But he knew these future teachers had to be better prepared. So, Levine recruited thirty-one universities in six states and gave them substantial funding to improve teacher preparation, which included a requirement that all candidates have a yearlong classroom internship, followed by three years of mentoring by a veteran educator. As of 2019, these consortium universities had collectively sent more than a thousand teachers into math and science classrooms in high-needs urban schools.[5]

When we sat down with Levine, he shared with us the results of that experiment. "What finally happened was the schools changed their programs, and they are considerably better in most cases than the programs they started with," he told us. "But it became clear you can only go so far with existing schools of education. . . . The reality is that ed schools have a set of values that make teacher education—ironically, the reason they were created—the least prestigious of the activities they engage in. They don't care about practice. What they care about is academic research." All too often, this research is only intended for other academics and rarely offers useful insights for practitioners.

Levine went on to explain that he also thought "the era of time-based, process-fixed education at all levels" had passed. "We designed our educational institutions for an industrial society, and we based them on a very, very successful form of technology—the assembly line. The notion of the assembly line is you fix the process, and you fix the time. And we built schools where both the process and the time were fixed."

He came to believe that existing schools of education could be reformed but not transformed. For transformation to occur, education schools needed to be reinvented, he told us, and new models were needed as exemplars. In 2015, in partnership with MIT, Levine announced the creation of a new freestanding graduate school of education, one that would be competency based. It was initially called the Woodrow Wilson Academy and later renamed the High Meadows Graduate School of Teaching and Learning.

The goal of this new school of education was both to create a laboratory for innovation in STEM education and to better prepare future secondary science and math teachers through a competency-based approach that was not driven by the calendar. In other words, students would only become certified teachers by demonstrating proficiency rather than by merely serving the prescribed time taking courses and practice teaching, as was the case in all other teacher-prep programs in the country.

Levine spent several years raising start-up funds—about $25 million—from major foundations and corporations, while his team went to work designing a competency-based program. "It took us nearly three years to create this thing," he told us. "It was really hard to imagine what a time-independent school would be. How do you create an internship [that is] time independent when you're working with time-dependent schools?"

Realizing that heading the new program was a full-time job on top of the one he already had as president of the Woodrow Wilson foundation, Levine reached out to a former colleague, Deborah Hirsch, to become the executive director. She was later named president of High Meadows.

The fledgling program launched its first class in 2017 after receiving approval to grant degrees by the Massachusetts Board of Higher Education. Borrowing an idea from Olin College, with which the new graduate school had an informal affiliation, these first-year students paid no tuition. Instead, they were designated as "design fellows" and helped create the curriculum.

The work of developing the list of competencies and assessments was an iterative process. "Instead of trying to design it perfectly, we'd try something, sit back, and say, 'What did we learn?' It was about building a culture that could support innovation because we wanted to graduate students who could both function in the schools of today as well as help design the schools of tomorrow," Hirsch told us. "We don't even like the word 'mastery' because in some sense it's not about mastery. It's about continuous improvement and always trying to get better."

She went on to explain, "One of the difficulties in competency-based education is that people treat it as a checklist," but teaching demands flexibility and improvisation. "Maybe if you are going to be an accountant, with certain skill sets, [the checklist approach] works. For teaching, there are a number of specific skills and a knowledge base, but when a teacher is in a classroom, it's like an orchestration of it all. It's like a symphony playing."

The curriculum that Hirsch and her team evolved, with the help of students, defined a set of twenty-two competencies and the kinds of evidence that would indicate proficiency for each. They then mapped these competencies to specific challenges, which students undertook in lieu of courses. For example, one competency was fostering cooperative learning in the classroom. "You want to see it in small groups, [and] you want to see it in a large group environment," Hirsch said. "Same with project-based learning."

In addition to the specific competencies like those mentioned above, the program identified five core competencies. The program's students were required to show a high level of proficiency in each, multiple times and in varied circumstances.[6] They include the following:

1. Thinking like a designer
2. Grounding instruction in the science of learning and development
3. Teaching for justice

4. Relating to students
5. Creating a community of trust

Like the innovators we met in previous chapters, Hirsch took on the task of translating these challenges and competencies into the language of educational bureaucracies. "The Massachusetts Department of Elementary and Secondary Education asked for a curriculum to be presented in terms of courses," she told us. "Well, we didn't have courses. So we offered to create a syllabus for each of our challenges, and the state agreed. We did a translation of roughly what we thought each challenge would be equivalent to in terms of credit hours and created a transcript for that. We had to be translators all along."

Two Students' Perspectives

To further our understanding of the High Meadows approach, we wanted to hear from students who'd gone through the program. We talked to two recent graduates, Norbert "Bert" Hootsmans and Amir Davis, about their experiences at High Meadows and how a different kind of learning had impacted their teaching.

Their backgrounds are quite different. For Hootsmans, teaching is a second career. He earned his BA at Harvard and a PhD at MIT and had a career in industry until his retirement five years ago. Davis graduated from Xavier University with a degree in chemistry in 2019 and had planned to teach English in China for a few years, but COVID hit. Both graduated from High Meadows in 2021 and have been teaching full-time in the Boston area since then. Hootsmans teaches math at Cambridge Rindge and Latin High School; Davis teaches biology and chemistry at Lexington High School.

We asked both why they'd chosen the unorthodox teacher preparation program at High Meadows. "There had been a lot of research on what was working in ed schools and what was not," Hootsmans told us, referring to Arthur Levine's three reports. "The fact that it was an experimental program, based on that research, was appealing to me. I also really liked the fact that the program had a strong equity orientation and was looking at education more structurally."

"The huge thing I would say was that there was a genuine commitment to social justice while incorporating the competency style of learning," Davis explained.

We wanted to know in what ways they felt differently prepared because of the program. Both told us that they were far more student centered than many of their colleagues. "I am a social and emotional safe haven for all of my students," Davis said. "I feel at a real advantage compared to my colleagues. And I trust that when I use my teacher discretion, it will be the right decision."

Hootsmans also has a more personal relationship with his students. "I was concerned about the disparities I saw and still see in school among different racial, ethnic, and socioeconomic groups. I was especially concerned about Black students getting a bad rap and worked to develop a rapport with them. Now, they're constantly popping in during their free periods and bringing their friends. The students just join one of the tables working on a math problem and help out for a bit. Then they leave when their break is over."

We asked them to what extent they use a competency-based approach in their teaching. Davis said he doesn't believe in giving students deadlines, provided they complete their work by the end of the semester, which is a school requirement. He told us a story of one student who missed some assignments, but he gave her ample time to complete them and refrained from chastising or penalizing her. Later, he learned that her father was dying of cancer, and she had to travel to Iran to say goodbye to him. That was the reason her work was late.

"In the end it matters that people show competency, right?" Hootsmans said in answer to our question. "I have a lot of group work—maybe half the quizzes and exams, I allow people to do in pairs or groups. I basically tell people that it's their responsibility to make sure that everybody in their team develops competency. I'm also careful not to disincentivize through grading. Really, the point of a grade is to motivate people to close the gap and drive themselves toward competency. I also make all students revise their work. If it doesn't get a perfect smiley face, they have to do revisions because I believe revision is how you learn."

We wondered to what extent they had received criticism from colleagues for their unconventional approaches to teaching. "Oh yeah!" Davis exclaimed. "There's a handful of things. My quizzes are ungraded. And I do this thing called Philosopher Friday, where students discuss relevant, real-world topics. One of them was *Roe v. Wade.* I've had a lot of pushback on stuff like that. I have to negotiate with my department head. He's great. He's like, 'So if you want to do one of those topics, make it related to biology, so that if a mom calls me and says, *Hey, we shouldn't be talking about this,* I can say, *Well, actually, they're doing the reproductive unit.*'"

"My wife is always saying, 'They'll love you or fire you—or both,'" Hootsmans shared. "I have students do a final project about exponential growth. They have to find a trend that's important to them and explain why it's relevant and what will happen over time. And we talk about how we might change a trend in the future to achieve the new trend we'd like to have. Kids have a lot of opinions, but they haven't always done the data analysis behind it. So the challenges come when they come up with very controversial topics like abortion, Black-versus-white disparities in prison, impact of fast fashion on the environment, LGBTQ discrimination and social-emotional well-being, suicide."

Because of the very different way Hootsmans and Davis were trained as teachers, they are consistently reaching students personally, motivating them to master core concepts and to apply their skills and knowledge. They are redesigning their curricula to make difficult academic material relevant and interesting. And they are ensuring that students leave their classrooms having achieved a level of proficiency in the subjects they are teaching. In a very real way, Hootsmans and Davis are teaching to the three goals of mastery learning that we outlined at the beginning of the book: preparing all students with the skills and attitudes they need for twenty-first-century work, civic life, and personal growth and well-being.

They are preparing these students for civic life by creating frequent opportunities for discussion of the critical issues of our time. They demand that students cite evidence to back up their opinions. They are strengthening students' personal health and well-being by creating a culture of care and trust in their classrooms, as well as developing students' sense of agency by reinforcing the idea that their opinions and actions matter. Students learn that they can improve and achieve mastery through sustained effort, developing the habit of grit and a growth mindset.

Of course, other teachers do some of these things too. But often these classroom practices evolve randomly and vary enormously from one teacher to the next. Imagine if every teacher in America was trained in the ways Hootsmans and Davis were.

Not content with only preparing future STEM teachers, the High Meadows team in 2021 developed an in-service online master of education program in justice, equity, design, and innovation, which was also entirely competency based. Created for existing teachers in all subjects, the program was designed to be accessed in several ways: as a degree program, in "stacks" as certificates or microcredentials, or as stand-alone professional development.

The faculty never got to implement the new program, though. Levine, Hirsch, and their colleagues determined that High Meadows could not continue as a boutique independent graduate school. "We could never make this affordable," Levine explained. "If we could have gotten our enrollments up to say two hundred, then we could have done it, but we weren't at all close."

Hirsch elaborated, "Our intention had always been to scale our innovations and not just be a one-off. We realized we had to find a partner to do that. And so we spent a year looking."

They had a lot of help from their board of advisers, which included some of the most innovative deans from education schools around the country. One of them was Rick Ginsberg from the University of Kansas. As it turned out, Ginsberg was very interested in bringing High Meadows to his university.

Ginsberg has been dean of the School of Education and Human Sciences at the University of Kansas since 2005. He served three years as the chair of the Kansas Professional Standards Board, is past chair of the board of directors of the American Association of Colleges for Teacher Education, and is a member of the board of directors for the Council for the Accreditation of Educator Preparation.

We asked Ginsberg why he wanted to bring the concept of mastery-based learning to all his programs at the KU graduate school of education and, by extension, to all the future students whom his graduates would teach. "Benjamin Bloom's idea of mastery learning [as we discussed in Chapter 2] is that if material is taught properly, all kids should learn it," he told us. "You don't move up until you've mastered what's below. And it just seems so basic and so logical, and we just never do it."

Ginsberg didn't have the money to bring High Meadows to KU, so he reached out to his new provost, Barbara Bichelmeyer, who, as you'll recall from Chapter 5, had created a Center for Certification and Competency-Based Education at the university. "When I heard about High Meadows," Bichelmeyer told us, "I thought their expertise filled a gap for us while we built out the rest of an infrastructure that we needed for competency-based education at scale."

High Meadows and its nine experienced faculty could become the engine to help KU transform. Today, High Meadows' groundbreaking approaches to developing teacher mastery continue at KU.

Improving Learning in Finland: A Systemic Approach

As we've seen with High Meadows' and now KU's teacher mastery programs, overhauling the preparation and supervision of teachers is a first step and a necessary element of adopting a mastery approach in K–12 education and beyond. However, this change alone is not sufficient to bring about the fundamental transformations in learning that are required today. Many other changes are required to produce a true mastery-based education system. The story of education in Finland suggests what some of these changes must be.

In the 1960s, Finland was a comparatively poor, predominantly agrarian country with a weak education system. The country had just one natural resource: trees. Twenty-five percent of its economy was forestry related, and trees were being harvested at an unsustainable rate. The country's leaders at the time realized that to bring Finland into the twenty-first century and create greater prosperity for everyone, they needed a new national resource: the minds and hearts of all their children.

The leaders initiated a nonpartisan national dialogue on the Finns' hopes and dreams for the future of their children and their country and began to research how their education system could be transformed. (Ironically, Finnish educators have said that their best ideas came from American education reformers such as John Dewey.)

The country committed to eliminating all forms of tracking or streaming in the primary and early secondary grades and, instead, to providing the same high-quality education for all students. But this commitment created a new problem: teachers had no idea how to work with students of differing abilities in the same classroom. So, Finland radically overhauled teacher preparation at every level.

Tony had an opportunity to visit Finland in 2010 to learn how teachers are trained there. What he saw was an incredibly sophisticated system of improving teaching through careful observation, deliberate practice, discussion of problems of practice, and expert coaching. For example, all student teachers in Finland are required to enroll in a master's degree program, where, in addition to their academic work, they spend a year with a master teacher as a part of a team of five or six student teachers. The team regularly observes both the master teacher's and each other's classes, debriefs after every class, and together iterates future lesson plans. Many believe this radical improvement in the preparation of teachers instituted in the 1970s has enabled Finland to greatly improve its education outcomes in a relatively short period of time.[7]

But Finland did much more to transform education. The country radically overhauled its curriculum and transformed the culture of schools and the conditions under which teachers and students work. Contrary to what was happening in most of the industrialized world, the Finns eliminated most forms of standardized testing, believing that such tests created unnecessary stress and did not contribute to better learning and teaching.

In fact, students don't take their first standardized test until the end of secondary school, and they have two, three, or four years to prepare for this matriculation exam. Students can also choose which exams to take, other than one of the required native-language exams; they can also take the tests over if they aren't satisfied with their scores. The exams are all essay based and assess students' critical thinking skills. Teachers create their own exams. And teachers from neighboring municipalities score one another's exams.

Rather than being shielded from controversial issues, students are asked to show their ability to deal with these topics, such as "evolution, losing a job, dieting, political issues, violence, war, ethics and sports, junk food, sex, drugs, and popular music," according to Pasi Sahlberg, a world-renowned Finnish educator and researcher. Writing about such issues requires multidisciplinary knowledge and skills, he added.[8] It also prepares students for dealing with the complexities of citizenship and adult life far better than even the most rigorous conventional academic curriculum. Sahlberg went on to explain that Finland's educational philosophy is based on a commitment to developing students' knowledge, skills, values, and attitudes, which are called "transversal competencies":

1. Thinking and learning how to learn
2. Interaction, self-expression, and cultural understanding
3. Life skills and taking care of oneself
4. Multiliteracy and technological literacy
5. Participation and influencing[9]

These competencies clearly incorporate the three education goals that we consider most important: preparation for work, citizenship, and personal health and well-being.

However, unlike almost every other industrial democracy, Finland's Ministry of Education and Culture has not created a standardized curriculum. The country's national education motto is "Trust Through Professionalism." The ministry trusts municipalities to adapt and adopt the curriculum guidelines as needed. Local governments trust their teachers, who, in turn, trust their students. When Tony visited Finland, he saw numerous examples of students hard at work on their projects when the teacher was absent from the classroom, and there were no Internet filters on any school computers.[10]

It is not merely their excellent training that enables educators to successfully meet the challenges of a classroom with different ability levels and ethnicities. In Finland, teachers spend an average of six hundred hours a year in front of students; in the United States, it is 1,100 hours.[11] This gives teachers in Finland much more time to work collaboratively and to learn from one another, both within their schools and at neighboring schools. This is time that US educators wish they had. Andreas Schleicher, the creator of the PISA assessments at the OECD, has stated, "Building networks among schools to stimulate and spread innovation helps explain Finland's success in making strong school performance a consistent and predictable outcome throughout the education system, with less than 5% variation in student performance between schools."[12]

The Finns have also created a system that educates all students to high levels without turning schools into pressure cookers. In addition to Finnish schools having almost no standardized testing, the state-sponsored preschools are play based, and there is no expectation that students will read before they leave kindergarten. In grades one through nine, there are fifteen minutes of recess and outdoor play for every hour of academic work.[13] Arts, music, and crafts are an integral part of the curriculum. And young people make meaningful choices about what and how they learn; 25 percent of courses in upper secondary are electives.

Finland also has shorter school days and assigns less homework than any other industrial country, so that students can participate in a rich assortment of extracurricular activities, which the Finns understand to be an important source of learning. They believe that education must contribute to students' personal health and well-being by giving them meaningful choices of what to learn with reduced stress.

Finland also created an upper-secondary school system in which all students choose between career and technical education, a more academic track, or some combination of the two. About 45 percent of students at the upper-secondary level in Finland enroll in CTE programs, which are developed in close collaboration with employers and prepare them for both higher education and a good job right out of high school. This compares with about only 5 percent of students in the United States. Also worth noting is the fact that Finland spends 1 percent of GDP on job training, while the United States spends only 0.1 percent.[14]

The result of this reimagination of learning and school is the creation of a truly equitable education system, which has consistently performed well above the average of all countries participating in PISA, whose work you learned about in the last chapter. Because its citizens are so well educated, the country today enjoys a robust, entrepreneurial, and innovation-driven economy that's no longer dependent on the lumber industry. These days, the running joke is: if you want to enjoy the American way of life, move to Finland.

The country has what many consider to be an outstanding quality of life and has ranked number one for the last seven years in a row as the country where people are happiest, according to the *World Happiness Report,* sponsored by a consortium of organizations including the United Nations and Gallup.[15] Another country that has pursued similar education transformations, Denmark, ranks number two in the latest survey. The US ranking has slipped to twenty-third, largely because youth "have become drastically less happy in recent years," according to a March 2024 article in the *New York Times.*[16] So the evidence suggests that a mastery approach to learning not only contributes to a strong economy but also to citizens' personal health and well-being.

We are not holding Finland up as a perfect solution, or the one right way to redesign a country's education system. Factors such as Finland's small size and comparative lack of cultural diversity make its results hard to replicate in other countries, particularly a large, diverse, and polarized nation like the United States, as many critics have pointed out. But we believe that Finland, as well as other countries like Denmark and Estonia, shows the possibilities of what can happen when a country takes the reimagination of education seriously and implements systemic rather than piecemeal change— change that begins with the preparation of teachers.

Workplace Educators: Training the Trainers

To complete our discussion of teacher education and preparation, we move from K–12 to adult learning and especially workplace training. As you know from our discussion in Chapter 6, much of the workplace education today tends to be largely seat time spent in a training session or static material presented in an online course. This has been the norm for years.

There is another influence at work here, and it mirrors what occurs in the K–12 classroom. Just as elementary and high school educators tend to teach the way they were taught, the same occurs with corporate trainers. They have little or no experience in what it means to teach adults, let alone to train them with a mastery approach. And so, they can't give to others what they themselves do not have.

Instead, in much of adult education—both workplace training and in enrichment pursuits such as sports, music, and other leisure activities—the focus is on ensuring teachers know the material or have the skills. A person with sales experience becomes a sales trainer. An IT professional with expertise in a particular technology or coding language trains others.

In the same way, a talented musician decides to make some money on the side by giving music lessons. But being proficient in musical performance does not mean someone has the skills to help a student pick up a guitar or place their fingers on the piano keyboard for the first time. Nor can a star athlete automatically coach others, particularly those who are new to a sport. Having the technical skills and competency is one thing; meeting learners where they are and helping them pursue mastery is quite another.

The same thing happens with trainers in the workplace. Someone may be a whiz at Excel and setting up spreadsheets to perform complicated calculations. But does that person know how to teach someone with absolutely no experience in Excel, who may feel too intimidated to admit how little they really know? Not necessarily. And yet, the norm is for so-called subject-matter experts within a company to train other employees. Few of them are educators by training.

When we discussed this observation with Cameron Hedrick, who now heads learning and culture at Citi (and whom you met in Chapter 6), he recalled his own background. At the time, he was working for another large financial services firm. When he moved into corporate education, he was giving two weeks of intensive training. "At the time, I thought it was normal. But it was extreme and rare," he recalled.

It's worth repeating. Even for corporate trainers at some of the leading companies, *two weeks* of intensive training is the outlier in terms of preparation. Far more common is someone being given a title and a new role, and off they go to train others. (To put that in perspective, to become a professional football or soccer coach would take *years* of training.)

Today, Hedrick has a vision for introducing mastery learning at Citi, helping employees to not only expand their knowledge and skills to perform the jobs they have today but also evolve their competencies for the jobs they will take on in the future. He is purposefully rolling out this new approach, starting with about one hundred learning advisers in his department. "That's a huge strategic priority for me this year," Hedrick told us. "I'm taking on learning advisory first." It's a strategic move to start with learning advisers, who typically develop and deliver learning to meet the needs of a company and its employees, such as through training programs, e-learning, and other formal and informal educational opportunities.

Hedrick is starting with the basics such as adult learning theory, learning standards and governance, and systems thinking to better equip his learning advisers. "We are running several approximately two-hour sessions to cover the various topics, utilizing the expertise of the more senior learning advisers to teach those who are new to the role," he told us. "Utilizing visual aids, role-plays, synchronous and asynchronous methods, our goal is to establish baseline knowledge for our one hundred or so learning advisers."

He added, "I think, perhaps naively, that improving their performance ever so slightly will have a remarkable downstream impact on these individuals, their teams, and the clients they serve. Over time we'll move to more advanced topics. We'll push the edges with generative AI skills and evolving measurement techniques."

The "Discounting" Effect

The challenge in changing the paradigm in corporate training—and the development of corporate trainers—can be attributed largely to a lack of value placed on much of workplace learning as it now exists. Given the preponderance of check-the-box training and lack of personalization in the memorize-and-regurgitate teaching methods (what Ulrik calls "one-size-fits-none"), it's no wonder that workplace learning does not receive more attention from senior leaders.

That reality, however, also points to what needs to be changed. Corporate leaders—and not just the chief learning officers like Hedrick who truly understand the importance of mastery—need to see workplace learning as an imperative. That means changing how this learning occurs and improving how the trainers are trained and by whom. "We have to turn [learning] into an economic benefit," Hedrick said.

Training is often used as a remedy to resolve and prevent costly or embarrassing business execution errors. Similarly, to grow revenues in today's highly competitive marketplace, sales training can no longer be limited to sales models and product features; the "human dynamics" and "emotional intelligence" must also be explored.

In short, Hedrick said, it's "leveraging the pain" of errors and opportunities. When corporate leaders realize that more effective workplace training—the kind that truly builds mastery of essential knowledge and skills—could make a difference, then workplace training will garner the attention it deserves. As this occurs, chief learning officers like Hedrick can make an even bigger push to improve the training of the trainers, ensuring that they are developed with a mastery approach that they can then deliver to others.

Preparing for the Future

Hedrick foresees the day when the quality of training and trainers is improved at Citi and learning is more closely integrated across talent development. "From selection to training to performance management to promotion—the whole thing," he said.

Although there is much talk in the corporate world about upskilling and reskilling, the reality does not always reflect the rhetoric. As Raffaella Sadun, a professor at Harvard Business School, said in an interview with *Harvard Business Review*, there can be resistance from employees to engage in training programs meant to change their jobs—not just adding a task or two but sometimes complete shifts in occupations. Sadun also cited "resistance at middle-managerial levels . . . middle managers that were very concerned about sending their own workers to get trained and especially trained to change occupations, very naturally because that's how you lose your talent."[17]

However, the risk of losing some valued employees who become upskilled may turn out to be a small price to pay for having a better-trained, better-equipped workforce overall. The inverse is a price that no organization can afford: a workforce that is not well trained and lacks the tools to compete in a technology-driven, rapidly changing marketplace.

Hedrick used the example of the cloud, which ten years ago would have been "the craziest thing I ever heard." But once the economic value of hosting applications and storing massive amounts of data on servers in the cloud became clear, companies raced to use this new technology. "That whole arc happened in just two, three years," he recalled. "And that's one of the reasons why I'm trying to push the envelope [at Citi]. If I wait for the organization to wake up to the impact of adaptive [learning] or generative AI, I'm way too late."

The learning agenda needs to move closer to the cutting edge. That way, as corporate leadership recognizes the importance of training workers to become more proficient with AI tools—and, perhaps even more important, becoming more skilled at what makes them valuable human employees, such as communication, creativity, and collaboration—training can be rolled out quickly and effectively.

For that to happen, the trainers themselves need to have a much deeper understanding of emotional intelligence and how adults learn and change. Over time, these trainers will be able to hone the skills and behaviors that make them able to personalize their approach to individual learners.

Conclusion

Most educators genuinely care about their students and want to do what's best for them. But if they have never experienced a different kind of learning and teaching, they cannot change. Too many education reform efforts mandate improvements in learning results without supporting teachers' learning. Without opportunities to learn new skills, educators will inevitably resist change. Along with assessment, transforming the preparation and continuing education of teachers is an indispensable element of the transition to mastery-based learning. As we learned from the example of Finland, this revolution requires both rethinking the preparation of teachers and dramatically increasing the time and quality of in-service learning. If we want students of all ages to be lifelong learners, so then must be their teachers.

CHAPTER 9

The Way Forward: A System Redesign

WITH UNPRECEDENTED CHALLENGES facing countries around the world, education is at a crossroads. In the future, it will no longer be enough to have correct answers, because AI can already supply them far more quickly and reliably than most college graduates can. What will matter more is the ability to ask the right questions and imagine better solutions to new problems. Without dramatic change, an increasing number of adults who lack durable skills will be thrown out of work, and youth lacking these skills will be increasingly relegated to marginal employment. Then there are the growing threats to democracy precipitated by social and economic inequalities and AI that can be used to generate fake news and counterfeit images to sway a public who has not learned how to think critically. Finally, there is the deteriorating mental and physical health of many of our youth and a growing climate crisis.

Even if these challenges did not exist, we have learned in this book all the ways our century-old education model falls short. The waste of time and resources and the squandering of talent are reasons enough to fundamentally change the learning experience for children and adults. Mastery learning is simply a far superior model for education at every level.

At the crossroads, one path leads to more of the so-called education reforms that many countries have implemented in the last quarter century: required courses, formulaic compliance-driven adult learning, top-down accountability, high-stakes testing, and mounting stresses on students and adults alike, with no results to show. Or we can take the other path and truly reimagine learning and teaching for the twenty-first century. There is no in-between, no halfway measures that will work.

In this book, we have outlined the framework for a dramatically more effective way of learning: a new vision for education that is focused on continuous human growth and development that prepares individuals for productive work, engaged citizenship, and enhanced personal health and well-being. This is education that will enable individuals to thrive in a time of rapid change and equip them with the cognitive and character skills they need to tackle the challenges ahead. Mastery learning is a radically different approach at every age and level.

All the examples of mastery-based approaches to learning we have encountered in this book have three cornerstones in common. The first is the transition from measuring learning based on seat time and grades to measuring what students can do with what they know. The second is the prioritization of the continuous development of essential skills and character dispositions over mere acquisition of academic content knowledge. The third is a focus on strengthening intrinsic curiosity and motivation to learn by individualizing the learning process to the greatest extent possible.

The examples we chose are meant to be illustrative, not definitive. We could easily have written a book five times longer with many more compelling examples of mastery learning and new approaches to assessment that are proliferating around the world. We continue to learn of new ones every day. This is a movement that is growing exponentially.

At the same time, we cannot underestimate the roadblocks on this more daring path: parents and community members who think that schools and tests should look like the ones they remember, teachers who graduate from education schools lacking skills and wedded to the curricula and methods of the past, colleges that cling to the SAT and ACT for admissions decisions, HR executives who still rely on a college degree as a prerequisite for a job, employers who do little to develop the skills of their workforce, a media that feeds on sensational headlines about declining test scores and other bad news about schools, and national governments that mandate an obsolete testing regime, to name a few. Indeed, our list of roadblocks makes clear that everyone must play a role for this new vision of education to become a reality for all learners.

In the following sections, we will outline some of the other critical changes needed to create a new learning system.

The Heart of Change: Buy-In Versus Ownership

It is common to hear people in politics and senior management positions everywhere—not just in education—talk about the need to get "buy-in" for their latest initiative or effort at change. Such talk suggests that the real problem of change is merely to sell a new initiative or reform to a passive public. However, in an age of unprecedented political and social division and diminished social trust, we believe that the only way to create enduring change is to develop ownership of the goals of change.

Ownership starts with authentic dialogues around shared goals and important questions, versus trying to sell simple answers. In communities and states where the change process has endured political upheavals, such as Kentucky, visionary leaders like Jason Glass and others before him have created exactly such conversations. They began by engaging a broad cross section of citizens, including young people, first at the state level, and then at the community level, in conversations about what they want for their children, their community, and their country. Finland began its successful education change efforts in much the same way fifty years ago.

The first step, then, is to create a foundation for enduring change through the nonpartisan sponsorship of such dialogues at the local, state, and even national levels. The goal of such conversations must be to enable adults to construct a deeper understanding of the changes occurring in the world around them as the basis for rethinking the goals of education. Only then can individuals help create new and more meaningful profiles of a graduate, which must be the concrete outcome of such dialogues. For many people, and especially for educators and parents, change feels risky. It is only by understanding the risks of not changing, as well as by explicitly affirming shared goals, that individuals can feel inspired and supported to make the needed transformation.

Once a profile of a graduate has been developed by a community, the rigid boundaries between school and the real world need to be broken down so that young people can experience the relevance and reality of what they're learning beyond the walls of school. Students' motivation to achieve proficiency is greatly strengthened when they can explore knotty problems and meaningful topics in their academic work via projects that are relevant to their communities and to their own interests. They have far greater agency, choice, and voice and are much more deeply invested in their work as a result.

Another important way to break down school-community barriers is for students to periodically present their learning, growth, and achievement back to the community via public exhibitions. Such presentations dramatically increase students' motivation because they have a real audience for their work beyond their teachers. Like the students measuring water quality at Gibson Ek in Chapter 4, students will do stronger work when they know it matters to their community. Also, just as a chorus teacher cannot hide a bad student performance and a team coach cannot gloss over repeated losses on the athletic field, students and teachers put their work on display with public defenses of learning and exhibitions of student portfolios. These presentations, like the one we described at the beginning of Chapter 7, allow the community to engage with what their young people are learning.

Kentucky calls this engagement-reinforcing cycle "reciprocal accountability." The community involves itself in the development of its young people, and young people understand that they are learning to become part of the community through their daily work in school. We already have this sort of reciprocal accountability to a degree in the arts and sports. We believe that student and teacher academic work needs reciprocal accountability as well. Far more important than a district's test scores, public displays of quality student work are the best evidence that our schools are succeeding and are much more likely to sustain public support.

Creating a New Curriculum for the Twenty-First Century

A second critical element of a system redesign is the development of clear performance objectives for student work. As we saw with Gibson Ek in Chapter 4, the most effective communities and states with graduate profiles have also created competency progressions that define the expectations of growing mastery. Educators—working with their communities, their colleagues, postsecondary educators, and employers—are creating strong pathways that make clear what mastery means.

For example, what does it really mean to be an effective communicator? What different forms of communication should graduates have to master and to what levels? Is it enough that high school graduates can write a five-paragraph essay, which is all that is tested in even the most rigorous accountability systems? Or should they have to meet the higher standard of being able to research a topic of deep interest to them and write a coherent analysis of what they've learned? Should high school graduates also demonstrate that they can deliver an effective speech? Write a concise summary and critical analysis of a news article? Compose and mail a letter to the editor on a topic of their choice? Participate in a respectful debate on a controversial topic? Show evidence of the habit of listening respectfully to others?

What does effective communication look like for the youngest of children, and then what does it look like in the middle school years, and then for adults? As we saw with Red Bridge in Chapter 3, four- to seven-year-olds can be taught to listen and respond attentively and empathetically. And they continue to grow their sophistication and nuance in listening and communicating as they grow older.

Mastery learning is never one-and-done; it is a dynamic progression. True mastery learning entails clear, high expectations of excellence with progressing levels of skills and competence that are developed over years. Once these competence expectations are fully spelled out, the expectations then need to be integrated into interdisciplinary learning opportunities and translated to the youngest children—or traced from the youngest children up through high school graduation.

Along the way, educators working collaboratively will need to decide what is critical, foundational content knowledge in the different academic disciplines. What should students know in math, for example? Why is calculus still a requirement for college? Why not require all students to show proficiency in statistics, probability, estimation, computation, and financial literacy? These are essential competencies that every citizen needs but which are rarely taught.

What about science and history? Why ask high school students to memorize a vast quantity of scientific facts—like the periodic table—that are forgotten as soon as the test is over? Why not ask students to demonstrate a deep understanding of the interdependence of all life and of the scientific method, something almost no high school does? Why not ensure that students who have studied history know how to weigh historical evidence and have become proficient at comparing and evaluating primary sources?

And other required courses? Why not create a civics education that develops media literacy and engages students with institutions beyond the walls of school, in addition to ensuring that they understand how our government works? Why not enable students to practice democracy through forms of self-governance, as SEEQS does with their regular town hall assemblies, described in Chapter 3? Why not create a health and wellness curriculum where students gain the knowledge and skills they need to attend to their mental and physical health? Why not yoga instead of dodgeball?

Decisions about what is essential knowledge should not be left up to college professors, who have traditionally dominated K–12 curriculum review committees. Too many merely argue for the inclusion of their special little corner of academic knowledge in an already overstuffed curriculum. Citizens must have a real voice in what students need to know and be able to do, as they have in Kentucky and elsewhere.

Today's problems often require solutions that stretch the bounds of the academic disciplines from the nineteenth century. There is not a single important challenge today that can be understood, let alone solved, within the constraints of an individual academic subject silo. How might we institutionalize interdisciplinary, problem-based learning, where students are learning content not for its own sake but to understand and contribute to solving real-world challenges? One such challenge students could embrace is the United Nations' Sustainable Development Goals, which necessitate solutions designed with knowledge and methods from multiple disciplines.

To create space for these additions, we will need to subtract from what we're currently doing. Today, as the world changes, legislators keep mandating more and more required content knowledge and courses to the curriculum, in the hopes of keeping up with changing times. In many states, the required subjects and topics are greater than the number of hours in the school day or week.

A shorthand way of thinking about how to pare down our bloated curriculum is to ask: What do we want students to know and be able to do a year after they have completed a particular learning experience? And then: What do we know about how students learn that will enable us to design curricula that will motivate them, help them to retain essential knowledge, and teach them to apply it in ways that are meaningful and relevant to today's world?

The evidence of proficiency in such a system is not merely seat time served. Nor is it a grade, test score, or GPA. It is the products that students produce in conjunction with their reflections on what they have mastered and their teachers' qualitative assessments. In our view, every student should have a digital portfolio that follows them through school, and the quality of work demonstrated should be the basis for determining whether students are ready to move to the next level of learning. Such digital portfolios, as we saw in the example of the mastery transcript described earlier, can include students' written work, videos of oral presentations, examples of works of art, peer reviews of work done collaboratively, and assessments from service-learning or internship supervisors, as well as teachers.

The hard work of creating a K–12 competency-based curriculum that integrates essential content knowledge with meaningful assessments of core skills is well underway. Several nonprofits in the United States have led in these curriculum redesign efforts, including Building21, reDesignEd, and the Aurora Institute. Another organization also called Aurora, which is sponsored by the European Union, has created competency frameworks for college subject area courses. And Getting Smart, an organization led by Tom Vander Ark, provides a wealth of information and resources for many of the school and curriculum redesigns we have described in this book. Finally, the Learning Policy Institute, led by Linda

Darling-Hammond, has produced numerous policy briefs on what must be done to better prepare educators and transform assessments, among many other topics. (Tony is a senior research fellow at the Learning Policy Institute.)

Similar work needs to be done in higher education, as Brandon Busteed of BrandEd, formerly of Kaplan, has argued. Every college student should be required to do at least one long-term, interdisciplinary project, earn a workplace certification, and complete an internship as a part of their college experience. According to Busteed, "College graduates who complete an internship applying classroom learning in the workplace and those who work on a long-term project (spanning a semester or longer) are twice as likely to be meaningfully engaged in their work later in life. Further, students with a college internship double their odds of having a good job upon graduation."[1]

Transforming the Teaching Profession

For the most part, we teachers teach in the ways we have been taught. The transformations of education that we have described cannot take place without a very different kind of teacher preparation and continuing professional development. The excellent work of the High Meadows Graduate School of Teaching and Learning, now a part of the school of education at the University of Kansas, and the ways in which Finland has transformed its preparation of teachers point the way toward what a truly competency-based teacher training program needs to look like.

Teachers' ongoing professional development must also be reimagined. Teaching is one of the most isolated professions in modern work life, with educators working alone with their students all day every day. Isolation is the enemy of improvement and innovation. Collaborative problem-solving is the true engine of change. It is our belief, as we mentioned earlier, that all educators need to have time to collaborate and be a part of communities of practice who work together to identify and solve the problems of practice in their schools. They also need time and space to collaborate with those outside of education, in the jobs and industries where their students will build careers.

Finally, it is not just the teachers in schools and colleges that need a different preparation. We need to pay the same amount of attention to the preparation of educators of adults. They must work together to understand what kinds of pedagogies and curriculum approaches will lead to mastery for adults and receive regular feedback on their work.

Lab Schools for Educational R&D

Anyone in business will tell you that there is no innovation without substantial investment in research and development. Yet education has no real R&D capability. Most of the innovative schools and programs that we have described in this book are outliers and are not known to many outside of a small circle of educators and community members.

Several states—including Colorado, Kentucky, Massachusetts, Nevada, and New Mexico—have established what they call "innovation zones," where individual schools or districts are granted some flexibility with respect to regulations, curricula, or staffing. However, the flexibility these schools or districts have is often limited in both time and scope, and there is frequently no support for ongoing research about what can be learned from these efforts.

What is needed is substantial additional funding from both private foundations and state and federal governments to establish more visible networks of lab schools, where new curricula can be developed, new teachers can be trained, and new methods of learning and teaching can be tested. Equally important, these lab schools can provide visible proof to skeptics who have never seen or experienced new approaches to learning.

It is our view that every school district should have a kind of lab school of choice—like the ones we've described in this book—that can serve as a learning and R&D hub for the community. In addition, schools of education should sponsor lab schools for the preparation of future teachers and as sites for education research, much like the one John Dewey established at the University of Chicago in 1896. (It was closed in 1904, due to disputes with university administrators.) While some universities sponsor so-called lab schools today, they often act more like selective private schools for the children of faculty and elites and are rarely innovative or connected to research efforts.

Accountability at the State and National Levels

These lab schools, like all other schools, would be accountable for student results. However, what needs to be layered on top of the local accountability described earlier are new approaches to systems accountability to ensure that all students are progressing over time. Tests like the CCRA developed by the Council for Aid to Education and the PISA tests created by OECD are examples of dramatically better ways to assess competencies rather than mere content knowledge acquisition. They measure the ability of students to apply their knowledge, not just regurgitate it. Preparation for such tests demands much higher levels of teacher skillfulness, as we've seen. So they become an additional incentive for teachers to improve their practices continuously and collaboratively.

Critics of such tests argue that it is more difficult to objectively assess something like critical thinking, for example, than it is to test facts about the branches of government. Assessments of durable skills are also more expensive to develop, administer, and score. If such tests were widely used, it would no longer be economically feasible to test every student. Some individuals who are deeply concerned about the education inequities in the United States believe that to not test every student at regular interviews weakens account-ability efforts.

Opponents to changes in testing need to understand that we currently test only what's easy to measure rather than what's most important to know and do. The United States and many other countries squander vast sums of money on testing that does not produce any information of real value and that creates enormous stress for students and teachers. Imagine the savings if we were to only test sample populations every few years, as do many countries that have the best education systems, such as Finland. The money saved could be used to develop better assessments, improve school facilities and teacher salaries, reduce class size, and provide teachers with more time for professional development.

The use of tests in Finland is also very different from how standardized tests are used in the United States and many other countries. Finland's tests are not punitive, with scores publicly proclaimed and compared. Instead, they are a diagnostic tool the Ministry of Education and Culture uses to determine the kinds of supports that are needed to improve learning. The result is a dramatic reduction in the stresses on both teachers and students, as well as more actionable knowledge to drive real improvements in learning for all students.

Using a sampling strategy with better assessments, along with individual student portfolios and exhibitions that are evaluated by both the community and skilled teams of educators, greatly reduces the likelihood of bias and will give a far more complete picture of what students truly know and can do. When it comes to assessing durable skills, collective human judgment, informed by evidence, will always beat out even the most sophisticated computer-scored tests.

What Employers Must Do

For the past twenty years or more, employers have complained about how ill prepared our graduates from both high school and colleges are for the world of work, but they have done very little to solve the problem other than to advocate for requiring students to take more of the same mind-numbing STEM courses.

As we learned in the chapter on adult learning, most employers do not develop the talents of their own workforce; instead, they have made many jobs more routinized. Now, however, AI can take over routine blue- and white-collar tasks, and the jobs that remain demand higher levels of skills. Because of the increased costs of attracting and retaining talent, every employee will need an individualized plan for continuous learning and improvement. The nature of the learning experiences for adults needs to be radically different as well, and in line with the best kinds of learning we've described in schools and colleges.

Employers must also be more actively involved as advocates for fundamental change in K–12 education and beyond. In the 1980s, CEOs like IBM's Lou Gerstner and Xerox's David T. Kearns were among the corporate leaders actively involved in education reform efforts, including sponsorship of national education summits and serving on commissions. Today, America Succeeds is an excellent example of a coalition of business and education leaders undertaking this important work in their advocacy for the teaching and assessment of durable skills. However, America Succeeds is the exception rather than the rule. In recent years, corporate leaders have become far more reluctant to speak out about needed changes. C-suite executives whom we've spoken to say they are reluctant to take stands that might be politically controversial. But we cannot move to a competency-based system without the active involvement of employers.

In addition to helping their local communities better understand the cognitive and character skills that matter most today, employers must demand assessments that will measure those skills, and they need to lobby Congress for needed changes in the education accountability laws. Onetime tests must be replaced by ongoing formative assessments that both monitor progress and help improve mastery-based learning. Finally, businesses must work with government to create meaningful paid internships and apprenticeships for high school students and graduates, as is the case in much of Europe. And policymakers and business leaders at the state and national levels need to educate the media about these new approaches to learning and assessment.

What Parents Can Do to Help Their Children

Parents today see a world that is much more competitive than the one they grew up in, and so they understandably want to give their children every possible competitive advantage. Many believe that the best way to do this is to urge their children to excel academically. They also coach their children to always be thinking of what will look good on their college applications so that they can get into a name-brand university and then have a better shot at a stable and lucrative career.

All too often, though, this insistent parental push becomes a source of greatly increased stress and anxiety in children's lives. Many young people become frightened of getting a low grade or making the slightest mistake that might harm their chances for future success. They grow increasingly risk averse—not a helpful trait to have in a world of change and innovation where one must take responsible risks and learn through trial and error.

Employers today care far more about competencies than credentials, and in the world of AI there are no longer any guarantees of stable careers. The best way that parents can support their children's future happiness and well-being is to actively encourage their curiosity and intrinsic motivation through exploration of their interests. Young people begin to master genuine self-discipline and other essential character skills through the pursuit of their passions, whether in sports, the arts, a hobby, or taking on problems in the real world. In the future, there will be many exciting opportunities for young people who have developed cognitive and character skills and can show evidence that they are self-aware, care deeply, take initiative, and seek to work with others to make a meaningful contribution.

A Call to Action

There is a great deal at stake and time is running short. The brilliant work of many education innovators has shown us the way. Now, with courageous leadership and a sustained commitment from all of us, we can—and must—revolutionize learning so that future generations thrive, are prepared for a transformed workplace, and can meet the complex challenges of citizenship in the twenty-first century.

Acknowledgments

A popular saying affirms that it takes a village to raise a child. We could say the same about this book as well. A number of people have contributed in different ways to its creation. First and foremost is Sujata Bhatt. In every meaningful sense, she has been a coauthor, having researched and taken the lead on writing three chapters and contributing important ideas and edits to others. We are deeply indebted to Sujata for her many significant contributions.

We are also grateful to Patricia Crisafulli for her faithful and timely edits of every chapter. Patricia and Pat Commins also assisted with extensive research for the book.

Several other people have reviewed drafts of this book and made many helpful suggestions. Flemming Juul Christensen—a lifelong, retired educator—contributed extensive comments and feedback to the early manuscript. P. J. Blankenhorn read and critiqued every draft of each chapter, as she has with all of Tony's other books. She plays an essential role as Tony's thought partner in all his work.

Esmond Harmsworth, our agent, deserves a special shout-out. He assisted in the early development of the book, found us the right publisher, reviewed and contributed edits to the manuscript, and was a vital link in communications with our colleagues at Basic Books. At Basic, publisher Lara Heimert and Emily Taber, executive editor, helped to shape and strengthen the book in important ways. Emily was also a very thoughtful and thorough editor, and Liz Dana did an outstanding job copyediting the book.

Finally, we wish to express our thanks to the many people who gave their time for interviews and site visits. Their work on mastery-based learning is a true inspiration.

Notes

Introduction

1. Tony Wagner, *The Global Achievement Gap: Why Even Our Best Schools Don't Teach the New Survival Skills Our Children Need—and What We Can Do About It* (New York: Basic Books, 2008).

Chapter 1: What Is Mastery Learning?

1. "From Apprentice Artist to Master: Art Lessons from Da Vinci," Milan Art Institute, November 10, 2020, www.milanartinstitute.com/blog/art-lessons-from-da-vinci.

2. "Camping Merit Badge Requirements," Boy Scouts of America, accessed May 7, 2023, www.scouting.org/merit-badges/camping/.

3. Girl Scouts, *Your Guide to Going Gold: How to Become a Gold Award Girl Scout* (New York: Girl Scouts of the USA, 2020), www.girlscouts.org/content/dam/girlscouts-gsusa /forms-and-documents/GSUSA_Your-Guide-to-Going-Gold.pdf.

4. "Gold Award," Girl Scouts, accessed May 7, 2023, www.girlscouts.org/en/members /for-girl-scouts/badges-journeys-awards/highest-awards/gold-award.html.

5. Anders Ericsson and Robert Pool, *Peak: Secrets from the New Science of Expertise* (Boston: Houghton Mifflin Harcourt, 2016).

6. K. Anders Ericsson, Michael J. Prietula, and Edward T. Cokely, "The Making of an Expert," *Harvard Business Review*, July–August 2007, https://hbr.org/2007/07 /the-making-of-an-expert.

7. Jill Elish, "World's Top Expert on Expertise Wins Elite Honor," Florida State University, June 24, 2020, www.fsu.edu/indexTOFStory.html?lead.ericsson.

8. Anders Ericsson, Ralf Krampe, and Clemens Tesch-Römer, "The Role of Deliberate Practice in the Acquisition of Expert Performance," *Psychological Review* 100, no. 3 (1993): 363–406, https://doi.org/10.1037/0033-295X.100.3.363.

9. Carol Dweck, "The Power of Believing that You Can Improve," TED video, TEDxNorrkoping, November 2014, www.ted.com/talks/carol_dweck_the_power _of_believing_that_you_can_improve.

10. Catherine Cote, "Growth Mindset vs. Fixed Mindset: What's the Difference," *Business Insights* (blog), Harvard Business School Online, March 10, 2022, https://online .hbs.edu/blog/post/growth-mindset-vs-fixed-mindset.

11. "Transcript for Carol Dweck on the Psychology of Failure and Success," *To the Best of Our Knowledge*, April 13, 2020, www.ttbook.org/interview/carol-dweck-psychology-failure-and-success.

12. David Yeager et al., "A National Experiment Reveals Where a Growth Mindset Improves Achievement," *Nature* 153 (September 2019), https://doi.org/10.1038/s41586-019-1466-y.

13. Angela Lee Duckworth, "Grit: The Power of Passion and Perseverance," TED video, TED Talks Education, April 2013, www.ted.com/talks/angela_lee_duckworth_grit_the_power_of_passion_and_perseverance?language=en.

14. Angela Duckworth, "Angela Duckworth Explains What Teachers Misunderstand About Grit," *Education Week*, September 29, 2023, www.edweek.org/leadership/opinion-angela-duckworth-explains-what-teachers-misunderstand-about-grit/2023/09.

15. Duckworth, "Angela Duckworth Explains."

16. "How Do You Define Character?," Character Lab, https://characterlab.org/character/.

17. "Alison Gopnik," UC Berkeley Research, https://vcresearch.berkeley.edu/faculty/alison-gopnik.

Chapter 2: The Case for Reinventing Our Education System

1. GreatSchools, "Warrensville Heights High School," accessed September 15, 2022, www.greatschools.org/ohio/warrensville-heights/1615-Warrensville-Heights-High-School/.

2. National Center for Education Statistics, "College Enrollment Rates," in *The Condition of Education 2020*, May 2020, https://nces.ed.gov/programs/coe/pdf/coe_cpb.pdf.

3. Postsecondary National Policy Institute, "Black Students in Higher Education," last modified November 2023, https://pnpi.org/black-students/.

4. Alicia Hahn and Jordan Tarver, "2024 Student Loan Debt Statistics: Average Student Loan Debt," last modified April 18, 2024, www.forbes.com/advisor/student-loans/average-student-loan-statistics/.

5. "The Labor Market for Recent College Graduates Versus Other Groups," Federal Reserve Bank of New York, July 18, 2024, www.newyorkfed.org/research/college-labor-market?t&utm_source=perplexity#—:explore:unemployment.

6. Statista Research Department, "Percentage of Recent College Graduates in the United States Who Are Underemployed from June 2017 to June 2024," Statista, November 15, 2022, www.statista.com/statistics/642037/share-of-recent-us-college-graduates-underemployed/.

7. Vanessa Fuhrmans, "Half of College Grads Are Working Jobs That Don't Use Their Degrees," *Wall Street Journal*, February 22, 2024, www.wsj.com/lifestyle/careers/college-degree-jobs-unused-440b2abd.

8. Statista Research Department, "Unemployment Rate of Recent Graduates in the United States from January 2016 to May 2024," Statista, September 14, 2024, www.statista.com/statistics/633660/unemployment-rate-of-recent-graduates-in-the-us/.

9. North Carolina State University, "Two-Thirds of U.S. Adults Receive Parental Support into Their 40s," news release, *Newswise*, September 23, 2023, www.newswise.com/articles/two-thirds-of-u-s-adults-receive-parental-support-into-their-40s.

10. Abigail Johnson Hess, "College Costs Have Increased by 169% Since 1980—but Pay for Young Workers Is up by Just 19%: Georgetown Report," CNBC, November 2, 2021, www.cnbc.com/2021/11/02/the-gap-in-college-costs-and-earnings-for-young-workers-since-1980.html.

11. Marianne Power, "Generation Who Refuse to Grow Up: No Mortgage. No Marriage. No Children. No Career Plan. Like So Many 30-somethings, Marianne Power Admits She's One of Them. . .," *Daily Mail*, July 19, 2012, www.dailymail.co.uk/news/article-2176281/Generation-refuse-grow-No-mortgage-No-marriage-No-children-No-career-plan-Like-30-somethings-Marianne-Power-admits-shes-.html#ixzz3YR22hH2y.

12. Katelynn Harris, "Forty Years of Falling Manufacturing Employment," *Beyond the Numbers* 9, no. 16 (November 2020), www.bls.gov/opub/btn/volume-9/forty-years-of-falling-manufacturing-employment.htm.

13. Thomas B. Edsall, "Elites Are Making Choices That Are Not Good News," *New York Times*, November 2, 2022, www.nytimes.com/2022/11/02/opinion/artificial-intelligence-automation-jobs-populism.html.

14. Aimee Picchi, "The Value of a High School Degree Has Collapsed Since 1980," CBS News, November 11, 2019, www.cbsnews.com/news/the-value-of-a-high-school-degree-has-collapsed-since-1980/.

15. Heather Barrett and Ryan Pendell, "72% of Top CHROs See AI Replacing Jobs—and Workers Aren't Ready," Gallup, August 21, 2023, www.gallup.com/workplace/509540/top-chros-replacing-jobs.aspx.

16. Will Rinehart and Allison Edwards, "Understanding Job Loss Predictions from Artificial Intelligence," American Action Forum, July 11, 2019, www.americanactionforum.org/insight/understanding-job-loss-predictions-from-artificial-intelligence/.

17. Adam Grant, "In Head-Hunting, Big Data May Not Be Such a Big Deal," *New York Times*, June 19, 2013, www.nytimes.com/2013/06/20/business/in-head-hunting-big-data-may-not-be-such-a-big-deal.html.

18. Steve Lohr, "A 4-Year Degree Isn't Quite the Job Requirement It Used to Be," *New York Times*, April 8, 2022, www.nytimes.com/2022/04/08/business/hiring-without-college-degree.html.

19. Kevin Gray, "What Are Employers Looking for When Reviewing College Students' Resumes?," National Association of Colleges and Employers, December 9, 2024, www.naceweb.org/talent-acquisition/candidate-selection/the-key-attributes-employers-are-looking-for-on-graduates-resumes.

20. Susan Caminiti, "No College Degree? No Problem. More Companies Are Eliminating Requirements to Attract the Workers They Need," CNBC, April 25, 2022, www.cnbc.com/2022/04/25/companies-eliminate-college-degree-requirement-to-draw-needed-workers.html.

21. Scott Belsky, "Creativity Will Be Key to Competing Against AI in the Future Workforce—Here's How," World Economic Forum, November 10, 2020, www.weforum.org/agenda/2020/11/ai-automation-creativity-workforce-skill-fute-of-work/.

22. World Economic Forum, *Future of Jobs Report 2023*, May 2023, 38, www3.weforum.org/docs/WEF_Future_of_Jobs_2023.pdf.

23. Amy Blaschka, "The Number One Soft Skill Employers Seek—and Five Ways Top Leaders Say to Cultivate Yours," *Forbes*, February 20, 2019, www.forbes.com/sites

/amyblaschka/2019/02/28/the-number-one-soft-skill-employers-seek-and-five-ways-top-leaders-say-to-cultivate-yours/.

24. World Economic Forum, *Future of Jobs Report 2023*, 40.

25. Elena Silva, Taylor White, and Thomas Toch, *The Carnegie Unit: A Century-Old Standard in a Changing Education Landscape*, Carnegie Foundation for the Advancement of Teaching, January 2015, www.carnegiefoundation.org/wp-content/uploads/2015/01/Carnegie_Unit_Report.pdf.

26. Thomas D. Snyder, ed., *120 Years of American Education: A Statistical Portrait* (Washington, DC: National Center on Education Statistics, 1993), 27, https://nces.ed.gov/pubs93/93442.pdf.

27. Commission on the Reorganization of Secondary Education, *Cardinal Principles of Secondary Education* (Washington, DC: US Government Printing Office, 1928), www.google.com/books/edition/Cardinal_Principles_of_Secondary_Educati/-KgWAAAAIAAJ?hl=en&gbpv=1&printsec=frontcover.

28. Nicolas Serge et al., "Sick? Or Slow? On the Origins of Intelligence as a Psychological Object," *Intelligence* 41, no. 5 (September–October 2013): 699–711, www.sciencedirect.com/science/article/pii/S0160289613001232.

29. US Congress, Office of Technology Assessment, "Lessons From the Past: A History of Educational Testing in the United States," in *Testing in American Schools: Asking the Right Questions* (Washington, DC: US Government Printing Office, 1992), www.princeton.edu/~ota/disk1/1992/9236/923606.PDF; William G. Wraga, "The *Cardinal Principles* Report Revisited," *Education and Culture* 11, no. 2 (Fall 1994): 6–16, https://docs.lib.purdue.edu/cgi/viewcontent.cgi?article=1401&context=eandc#:~:text=Scholars%20looking%20back%20on%20the,the%20age%20cohort%20than%20had.

30. Thomas R. Guskey, "Lessons of Mastery Learning," ASCD, October 1, 2010, www.ascd.org/el/articles/lessons-of-mastery-learning.

31. Veera Korhonen, "Education Attainment Distribution in the United States from 1960 to 2022," Statista, August 22, 2024, www.statista.com/statistics/184260/educational-attainment-in-the-us/; Anya Kamenetz, "What 'A Nation at Risk' Got Wrong, and Right, About U.S. Schools," NPR, April 29, 2018, www.npr.org/sections/ed/2018/04/29/604986823/what-a-nation-at-risk-got-wrong-and-right-about-u-s-schools.

32. National Commission on Excellence in Education, *A Nation at Risk: The Imperative for Educational Reform*, April 1983, archived at the Wayback Machine, October 29, 2020, https://web.archive.org/web/20201029222248/https://www2.ed.gov/pubs/NatAtRisk/index.html.

33. "Student Performance Across Subjects," Nation's Report Card, accessed October 1, 2024, www.nationsreportcard.gov.

34. "For Nearly 50 Years Student Achievement Gap Fails to Close," *Education Next*, March 11, 2019, www.educationnext.org/nearly-50-years-student-achievement-gap-fails-close/.

35. Matthew Kraft and Melissa Arnold Lyon, "The Rise and Fall of the Teaching Profession: Prestige, Interest, Preparation, and Satisfaction over the Last Half Century" (EdWorkingPaper no. 22-679, Annenberg Institute, Brown University, April 2024), https://edworkingpapers.com/ai22-679.

36. Alliance for Excellent Education, *On the Path to Equity: Improving the Effectiveness of Beginning Teachers*, July 2014, https://all4ed.org/wp-content/uploads/2014/07/Path ToEquity.pdf.

37. Ross Brenneman, "Gallup Student Poll Finds Engagement in School Dropping by Grade Level," *Education Week*, March 22, 2016, www.edweek.org/leadership /gallup-student-poll-finds-engagement-in-school-dropping-by-grade-level/2016/03.

38. "The Startling Evidence on Learning Loss Is In," editorial, *New York Times*, November 18, 2023, www.nytimes.com/2023/11/18/opinion/pandemic-school-learning-loss .html.

39. April Rubin, "15 Million Students Chronically Miss School in Post-COVID Spike," *Axios*, November 21, 2023, www.axios.com/2023/11/21/student-chronic -absenteeism-covid-recovery.

40. Jerusha O. Conner and Denise C. Pope, "Not Just Robo-Students: Why Full Engagement Matters and How School Can Promote It," *Journal of Youth and Adolescence* 42 (2013): 1426–1442, https://doi.org/10.1007/s10964-013-9948-y.

41. Matt Richtel, "The Surgeon General's New Mission: Adolescent Mental Health," *New York Times*, March 21, 2023, www.nytimes.com/2023/03/21/health/surgeon-general -adolescents-mental-health.html.

42. Nicole Willcoxon and Stephanie Marken, "K–12 Schools Struggle to Prepare, Excite Gen Z About Learning," Gallup, June 14, 2023, https://news.gallup.com/opinion /gallup/507053/k12-schools-struggle-prepare-excite-gen-learning.aspx.

43. Thomas Ehrlich, ed., *Civic Responsibility and Higher Education* (Phoenix, AZ: Oryx Press, 2000), vi.

44. Ehrlich, *Civic Responsibility*, xxvi.

45. Shawn Healy, "Momentum Grows for Stronger Civic Education Across States," American Bar Association, January 4, 2022, www.americanbar.org/groups/crsj /publications/human_rights_magazine_home/the-state-of-civic-education-in-america /momentum-grows-for-stronger-civic-education-across-states/.

46. "Civics (History and Government) Questions for the Naturalization Test," US Citizenship and Immigration Services, last modified January 2019, www.uscis.gov/sites /default/files/document/questions-and-answers/100q.pdf.

47. Sarah Shapiro and Catherine Brown, "The State of Civics Education," Center for American Progress, February 21, 2018, www.americanprogress.org/article /state-civics-education/.

48. National Center for Education Statistics, "Table 303.90. Fall Enrollment and Number of Degree-Granting Postsecondary Institutions, by Control and Religious Affiliation of Institution: Selected Years, 1980 Through 2020," *Digest of Education Statistics*, accessed August 20, 2023, https://nces.ed.gov/programs/digest/d21/tables /dt21_303.90.asp.

49. SHAPE America, "New National Health Education Standards," accessed July 16, 2024, www.shapeamerica.org/MemberPortal/standards/health/new-he-standards .aspx.

50. M. Elaine Auld et al., "Health Literacy and Health Education in Schools: Collaboration for Action," National Academy of Medicine, July 20, 2020, https://nam.edu /health-literacy-and-health-education-in-schools-collaboration-for-action/.

51. "Childhood Obesity Facts," CDC, April 2, 2024, www.cdc.gov/obesity /childhood-obesity-facts/childhood-obesity-facts.html.

52. Sam Wineburg et al., "Evaluating Information: The Cornerstone of Civic Online Reasoning," Stanford Digital Repository, November 22, 2016, http://purl.stanford.edu /fv751yt5934.

53. Jonathan Haidt, "End the Phone-Based Childhood Now," *The Atlantic*, March 13, 2024, www.theatlantic.com/technology/archive/2024/03/teen-childhood-smartphone -use-mental-health-effects/677722/.

54. US Department of Health and Human Services, "Surgeon General Issues New Advisory About Effects Social Media Use Has on Youth Mental Health," news release, May 23, 2023, www.hhs.gov/about/news/2023/05/23/surgeon-general-issues -new-advisory-about-effects-social-media-use-has-youth-mental-health.html.

55. Haidt, "End the Phone-Based Childhood."

56. Jal Mehta and Sarah Fine, *In Search of Deeper Learning: The Quest to Remake the American High School* (Cambridge: Harvard University Press, 2019).

Chapter 3: Mastery Learning in K–8

1. Arianna Prothero, "The School Counselor–Student Ratio: There's Good News and Bad News," *Education Week*, January 5, 2023, www.edweek.org/leadership/the-school -counselor-student-ratio-theres-good-news-and-bad-news/2023/01.

2. "How Do You Define Character?," Character Lab, accessed October 1, 2024, https://characterlab.org/character/.

3. "Teacher-Powered Schools," Education Evolving, accessed October 1, 2024, www .teacherpowered.org/.

4. Hailey Hardison, "Wait, Some Teachers Have to Pay to Wear Jeans?," *Education Week*, March 4, 2022, www.edweek.org/teaching-learning/wait-some-teachers-have -to-pay-to-wear-jeans/2022/03.

5. Joanne W. Golann, "I Spent a Year and a Half at a No-Excuses Charter School—This Is What I Saw," Princeton University Press, May 19, 2021, https://press.princeton.edu /ideas/i-spent-a-year-and-a-half-at-a-no-excuses-charter-school-this-is-what-i-saw; Joanne W. Golann, "Why Are No-Excuses Schools Moving Beyond No Excuses?," *Hechinger Report*, June 10, 2021, https://hechingerreport.org/opinion-why-are-no-excuses-schools -moving-beyond-no-excuses/; Robert Pondiscio, "No Apologies for 'No Excuses' Charter Schools," Thomas B. Fordham Institute, July 24, 2019, https://fordhaminstitute.org /national/commentary/no-apologies-no-excuses-charter-schools.

6. Joanne Golann and Mira Debs, "The Harsh Discipline of No-Excuses Charter Schools: Is It Worth the Promise?," *Education Week*, June 9, 2019, www.edweek .org/leadership/opinion-the-harsh-discipline-of-no-excuses-charter-schools-is-it -worth-the-promise/2019/06.

7. "Results: How We Measure Success," KIPP, accessed August 1, 2023, www .kipp.org/results/national/#question-4:-are-our-students-climbing-the-mountain -to-and-through-college.

8. Shawn Malia Kanaiaupuni and Koren Ishibashi, *Left Behind? The Status of Hawaiian Students in Hawai'i Public Schools* (Honolulu, HI: Kamehameha Schools, 2003), www.ksbe.edu/assets/research/collection/03_0204_kanaiaupuni.pdf.

9. "Hawaiian Word of the Day: Kuleana," Hawaii News Now, April 17, 2015, www
.hawaiinewsnow.com/story/28832829/hawaiian-word-of-the-day-kuleana/.

10. "Why We Sail," Wa'a Honua, accessed June 10, 2023, https://waahonua.com
/why-we-sail/.

11. Kamali'iokekai Akiona, "An Experience to Remember," *Ka Wai Ola o
OHA*, September 1, 2021, https://kawaiola.news/columns/he-leo-hou-a-new-voice
/an-experience-to-remember/.

Chapter 4: Growing Mastery in Secondary School

1. Heidi Borst, "The Rise of High School Internships," *US News & World
Report*, January 14, 2022, www.usnews.com/education/k12/articles/the-rise-of-high
-school-internships.

2. Samantha Selby, "Insights into How & Why Students Cheat at High Performing
Schools," Challenge Success, March 24, 2019, https://challengesuccess.org/resources
/insights-into-how-why-students-cheat-at-high-performing-schools/.

3. "Competencies," Gibson Ek High School, accessed September 22, 2023, https://
gibsonek.isd411.org/academics/competencies.

4. "Vocational Education Statistics," Eurostat, September 2024, https://ec.europa.eu
/eurostat/statistics-explained/index.php?oldid=578213.

5. "Career and Technical Education," Fast Facts, National Center for Education Statistics, accessed May 9, 2024, https://nces.ed.gov/fastfacts/display.asp?id=43.

6. Advance CTE, "States Increase Funding for Secondary Career Technical Education," news release, August 29, 2023, https://careertech.org/news/states-increase
-funding-for-secondary-career-technical-education-by-average-of-182-million-over-last
-decade/.

7. Stephanie Aragon and Emily Workman, *Emerging State Turnaround Strategies*
(Denver, CO: Education Commission of the States, 2015), www.ecs.org/wp-content
/uploads/12139.pdf.

8. Emily Hanford, "The Troubled History of Vocational Education," *APM Reports*,
September 9, 2014, www.apmreports.org/episode/2014/09/09/the-troubled-history
-of-vocational-education.

9. "CMS CTE," Charlotte-Mecklenburg Schools, accessed October 1, 2024, https://
discovercte.com/filter-options/?search=pathway.

Chapter 5: Postsecondary Education

1. Edge Research, *Exploring the Exodus from Higher Education*, May 2022, https://
edgeresearch.com/exploring-the-exodus-from-higher-education/.

2. "Franklin W. Olin College of Engineering," College Scorecard, US Department of Education, accessed May 28, 2023, https://collegescorecard.ed.gov/school
/?441982-Franklin-W-Olin-College-of-Engineering.

3. "Career Services," Olin College of Engineering, accessed May 28, 2023, www.olin
.edu/impact-research/career-services.

4. "Harrisburg, Pennsylvania," QuickFacts, US Census Bureau, accessed May
28, 2023, www.census.gov/quickfacts/fact/table/harrisburgcitypennsylvania/PST0
45222.

5. Wikipedia, s.v. "Harrisburg, Pennsylvania," accessed May 28, 2023, https://en.wikipedia.org/wiki/Harrisburg,_Pennsylvania.

6. "Today's Students," Lumina Foundation, accessed May 28, 2023, www.luminafoundation.org/campaign/todays-student/.

7. Melanie Hanson, "College Tuition Inflation Rate," Education Data Initiative, September 9, 2024, https://educationdata.org/college-tuition-inflation-rate.

8. Amie Baisley, "The Influences of Calculus I on Engineering Student Persistence" (PhD diss., Utah State University, 2019), 122–126, https://digitalcommons.usu.edu/cgi/viewcontent.cgi?article=8734&context=etd.

9. University of Texas at Austin Charles A. Dana Center et al., *Launch Years: A New Vision for the Transition from High School to Postsecondary Mathematics*, 2020, www.utdanacenter.org/sites/default/files/2020-03/Launch-Years-A-New-Vision-report-March-2020.pdf; University of Texas at Austin Charles A. Dana Center, "Twenty States Join the Launch Years Initiative," news release, September 29, 2022, www.utdanacenter.org/twenty-states-join-launch-years-initiative.

10. Daniel Mollenkamp, "UCLA Life Sciences Revamped How It Teaches Math. Is It an Example Others Should Follow?," *EdSurge*, January 17, 2023, www.edsurge.com/news/2023-01-17-ucla-life-sciences-revamped-how-it-teaches-math-is-it-an-example-others-should-follow.

11. Erin Sanders O'Leary et al., "Reimagining the Introductory Math Curriculum for Life Sciences Students," *CBE Life Sciences Education* 20, no. 4 (Winter 2021), www.ncbi.nlm.nih.gov/pmc/articles/PMC8715777/.

12. Yash Rajpal, "Economics Department Offers New Math Sequence for Majors in Place of MATH 1400, MATH 1410," *Daily Pennsylvanian*, February 15, 2023, www.thedp.com/article/2023/02/penn-math-economics-requirement-change-major.

13. "About ABET," ABET, accessed May 28, 2023, www.abet.org/about-abet/.

14. Jon Marcus, "Colleges Are Now Closing at a Pace of One a Week. What Happens to the Students?," *Hechinger Report*, April 26, 2024, https://hechingerreport.org/colleges-are-now-closing-at-a-pace-of-one-a-week-what-happens-to-the-students/.

15. Gallup and Lumina Foundation, *The State of Higher Education 2023*, 2023, www.luminafoundation.org/wp-content/uploads/2023/05/State-of-Higher-Education-2023.pdf.

16. "The History of SNHU," Southern New Hampshire University, accessed May 29, 2023, www.snhu.edu/about-us/leadership-and-history/history.

17. "Our Story: Measuring Impact," About, Western Governors University, accessed May 29, 2023, www.wgu.edu/about/story/measuring-impact.html.

18. "Applying to Minerva," Univstats.com, accessed May 29, 2023, www.univstats.com/colleges/minerva-university/admission/#:~:text=Acceptance%20Rate%2C%20Yield%2C%20and%20Headcounts,been%20admitted%20to%20the%20school.

19. Sanjay Sarma et al., *Ideas for Designing an Affordable New Educational Institution* (Cambridge, MA: MIT Jameel World Education Lab, 2022), https://openlearning.mit.edu/ideas-designing-affordable-new-educational-institution.

Chapter 6: Adult Mastery Learning

1. R. T. Helmreich, A. C. Merritt, and J. A. Wilhelm, "The Evolution of Crew Resource Management Training in Commercial Aviation," *International Journal of Aviation Psychology* 9, no. 1 (1999): 19–32.

2. Josh Bersin, "Build vs. Buy: The Days of Hiring Scarce Technical Skills Are Over," JoshBersin.com, August 16, 2022, https://joshbersin.com/2019/10/build-vs-buy-the-days-of-hiring-scarce-technical-skills-are-over/.

3. Korn Ferry, *Talent Acquisition Trend Report 2024*, 2024, www.kornferry.com/content/dam/kornferry-v2/featured-topics/pdf/TA-Trends-Report-2024.pdf.

4. Accenture, *Future Skills Pilot Report*, 2021, www.accenture.com/content/dam/accenture/final/accenture-com/document/Future-Skills-Pilot-Report.pdf.

5. Will Rinehart and Allison Edwards, "Understanding Job Loss Predictions from Artificial Intelligence," American Action Forum, July 11, 2019, www.americanactionforum.org/insight/understanding-job-loss-predictions-from-artificial-intelligence/.

6. Accenture, *Future Skills Pilot Report*.

7. National Transportation Safety Board, "Aircraft Accident Report: Runway Overrun During Landing American Airlines Flight 1420 McDonnell Douglas MD-82, N215AA Little Rock, Arkansas, June 1, 1999" (Accident Report NTSB/AAR-01/02, Washington, DC), www.ntsb.gov/investigations/AccidentReports/Reports/AAR0102.pdf.

8. National Transportation Safety Board, "Aircraft Accident Report."

9. "About PISA," Programme for International Student Assessment, OECD, accessed December 18, 2023, www.oecd.org/pisa/.

10. Ulrik Juul Christensen, "Identity Saved the Day for Danish Men's Soccer Team: What Business Leaders Can Learn," *Forbes*, September 22, 2021, www.forbes.com/sites/ulrikjuulchristensen/2021/09/22/identity-saved-the-day-for-danish-mens-soccer-team-what-business-leaders-can-learn/.

11. Christensen, "Identity Saved the Day."

12. Melissa Reddy, "How Denmark's 'Incredible' Coach Kasper Hjulmand Has Empowered His Players to Keep Going," *The Independent*, June 27, 2021, www.independent.co.uk/sport/football/denmark-manager-kasper-hjulmand-euro-2020-b1873396.html.

13. Associated Press, "World Cup: Denmark Kit to Protest Qatar's Human Rights Record at 2022 Tournament," ESPN, www.espn.com/soccer/story/_/id/37632343/denmark-kit-protest-qatar-human-rights-record-2022-tournament.

14. Carol Dweck, "The Power of Believing that You Can Improve," TED video, TEDxNorrkoping, November 2014, www.ted.com/talks/carol_dweck_the_power_of_believing_that_you_can_improve.

15. Leah Fessler, "'You're No Genius': Her Father's Shutdowns Made Angela Duckworth a World Expert on Grit," *Quartz*, March 26, 2018, https://qz.com/work/1233940/angela-duckworth-explains-grit-is-the-key-to-success-and-self-confidence.

16. Ulrik Juul Christensen, "How Denmark Produced a Badminton Champion—and What That Teaches Business," *Forbes*, March 17, 2021, www.forbes.com/sites/ulrikjuulchristensen/2021/03/17/how-denmark-produced-a-badminton-champion---and-what-that-teaches-business.

17. Umair Bashir, "Most Popular Sports Activities in China as of September 2024," Statista, October 22, 2024, www.statista.com/forecasts/1388991/most-popular-sports-activities-in-china.

Chapter 7: Assessing Mastery

1. Jacob Perkins, "End of Virtual Commissioner's Listening Tour Will Begin Kentucky's Journey to a New Education System," *Kentucky Teacher*, May 6, 2021, www.kentuckyteacher.org/news/2021/05/end-of-virtual-commissioners-listening-tour-will-begin-kentuckys-journey-to-a-new-education-system/.

2. "Academics," Allen County Schools, accessed October 9, 2023, www.allen.kyschools.us/academics.aspx.

3. "Backpack Defenses—Bloom Elementary School," Jefferson County Public Schools, YouTube video, April 12, 2019, www.youtube.com/watch?v=L1uph8C_gj4&list=PLqh7c7rfeyEO6UP1xzET4xbvFJYHiT4Kq&index=10.

4. Claire Cain Miller, "New SAT Data Highlights the Deep Inequality at the Heart of American Education," *New York Times*, October 23, 2023, www.nytimes.com/interactive/2023/10/23/upshot/sat-inequality.html.

5. "List of Colleges Dropping & Reinstating the SAT/ACT Requirements," Horizon Education, May 3, 2024, https://horizoneducation.com/blog/colleges-dropping-reinstating-act-sat-requirements#:~:text=Notable%20schools%20that%20have%20reinstated,a%20student's%20readiness%20in%20college.

6. "Test Optional and Test Free Colleges," FairTest, accessed April 23, 2023, https://fairtest.org/test-optional-list/.

7. Scott Jaschik, "Making the Case for Test Optional," *Inside Higher Ed*, April 27, 2018, www.insidehighered.com/news/2018/04/27/large-study-finds-colleges-go-test-optional-become-more-diverse-and-maintain.

8. Council of the Great City Schools, *Student Testing in America's Great City Schools: An Inventory and Preliminary Analysis*, October 2015, www.cgcs.org/cms/lib/DC00001581/Centricity/Domain/87/Testing%20Report.pdf.

9. Matthew M. Chingos, *Strength in Numbers: State Spending on K–12 Assessment Systems* (Washington, DC: Brown Center on Education Policy at Brookings, 2012), www.brookings.edu/wp-content/uploads/2016/06/11_assessment_chingos_final_new.pdf.

10. Bryan Robinson, "2024 Graduates Lack Skills in Communication, Collaboration, and Critical Thinking, Study Finds," *Forbes*, June 17, 2024, www.forbes.com/sites/bryanrobinson/2024/06/17/2024-graduates-lack-skills-in-communication-collaboration-and-critical-thinking-study-finds/.

11. Coalition of Essential Schools, "Common Principles for Uncommon Schools," archived at the Wayback Machine, January 21, 2022, https://web.archive.org/web/20220121202648/http://essentialschools.org/.

12. "5 Habits of Mind: Deborah Meier," *21st Century Schools* (blog), June 28, 2011, https://21centuryschools.wordpress.com/2011/06/28/5-habits-of-mind-debroah-meier/.

13. "About Performance Assessment," Performance Assessment, Consortium, accessed May 2, 2023, www.performanceassessment.org/howitworks.

14. Michelle Fine and Karyna Pryiomka, *Assessing College Readiness Through Authentic Student Work: How the City University of New York and the New York Performance Standards Consortium Are Collaborating Toward Equity* (Palo Alto, CA: Learning Policy Institute, 2020), https://learningpolicyinstitute.org/product/assessing-college-readiness-authentic-student-work-report.

15. Johanna Alonso, "2 Architects of Traditional Assessment Embrace Competency," *Inside Higher Ed*, April 17, 2023, www.insidehighered.com/news/students/academics/2023/04/17/2-architects-traditional-assessment-embrace-competency#.

16. Ou Lydia Liu et al., *A New Vision for Skills-Based Assessment* (Princeton, NJ: Educational Testing Service, 2023), www.ets.org/content/dam/ets-org/pdfs/rd/new-vision-skills-based-assessment.pdf.

17. "Mastery Transcript and MTC Learning Record," Mastery Transcript Consortium, accessed May 4, 2023, https://mastery.org/what-we-do/mastery-transcript-and-mtc-learning-record/.

18. "MTC College Admissions List," Mastery Transcript Consortium, accessed May 13, 2024, https://mastery.org/college-acceptances/.

19. Educational Testing Service, "ETS and Mastery Transcript Consortium (MTC) Join Forces to Scale Skills Transcript," news release, May 15, 2024, www.ets.org/news/press-releases/ets-mastery-transcript-consortium-mtc-join-forces-scale-skills-transcript.html.

20. Tony Wagner, *The Global Achievement Gap*, 2nd ed. (New York: Basic Books, 2014), 115.

21. Wagner, *Global Achievement Gap*, 115–116.

22. "Authentic Assessments That Put Students' Abilities to Work," CAE, accessed April 29, 2023, https://cae.org/assessment-overview/#:~:text.

23. J. D. Singer, H. I. Braun, and N. Chudowsky, *International Education Assessments: Cautions, Conundrums, and Common Sense* (Washington, DC: National Academy of Education, 2018), https://naeducation.org/wp-content/uploads/2018/08/International-Education-Assessments-NAEd-report.pdf.

24. "PISA 2018 Global Competence," OECD, accessed April 29, 2023, www.oecd.org/pisa/innovation/global-competence/#.

25. A. J. Hess, "Ranking Workers Can Hurt Morale and Productivity. Tech Companies Are Doing It Anyway," *Fast Company*, February 16, 2023, www.fastcompany.com/90850190/stack-ranking-workers-hurt-morale-productivity-tech-companies.

26. Donald L. Kirkpatrick and James D. Kirkpatrick, *Evaluating Training Programs: The Four Levels*, 3rd ed. (Oakland, CA: Berrett-Koehler, 2006).

27. Lars W. Andersen et al., "In-Hospital Cardiac Arrest: A Review," *Journal of the American Medical Association* 321, no. 12 (2019): 1200–1210, https://doi.org/10.1001/jama.2019.1696.

28. IBM, History, "Education at IBM," accessed December 19, 2024, www.ibm.com/history/education-at-ibm.

29. Jean Matthews and Madhusmita Patil, "A Cognitive Framework for Enabling Talent Development and Learning," *Chief Learning Officer*, September 16, 2022, www.chieflearningofficer.com/2022/09/16/a-cognitive-framework-for-enabling-talent-development-and-learning/.

30. Sydney Lake, "'A Tipping Point for Higher Ed': Google Launches New, Low-Cost Online Programs for High-Demand Jobs," *Fortune*, October 13, 2022, https://fortune .com/education/articles/a-tipping-point-for-higher-ed-google-launches-new-low-cost -online-programs-for-high-demand-jobs/.

31. "Package Delivery Drivers," Search Jobs, UPS, accessed May 18, 2023, www .jobs-ups.com/package-delivery-driver.

Chapter 8: A Mastery Approach to Teacher Preparation

1. Étienne Wenger, "Communities of Practice: Learning as a Social System," *Systems Thinker*, June 1998, www.wenger-trayner.com/wp-content/uploads/2022/06/1998-EWT -Article-for-the-Systems-Thinker.pdf.

2. Maria Newman, "Levine Named 9th President at Teachers," *New York Times*, April 29, 1994, www.nytimes.com/1994/04/29/nyregion/levine-named-9th-president -at-teachers.html.

3. "The Education Schools Project," Woodrow Wilson National Fellowship Foundation, last modified September 18, 2006, http://edschools.org/.

4. Madeline Will, "Arthur Levine, Known for Harsh Critiques of Teacher-Preparation Programs, to Step Down," *Education Week*, June 18, 2019, www.edweek.org /policy-politics/arthur-levine-known-for-harsh-critiques-of-teacher-preparation -programs-to-step-down/2019/06.

5. Will, "Arthur Levine."

6. Meredith Moore, unpublished High Meadows Graduate School curriculum model working paper, June 2020 (shared with us by Deborah Hirsch).

7. See the documentary *The Finland Phenomenon: Inside the World's Most Surprising School System*, produced by Robert Compton, video, 2016, https://vimeo.com/ondemand /finlandphenomenon. See also books by Pasi Sahlberg.

8. Pasi Sahlberg, *Finnish Lessons 3.0* (New York: Teachers College Press, 2021), 43.

9. Sahlberg, *Finnish Lessons*, 61–62.

10. See *Finland Phenomenon*.

11. Elizabeth Christopher, "Teachers Need Our Support," *Harvard Ed.*, May 24, 2022, www.gse.harvard.edu/ideas/ed-magazine/22/05/teachers-need-our-support.

12. Sahlberg, *Finnish Lessons*, 65.

13. See Pasi Sahlberg and William Doyle, *Let the Children Play: How More Play Will Save Our Schools and Help Children Thrive* (New York: Oxford University Press, 2019).

14. Samuel E. Abrams, "Workforce Development in Finland and in the U.S.," Fulbright Finland Foundation, June 15, 2023, www.fulbright.fi/news-magazine /workforce-development-finland-and-us.

15. Gallup, *World Happiness Report 2024*, March 2024, www.gallup.com/analytics /349487/gallup-global-happiness-center.aspx.

16. Sopan Deb, "Led by Its Youth, U.S. Sinks in World Happiness Report," *New York Times*, March 20, 2024, www.nytimes.com/2024/03/20/us/world-happiness -report-finland-us.html.

17. Adi Ignatius, "How to Reskill Your Workforce in the Age of AI," *Harvard Business Review*, August 25, 2023, https://hbr.org/2023/08/how-to-reskill-your-workforce -in-the-age-of-ai.

Chapter 9: The Way Forward: A System Redesign

1. Brandon Busteed, "Your College Major Is Minor Compared to This," *Forbes*, last modified September 18, 2024, www.forbes.com/sites/brandonbusteed/2024/06/28 /your-college-major-is-minor-compared-to-this/.

Index

Credit: PJ Blankenhorn

Tony Wagner is senior research fellow at the Learning Policy Institute. He was formerly the expert in residence at the Harvard Innovation Labs and codirector of the Change Leadership Group at the Harvard Graduate School of Education. Wagner is the author of numerous books, including the bestsellers *Creating Innovators* and *The Global Achievement Gap*. He lives in New Hampshire.

Credit: Ulrik Jantzen

Ulrik Juul Christensen, MD, is the founder and CEO of Area9 Lyceum, a leader in personalized and adaptive learning systems. Formerly a member of the McGraw Hill board of executives, he is a frequent keynote speaker and regular contributor to *Forbes*, and he serves on a number of boards, including the Technical University of Denmark. He lives in Boston, Massachusetts.

RAISING READERS
Books Build Bright Futures

Thank you for reading this book and for being a reader of books in general. As an author, I am so grateful to share being part of a community of readers with you, and I hope you will join me in passing our love of books on to the next generation of readers.

Did you know that reading for enjoyment is the single biggest predictor of a child's future happiness and success?

More than family circumstances, parents' educational background, or income, reading impacts a child's future academic performance, emotional well-being, communication skills, economic security, ambition, and happiness.

Studies show that kids reading for enjoyment in the US is in rapid decline:

- In 2012, 53% of 9-year-olds read almost every day. Just 10 years later, in 2022, the number had fallen to 39%.
- In 2012, 27% of 13-year-olds read for fun daily. By 2023, that number was just 14%.

Together, we can commit to **Raising Readers** and change this trend. How?

- Read to children in your life daily.
- Model reading as a fun activity.
- Reduce screen time.
- Start a family, school, or community book club.
- Visit bookstores and libraries regularly.
- Listen to audiobooks.
- Read the book before you see the movie.
- Encourage your child to read aloud to a pet or stuffed animal.
- Give books as gifts.
- Donate books to families and communities in need.

BOB1217

Books build bright futures, and **Raising Readers** is our shared responsibility.

For more information, visit **JoinRaisingReaders.com**

Sources: National Endowment for the Arts, National Assessment of Educational Progress, WorldBookDay.org, Nielsen BookData's 2023 "Understanding the Children's Book Consumer"